Making Things Grow

THALASSA CRUSO

MAKING THINGS

A PRACTICAL GUIDE

ILLUSTRATIONS BY GRAMBS MILLER

GROW (INDOORS)

FOR THE INDOOR GARDENER

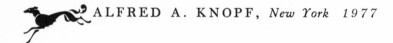

ALFRED A. KNOPF, New York 1977

THIS IS A BORZOI BOOK, PUBLISHED BY ALFRED A. KNOPF, INC.

ISBN: 0–394–73183–2
Library of Congress Catalog Card Number: 69–17238

Manufactured in the United States of America
Hardcover Edition Originally Published as *Making Things Grow*,

Paperback Edition Published April 28, 1976
Reprinted Once
Third Printing, May 1977

TO
the gardening heritage of my family
and to Francis who shares it
and Hugh who enjoys it

CONTENTS

✿ INTRODUCTION

NOT LONG AGO a distinguished horticulturist asked me where I had been trained. Taken by surprise, I answered that I had not had any professional training, for my work had been in archaeology. Now I think I gave the wrong answer. I may not have taken my degree in horticultural affairs, but, as I look back, I realize I had a vigorous and thorough apprenticeship at the hands of my innumerable gardening relatives.

Like many English people of my generation, I grew up taking gardens and gardening for granted. But just as some families were consistently church-oriented, and others interested in scientific matters, my family had always been scholars and gardeners with equal emphasis on both pursuits. I do, in fact, possess a fund of stories that deal with the gardening activities of my kin, many of whom I, of course, never knew. But my own experiences add up to quite a collection in themselves. As a small child I was forced by my grandmother to sit beside her for several mornings one summer watching the gardeners toil over an enormous bed that stretched the entire length of the croquet lawn. She had been away, fetching me for a visit, when the head gardener had planted it in the curves, ribbons, and blocks of bedded-out annual plants then in vogue. On her return, she disapproved of the way it had been done, and we sat there supervising the men as they reset every single plant (and there must have been thousands of them) into a pattern that pleased her more. My presence was required because Grandmama wanted me to understand why the changes were being made. She was enormously ahead of her time in realizing that blocks of a single color look best massed together.

Grandpapa was also interested in every aspect of the garden. I remember on another occasion listening with apprehension to some strong words being spoken to the gardener in charge of the vegetables about the quality of the gooseberries. I was well acquainted with the gooseberry bushes, and the gardener and I both knew why there had been so small a yield, and of such poor quality, that week. But friendship prevailed and respectful silence on both our parts averted a crisis.

I planted my first seeds in a tiny pocket handkerchief of a garden inside a cathedral close, under the supervision of a great-aunt. She directed my activities wearing full braided skirts that swept the ground, gloves, a feather boa, and an enormous hat, tied around with a purple motoring veil for fear of the sun. I also used to visit a hypochondriacal housebound great-aunt who wore a white lace cap, a black dress and shawl, and black buttoned boots. She used to sit me on a small stool and feed me seedcake, which I detested, while she explained the care of an enormous potted palm of which she was extremely proud. The secret rather curiously seemed to be tobacco ash, though, as she was unmarried, I cannot imagine where she got it!

I knew much better the inevitable spinster aunt who was a very good watercolor artist and a superb horticulturist. She used this combination of talents to produce herbaceous borders the like of which I have never seen since. Unfortunately, she had no skill with words and never could explain how she achieved the effects. There was another aunt who gardened fitfully, high-handedly, casually, and inexpertly, and managed, to my mother's annoyance, to grow the best roses in the family. Her husband, who was a poet, was regarded a little dubiously by some of the rest of my family. I now think his total disinterest in gardening may have been the black mark.

Both my parents were talented, though uninformed, gardeners. I am sure neither of them ever read a gardening book; they felt no need for instruction. But, by this time, World War I had made labor unobtainable, and my parents were the first of the family gardeners to do some of the physical work themselves rather than just supervise others. The same war forced a household move upon us. Today, in any such change, the status of the nearest schools would be of prime importance. I recall hearing my parents discussing the relative attractions of the houses they had seen, the decision turning on the merits of the gardens each possessed.

My earliest appreciation of plants is hazy yet vivid. The summer I was two, my family took a holiday by the sea. To reach the beach my carriage, I am told, was pushed over a sandy road across a salt marsh. I have no recollection of that summer except a bird's-eye panorama of rushes, poppies, and the sea, which I must have seen from the carriage as I was jounced along. My father was always a countryman at heart. During the short period we lived in London I recall him working in a small garden cleaning the green fly off the roses—no doubt in furious competition with his sister-in-law. I remember being lifted up by him to brush with a soapy toothbrush the infested stems of plants high above my head.

It was in London that I made my first garden. I was six by then. World War I had led to the temporary abandonment of many of the flower beds in the square to which we had access. I and my best friend, who I fear may have been dragooned by me into helping, weeded and planted one of those desolate plots with gleanings stolen from the garden of the casual aunt; any such pilfering would have been noticed instantly in my parents' garden. When it was finished we held hands and swore a solemn oath to remember our work forever—which in truth I have.

This gardening heritage was perhaps unusually intensive. I may have been a little more interested than most children of my age, but I also had many other pursuits. Gardening at that time was simply a part of the general pattern of everyday life for many people. It was considered a useful and entirely suitable hobby.

This, however, was all outdoor horticulture; indoor plants were something else again. Flowering or foliage plants indoors fell into the category of greenhouse gardening and, as such, belonged exclusively in the province of the paid, trained gardener. Superb plants were raised in greenhouses and were carried indoors. But these were for temporary display; they were never grown in the house. I doubt if even my hot-tempered grandfather would have interfered in any way with the work done under glass.

As I grew up all this began to change. Big greenhouses and conservatories and the men who understood them were becoming rare. Interest in gardening was as strong as ever, but the emphasis now had to change and the scope become more limited. The do-it-yourself period was on the way.

About the time I came to this country, houseplants grown indoors were coming strongly into the picture. Ironically, this at first proved quite hard to master. English houses until very recently were largely unheated, and plants that had flourished in warm greenhouses failed dismally indoors. It was, in fact, necessary to learn a new skill. I was not much surprised to hear that my parents found growing plants indoors "difficult" when the greenhouse had to be abandoned for lack of fuel in World War II. As a child, I had frequently done my homework by candlelight in the greenhouse, because it was so much warmer there than in my bedroom. I knew just how the plants felt! Gradually both the plant varieties and the new generation of gardeners came to an understanding, and in the postwar years houseplants have become enormously fashionable and exceedingly well grown.

In this country the relegation of houseplants to greenhouse growing also seems to have existed. But the next stage, learning to grow plants for oneself, took on a reverse twist. American houses have always been heated and attempts to grow greenhouse plants successfully indoors was made more difficult by too much, rather than too little, indoor heat. Also, by and large, there still seems to exist in America a kind of built-in resistance among many people to the idea of making things grow indoors, which I deplore. Plants can give so much pleasure that it seems a crime to forego this unnecessarily. Yet people who take on the care of an outdoor yard without a qualm still cringe at the idea of plants indoors and are willing to settle for dreary imitations.

Many people would like to grow plants, knowing that puttering around living things which cannot be hurried is a pleasant relief from the pressures of everyday life. But, more often than not, they are too afraid to try. Possibly they failed in their first attempts (and who of us did not?) and now believe that they have no place in which a plant will live. Or they may have fallen for that tiresome myth about a green thumb—the idea that to grow plants well you have to possess some mysterious, occult power that is given only to a chosen few. Some people feel that plants are too expensive and too demanding in their requirements for the average person to undertake. All these are very normal reactions if you have never been exposed to plant management, but none of them are, in fact, correct.

Former horticulturists who now live in apartments are another group of people who need encouragement about plants. Too many have come to feel that their gardening days are inevitably over. Many of them have given up too soon. I would like to show them that modern equipment has made it possible to carry on many gardening activities in our houses that once needed greenhouse treatment and the attention of trained gardeners. This book, therefore, has two purposes: to convince would-be gardeners that making things grow indoors is not too complicated for them to manage, and to bring gardening back for the gardenless gardener.

Success with houseplants is partly a state of mind. If you want to succeed you can, for there are no insuperable problems. In this book I hope to banish some unnecessary fears and dispose of some of the legends which have discouraged people from indoor horticulture. Gardening is not and never can be an exact science, for there is no one perfect way to approach any horticultural process. But there are some basic concepts that must be understood and certain skills that must be acquired if you want to be successful, even in so simple a venture as keeping a philodendron flourishing on a coffee table!

The fundamental rules are few and simple, and once they are mastered the door is open for endless pleasure.

Beginning gardeners should realize that there are easy, inexpensive plants that will be no great financial loss, even if they die while their owners are learning how best to care for them. Neglectable plants also exist, which allow us to go away; there are also methods by which we can take care of more demanding plants when we take a holiday. There are plants that will grow in the most unpromising locations, for artificial light has freed us all from the tyranny of the window sill. If these few facts are understood the first hurdle is taken.

The idea that it is necessary to possess a mysterious power in order to grow good plants is ridiculous. The only secret power the indoor horticulturist really needs is a true interest in plants. This will lead you to work a great deal around and among them. As you do so, you will breathe out carbon dioxide; this is a great stimulant to all plant growth and is probably the origin of the legend about the green thumb. Neither humans nor animals can thrive if basically they are unwanted. They sense this from the attitude of the people around them. I suspect that plants have something of the same capacity, for it is always obvious when they are grown only as part of the decor and not because the owner cares about them. If, at heart, you think plants a bore and a nuisance, throw them out and go back to plastic imitations. You'll be more comfortable with them!

Good gardeners are never born with an instinctive knowledge of what to do. Their skill evolves slowly; they learn from many failures along the way, and they enjoy success all the more when it comes. It is no coincidence that gardening parents almost always have children who are also interested in plants. The pleasures and skills of horticultural involvement pass imperceptibly from one generation to another. But it is important to realize that the abilities which bring these pleasures can easily be learned.

We now realize that people suffer if they are consistently deprived of contact with nature. People who have moved into apartments after having owned a garden do not need to be told this. And even those who have never had any interest in growing things are affected, whether they realize it or not, if they are completely divorced from the orderly progression of the seasons. The strains and tensions of modern life have, perhaps, made this more obvious. More and more people are discovering that they can relax when they work among plants, which, in a changing world, still carry on the old cycle of rest, rejuvenation, and fulfillment that has ordered their progress since time began. Once we become interested in the progress of the plants in our care, their development becomes a part of the rhythm of our own lives and we are refreshed by it. Artificial plants, no matter how beautifully made, cannot involve us in the same way; that is why they produce a lifeless, sterile feeling for many of us—and the more lifelike, the worse the letdown.

Indoor horticulture can become an engrossing and expensive hobby, but most of us gain the satisfaction we want without great expense or elaborate equipment. The tools and necessary supplies can normally be kept in a small carton.

This book is designed to follow the horticultural year as it affects the indoor gardener, from the time when plants have to come inside to avoid frost to the arrival of hot weather when we usually lose interest. Because most houses in America are kept at a temperature of about 70 degrees, the information is applicable to the whole country. The varieties of plants that may be used differ from area to area, but the essential skills and processes remain constant. Some of the horticultural methods that will be described have been in use for centuries. Other ideas are new and have come into use to help plants meet the challenge provided by our present style of living. Today even seasoned indoor horticulturists often feel like the Red Queen—they must run just to keep up with all that is new.

Houseplants themselves have been affected by modern life. They have been conditioned to show greater tolerance and flexibility so that they can handle the dry, intense heat of our houses in winter, icy air conditioning in the summer, and many entirely new growing materials. Some plants have fallen by the way; they have proven unable to take it. Some have dropped out of favor; others have been improved out of recognition; and there are also many new introductions. New growers need reassurance that they are not alone in being a little bewildered by the many plants now offered and the contradictory advice about their care that is so freely given.

In this book I discuss the basic rules for growing plants indoors as I apply them to my own collection. Everything described here has been done successfully in plant windows or under lights, not just for one experimental year but over a long period of time. Because the book deals only with plants that I grow indoors, the list of plants discussed seems short. My house is not suitable for some types of houseplants, and there are others I have never grown. My aim is to present only firsthand experience. Many plants that are suggested in other books for indoor use are omitted from this one. This is not due to a lack of appreciation of many other excellent plants which grow well in pots. They are not included because, over the years, I have found that they can no longer take our evenly heated houses and hermetically sealed windows throughout the winter. They must have periods of recuperation in greenhouses to do well. The tremendous alteration in the way we live which has come about since World War II has had a profound effect upon many plants that were household stand-bys, and it is time that we recognize this for a fact.

Indoor horticulture can be immensely rewarding if you have fun with your plants and refuse to allow them to take over your life. A firm but relaxed attitude, allied with a little common sense, usually provides exhilarating results for the novice horticulturist and the gardenless gardener alike. Why don't you go ahead and try?

Thalassa Cruso

Boston, 1969

Making Things Grow

1 ❧ BASIC CARE

Watering

If you are an eager beginner with houseplants, it is extremely frustrating to ask the experts how to water and get the answer, "It depends." There's nothing very helpful in that, but it is, in fact, the only proper answer. There is no single absolute rule that can be applied to watering; far too many factors are involved. But there are clues which anyone can learn that will help determine when water should be given or withheld. Once these are understood, one of the most baffling problems that haunts the indoor gardener vanishes.

Water is essential to all plant life; proper watering makes the difference between a thriving houseplant and a sickly misery. Identical plants can be grown in similar pots in the same location, but the way in which they are watered can make one flourish and the other pine. Even expert gardeners run into difficulties when they try to take care of someone else's collection. Plants are highly individualistic: they grow accustomed to their owner's particular treatment, and they resent any change. One of my children, an excellent gardener, summed up the situation when she said that any plant I gave her first had to understand that it was now living with her, not me—after that there was no more trouble.

Watering is, therefore, always a bit of a problem. This may comfort the beginner a little, but it is still exasperating to be told to water plants "when they need it," which is the advice usually handed out by gardening books. How is anyone to know when this mystical moment has arrived?

Even the newest gardener realizes that plants die without water; what is not so well known is that plants die equally decisively, though not quite so quickly, if they are overwatered. Beginners usually decide to play it safe and keep their potted plants thoroughly wet. In consequence, death by drowning is one of the commonest disasters to befall the plants of a new horticulturist. Plants wilt if they don't get enough water, and this draws attention to their problem. A plant that has been slightly underwatered so that it droops strikes terror into the heart of its new owner. But it will, in fact, recover completely, as long as rescue comes in time and the process is not repeated too often. Overwatered plants, unfortunately, do not give any such obvious signal; slowly they cease to thrive and the first visible indication of serious trouble is a yellowing-off of the lower leaves. Unless the overwatered pot soil is given a considerable period without water, during which time the plant will continue to look wretched, it will suddenly collapse in exactly the same way as an underwatered plant—but with no chance of being revived because the roots will have rotted away.

The best way to come to grips with the problem is to understand the process by which a plant lives. Plants in the ground or in a pot survive by having light fall upon their leaves. Light sets off an energy process called photosynthesis, which is the source of plant growth. To produce enough leaves and get them up where the light can strike them, plants have to have stems that are turgid, or full of water. To produce the stems, the plants must have a good root system through which moisture is conducted and which also serves to anchor the plant firmly in the soil. It's a little like the house that Jack built. Roots support the plant and conduct moisture that rises up into the stems so they, in turn, can produce and support the leaves on which the energizing light must fall. So far so good. What novice gardeners do not always realize is that this is not quite the whole structural story; there is a final "basement" level. Along the lower ends of every root strand there is a fringe of minute feeding roots, called hair roots. These hair roots are the backbone of every plant; only they can take in the nutrients that support the entire plant system; only they absorb moisture. Without properly functioning hair roots a plant will die. It's a situation not unlike the faulty ten-cent washer that prevents a space capsule from taking off.

Hair roots will work properly only if there is air as well as water in the soil; they need oxygen for stimulation. If the soil around a potted plant is allowed to dry out a little, oxygen will enter the areas opened up by the shrinking soil particles. This slight drying of the interior pot soil stimulates the root hairs in two ways. First, it provides them with oxygen, and then, because the earth is drying out, it sends them actively thrusting in all directions in search of any available moisture. Active root hairs are the key to all good plant growth: they feed the plant properly and keep the soil in good condition.

In overwatered soil, air is pressed out as the saturated soil mass packs down. Earth from a pot that has been lightly watered feels and looks quite unlike earth that has been given a daily drenching. If overwatering persists, the root hairs will die, usually from rot, and that will be the end of the plant. Every potted plant does better if it is allowed a short period of drying out between waterings.

But how dry is dry? How are we to know when to rewater? The drying-out period obviously cannot be carried to extremes. Plants wilt if they do not have enough moisture, and, if the process is continued too long, the root hairs will again shrivel and die. The trick is how to judge between allowing a plant to collapse, which will eventually be the death of it should it happen too often, and overwatering the pot. Here again the experts disagree on how to tell when the perfect moment arrives. Some people rap their pots with a spoon or their knuckles (or say they do); the resulting "ring" tells them when the pot is getting too dry. I have never been able to tell anything that way; besides, plastic pots don't ring, they "thunk." Other writers suggest you lift each pot and decide by the weight. This I would find time-consuming as well as impossible with really big pots. Besides, I don't think I know what the ideal weight is supposed to be. I suggest you use your eyes and fingers. Touch the top surface of the soil—if it feels as dry as it looks, then rewater.

The most important thing to learn is not to water every plant every day, regardless. Consider plants as individuals, not as a collection, and take into account the kind of place in which they grow wild. If a plant originated in desert conditions, it clearly needs less water than one whose forebears came from swampy ground. Shops now carry plants that originated all over the globe under very different living conditions. The only way to discover how to treat them is either to read the label carefully, which ought to be on all plants sold by good retailers, or else make sure of the name and look up its needs in one of the many plant books available. To do this it will be necessary to know the Latin name. A lot of people make extremely heavy weather over this, but, if the plant is unknown in the first place, there is no more trouble involved in having the retailer write down the Latin name than the common name. We will all grow better plants if we impress on those who want to sell them to us the need for good, accurate labeling.

Another consideration is the growth stage of the plant. If there are a great many flower buds, or much young fresh foliage, the pot will need more water than a plant in full bloom or one in which the leaves are all the same size and color. Still another point is the pot itself. Small pots dry out faster than large ones; plants in clay pots collapse faster than those in plastic pots. A hanging plant will need more water than a plant on the ground. Those displayed in a cool, sunless window will use up much less moisture than those in a warm, sunny place. There will also be a great variation in the watering needs of plants that are near house heating outlets and those that are not. This may all seem plain common sense, but it is surprising how many people treat all their plants in exactly the same manner no matter what the varieties are or the place they occupy indoors. I have many friends who give everything a daily slosh of water, like it or not. The surprise is how well their plants do under the circumstances.

Watering calls for very little special equipment. One necessity is a reasonably large watering can that is not too heavy to hold overhead and has a wide mouth and a straight spout. Finding one is not as simple as it sounds. Good indoor watering cans in reasonable colors are hard to find. Try to stay away from small, cute cans with curved spouts. It is an unchangeable law of home horticulture that debris

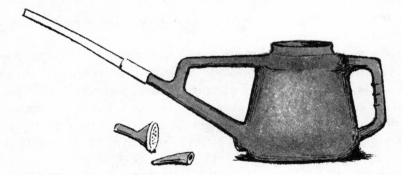

collects in watering cans. Small cans need endless refilling during the course of which something will get stuck in the curve of the spout. Most watering cans have too small an opening to get a hand inside to clean them out. Poking away with a curved wire or pecking at clogged leaves with kitchen tongs can be most irritating. A good can that is available is made of lightweight plastic with a high neck to prevent splashing. It holds plenty of water, the spout is straight and comes in sections for cleaning, and there is additional equipment for special needs like watering seeds. A mister is another essential piece of watering equipment. Most plants like a light spray occasionally, but it should be both light and in most cases occasional. No plant enjoys a daily drenching. Misters are available at all good garden centers, but they too have a tendency to get clogged—so don't expect a long working life. Don't worry too much about the temperature of the

water; plants need moisture not therapy. In areas where there is heavy chlorination, it's a good idea to draw the water overnight and let the chlorine evaporate. In exceedingly bitter weather I do sometimes fill my cans before going to bed so as to have water at room temperature the next morning.

If the soil in any pot looks unnaturally sodden, and you know the plant has not been regularly overwatered, poke a finger deep into the pot. If the saturated condition exists far down, something is seriously wrong. To find the trouble, knock out the plant and take a look at the root ball. Knocking out, which consists of getting the plant unharmed out of its pot, is an essential skill for every indoor gardener. Nothing frightens people more as they watch others do it—and nothing is simpler to learn. For right-handed people turn the pot upside down and spread the left hand over the top of the pot; if there is a single stem, slide that between the fingers. Hold the bottom of the upturned pot in your right hand and rap the rim of the pot on something hard—the edge of a table is excellent. The first time the process may call for several raps, for any novice to the game is going to be timid and give cautious little taps when what is needed is a really good hard thump. Sooner or later the plant will drop intact into the hand spread over the foliage—and that's all there is to the mystery of knocking out. Difficulties will occur only if the plant was put originally into a dirty pot that had old soil clinging to the pot sides. In that case, the root hairs will have grown into the hard-caked residue and will have to be broken out with very hard banging; this does do damage and is why good gardeners harp upon the need for clean pots.

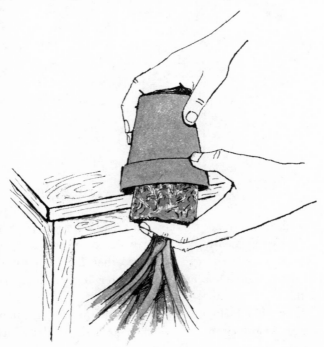

If the sodden state of the soil comes only from a little temporary overactivity with the watering can, no real harm will have been done. The root ball will still be strong and white. If the sodden soil has existed for a long time, the roots will be soft, brown, rotted, and will

9

smell sour. A plant that has got into that state cannot be saved. Throw it away. Anyone who loses a plant through root rot should re-evaluate his methods. If one plant rots, the chances are excellent that others may be in trouble too.

Never allow a pot to stand in a saucer with water over the base of the pot. Plants, after absorbing all the water they need, drain the rest out through the holes that are in the bottom of every pot. If a plant is standing in a saucer, the surplus water remains there and may, in fact, increase the next time water is given. Ideally every saucer under a plant should be checked about an hour after watering and any excess emptied out. This is a fearful nuisance, and it is the rare indoor gardener who can be bothered. It will save a lot of work and do the plant a great deal of good if the saucer is filled with pebbles and the pot stood on them to make a dry well. Surplus water will then drain into

Dry well of pebbles

the dry well and can be allowed to rise to the top layer of pebbles but never over them. The warm house air evaporates water contained in the stone layer; the extra humidity rises up and through the foliage of the plant and is extremely good for it.

Many books advise watering certain plants only from below—African violets and cyclamen being the most usual cases. This is a dangerous practice. To be watered adequately from below, the topsoil of the pot must show moisture. This takes a long time to occur and calls for a lot of water. The rushed housewife hardly ever remembers to empty the saucers after this operation is over, and saturated soil results. I am all for owning, not being owned by, plants; constantly checking on plant saucers is not my idea of constructive gardening, and I have had no trouble watering all my plants from above.

Plants sometimes look miserable and have wet soil without having been the victim of any of these mistakes. In that case it is possible that the drainage vents are clogged; earth often works into them and blocks the free passage of surplus water. Turn the pot over and clean the vents out with a small stick. If the stick does not hit something hard but goes right inside the pot, the trouble lies right there. It is an unfortunate modern labor-saving device among plant wholesalers to pot plants without any internal drainage. This is bad for the home horticulturist. Uncrocked pots, which is their technical name, are extremely liable to rot. If no crocks can be felt inside, knock out the plant, scrape off some of the bottom sodden soil, and recrock the pot.

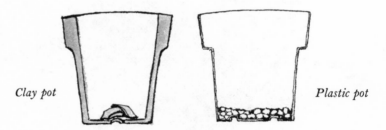

Clay pot *Plastic pot*

A couple of overlapping shards, which is the rather elaborate name used for pieces of broken clay pot, will suffice over the drainage holes in a clay pot. Plastic pots should have an inch of smaller broken-up pieces of pot covering the entire base. No shards? Buy a bag of pebbles from the florist and spread a layer of them. Put back the plant and settle it with a sharp bang; it will probably recover if you allow the soil time to dry out.

Another source of trouble for potted plants are the elegant containers in which we put them. Jardinieres shouldn't be form-fitting. This prevents circulation of air within the soil in the pot and may also hide the fact that the waters are steadily rising within the container and drowning the plant. Any plant in a solid container should have at least an inch of air space all around it. There should also be a pad of pebbles inside on the bottom. Another enemy of keeping plants in good condition is that dreadful foil. What is there about crumpled red or green paper with an embossed silver pattern inside that is supposed to

improve the appearance of a plant? The material crackles and slips about and, as an additional insult, is often pegged in place with an enormous bow wired to a stick. In my innocence I first thought that foil, which is a postwar treat, had appeared as a labor-saving device to save growers the bother of cleaning their clay pots. But foil is also wrapped around plastic pots, which are always clean. I considered the possibility that foil was added as a temporary convenience so that the

BASIC CARE

purchaser could set the plant safely on a piece of furniture while looking for a saucer. It certainly cannot be used for permanent protection, for water inevitably leaks through pinholes and along the seam. Furthermore, a plant that is left tightly encased in foil will drown unless a hole is torn in the bottom to let the surplus water out. This means there must be a saucer, and I don't approve of the esthetic appearance of a foil-wrapped plant sitting in a plastic saucer. Maybe we should wrap the saucer to match. Any claim that foil minimizes the drying out of houseplants won't do; plastic pots do that much better. Cleaner to carry home? What's wrong with old-fashioned wrapping paper? There is only one conclusion—foil is now a horticultural status symbol. The plant will seem more desirable if it is blanketed in crinkled metallic paper. Foil has many good uses but it is expensive. Nothing in the world is given away, and the price of this disfiguring material is undoubtedly passed on to us in higher prices. I would far rather pay the extra price to have my plants properly crocked instead. And I cannot think that any harm will be done if those of us who feel the same way make this point to the retailers. People who sell plants want us to come back for more. They should be told when an expensive or even a cheap plant has been potted up in such a slipshod manner that it will have a hard time just staying alive. I upend any plant I may buy and look at the drainage holes. This has not always endeared me to the grower nor does it normally meet the approval of the retailer. But nowadays I very rarely get offered a plant wrapped in foil or one potted without any drainage, and I am still buying my plants from the same sources.

It is often suggested that plants should never go into the night with wet foliage; morning watering is recommended. I think our dry house air takes care of wet leaves, but I do water in the morning because that is when the interaction of root and top growth is at its best. Don't give a thought to the legend that sun shining on a droplet of water will act as a magnifying glass and burn the leaves—it won't.

To sum up. Watering will become much easier if each plant is considered as an individual and attention is paid to where it is and its stage of growth. Make sure there is a free run-off of surplus water and always look at and touch the pot soil before rewatering. When and how to water is the toughest hurdle in the whole art of growing plants. Follow these rules and soon you'll be telling someone to water their plants when they need it!

Soils

Sooner or later all indoor gardeners find themselves in need of soil. Plants fall over and break their pots or outgrow the size they are in, or some other horticultural problem arises. Then even the most reluctant gardener has to face the necessity of finding something to put around the plant in the new pot.

Novice gardeners are usually anxious to do the right thing, but any search for simplified instructions about potting soil usually leaves them depressed and bewildered. To begin with, most books generally assume that everyone has access to that somewhat mysterious product called "good garden loam." Gardening articles are also full of information about humus and well-rotted manure, neither particularly accessible to the apartment dweller, or else they launch into scholarly research about something called the "pH" factor. It also isn't much help to the novice to run into furious arguments about the relative merits of organic versus chemical fertilizers. This is not what a beginner with a broken pot is looking for; it makes everything seem far too difficult, and the usual effect is to put the searcher off gardening forever. This is a great pity. Budding gardeners ought to know something about soil and how to use it to the best advantage.

To do their best, potted plants do need soil suited to their particular needs. And although elementary basic information about what is best for what plant is extraordinarily hard to come by, there is really no need for any very erudite approach. Anyone can learn how to make good potting soil even if they live in a high-rise apartment, and the end result is usually perfectly satisfactory.

When it is absolutely necessary to have something to put around a plant, a normal, sensible reaction is to buy a packaged soil, sometimes called "African Violet Soil" and sometimes labeled "General-Purpose Soil." This sterile, weed-free material is perfectly acceptable for small indoor horticultural jobs, but it has some disadvantages, particularly if you are going to use it for a great many of your plants. For one thing, the material has no texture but is powder fine. Fine soil of this consistency has a poor capacity to hold or absorb water, and it also packs under constant overhead watering. There is not enough structural "bounce" in it, and it will sink into a tight wad from which all air is excluded. Horticulture is very repetitious, but it must be stressed that lack of air in pot soil means a lingering death to the plant it is supposed to be nourishing. The lack of texture is another drawback. All mature plants need coarse material in their pots around which they can anchor their roots.

Potted plants have a hard time, confined as they are to such a limited root area. They also come from many different climates and growing conditions, and they are not all suited by the same soil mixture. You will get much better results if you can make them a soil mix which will suit their particular needs. If you are a gardener with access to a garden, your basic planting soil will automatically have in it much of the material needed for good growth. But even when good garden soil is available almost every potted plant will still grow better if it has, in the horrid modern term, "personalized" soil. If you have to buy a packaged mix, modification is really essential.

The best soil that can possibly be used for houseplants is natural leaf mold. This is a crumbly, extremely rich earth made over a long period by a natural accumulation of rotting leaves and other vegetable matter in some damp place. It is also impregnated with gritty particles of abraded rock and sand. With our suburban explosion, leaf mold has almost vanished. It can now be found, occasionally, deep in undisturbed woodland, but, even were you to tumble upon a cache, it is highly unlikely that the owner would give any away. Most good gardeners with access to the outdoors make their own version of leaf mold by a process known as composting. Compost is a man-made accumulation of vegetable debris of all kinds: weeds, hay, vegetable trimmings, seaweed—you name it. This accumulation is piled up into heaps, where it decomposes under the influence of water, internal heat, and bacterial activity into a very good equivalent of natural leaf mold. How you make your compost work leads to some of those furious arguments about the chemical or organic activators that can be added to the pile to set it throbbing, rather along the lines of an atomic reactor.

If compost were screened, that is, rubbed through fine mesh, it would look very like the commercially packaged mixtures, dark and rich and of a powder consistency. The nutritional value of the two materials is often very much the same. What distinguishes compost

Potting soil + spagnum moss (chopped)
+ sharp sand or perlite
all = parts

from store-bought soil is the rough debris that remains in it after the breakdown of the soft waste vegetable products. Small bits of stalk, strands of seaweed, and occasional pads of extra-tough leaves form roughage in most compost. This roughage makes the material springy and full of air in addition to its basic quality, which is to be absorbent and friable. Friable is the term applied to soil that is loose and crumbling and not able to be pressed into a sodden paste. Compost is an excellent product to have at hand, but there is no need to despair if you don't have access to any. It is quite easy to change packaged soil into a reasonable facsimile of it.

The first requirement is to add bulky material that will provide the necessary roughage for the root system and also give extra absorbency and air to the mix. There are two materials that can be used, both of which are readily available in small quantities. The first is chopped sphagnum moss, a rough, fibrous, and very tough vegetable produce that comes to us dry. There are three stages in which sphagnum moss is commercially available: long strand, chopped, and milled. The chopped version is what you want. Long-strand sphagnum moss is used alone in pots by some growers in place of soil, and it is also extremely popular as an addition to any soil mix. For some reason I do not manage it well; my plants don't seem to thrive on it. The fault lies in me, not the material, because I have seen it in successful use many times. Dried sphagnum moss is hard to get wet. A handful will float obstinately on top of a bowl of cold water, sternly repelling the moisture. The trick is to use a kettle of boiling water, pouring that over dried sphagnum in a plastic bowl. But mind your hands—the sphagnum takes up the boiling water instantly, but, perhaps to punish you, remains red-hot far longer than you might expect! When you are incorporating sphagnum moss into any other soil, have it wet but not soaking. Wring out the surplus water as you would a dishcloth before you start to mix it in. Another excellent addition to any soil is peat moss. This has all the advantages of sphagnum, good water-storing properties, and a coarse texture. It also confers another benefit on soil that is not totally understood. When incorporated in soil, peat moss has the power to stimulate additional growth from the all-important root hairs. It is also the essential material to add if you are making a soil mix for a plant like an azalea that needs an acid condition—the famous pH factor! Like sphagnum moss, peat moss is very tiresome about taking up water in a dry state, but it also gives way instantly under the

BASIC CARE

boiling-water treatment. It is of vital importance that peat moss is never incorporated into soil in a dry state. If that happens it will not absorb any moisture and the dry particles will eventually destroy the structure of the soil. Peat moss varies in quality, but a small bag has unlimited uses for every gardener.

All natural soils always have a slightly gritty feeling. This comes from the gradual breakdown of rocks and stones. Grit in soil is very important. It provides air space by making tiny pockets within the earth around which air forms. The minute pockets give the soil free drainage, for surplus water that cannot be absorbed runs out of the pot through them. The way to add grit to a homemade mix is to add sharp sand. This is not soft sea sand that packs down (a cardinal sin in pot soil) but quarry sand full of hard particles. It used to be difficult to get in small quantities, but now farsighted garden centers are packaging it. Sharp sand is vital to any soil mix that is being improved with either sphagnum or peat moss, because these products are so spongy by nature that the mixture might become waterlogged unless additional means of fast drainage is added. If you can't get sharp sand, substitute perlite or perloam. This is an expanded volcanic rock that also absorbs moisture. It comes in the form of small particles that do not lose their firmness when wet. Perlite therefore provides both excellent roughage and first-class drainage to any soil mixture. For me it has the slight disadvantage of being white. I don't happen to like the look of it in the pot. But I realize that this is a totally unworthy reaction to a fine product.

Good horticulturists improve any soil they use, whether it is their own compost or a packaged mix, in order to make the mixture right for specific plants. The ground rules for doing this for differing plant families are very simple. I am always going to suggest sand when I describe the mix, but perlite would be as good a substitute. I shall also always speak of peat moss where, again, sphagnum moss would do as well.

The plants we grow indoors come to us from all over the globe, but many of them are very undemanding in their soil needs. Chrysanthemums, cyclamen, poinsettias, and geraniums originated on four different continents, but they will all thrive in an identical soil mix. This is an all-purpose soil which, if you are using compost, should have one quarter of a handful of sand added to one part compost. If you are improving a packaged soil, the proportions should be equal quantities of packaged soil, peat moss, and sand. Plants that originate where there is very little water don't want a pot soil that holds water too long. A cactus, for instance, has adapted itself to surviving in a climate with very little rain; it needs a quick-draining, fast-drying soil. A good mix would be one part sand and half a part compost—or one part prepackaged mix, enough peat moss to provide some root anchorage, and enough sand to make the mixture light in color. Plants like the Christmas cactus and all the bromeliads that live naturally in crotches of trees need rich material that sheds water fast for their roots. Their mixture would be two parts compost to one part sand—or two parts packaged mix to one part peat moss and one part sand. The final class are plants that enjoy damp feet, that is, soil that stays evenly moist but not sodden. The spathe flower is such a plant and so are members of the primrose family. For them add one half part peat moss to one part compost and one half part sand—or two parts packaged soil, two parts peat moss, and one half part sand.

That's all there is to very simplified soil mixing. Naturally this is far from the whole story, but it does for the average indoor grower. And don't take the instructions too literally; they are intended only as basic guides to give the grower an idea of the varying proportions of water-holding and water-draining materials each type of plant prefers. As you get more experienced your eye and the subsequent behavior of your plant will turn you toward personal modifications of these outlines. One thing I would stress: you will never go wrong adding sharp sand. Except for water lilies, I can't think of any plant that is not improved with good drainage.

You may remember that one of the advantages of compost is its richness that comes from the fact that it is a breakdown of concentrated vegetable matter. The packaged soil you buy is usually also well fortified with the proper nutrients and what are called trace elements, the minerals vital to plant growth. If you use packaged mix just as it comes from the bag, it will need no extra fertilizer. If you change its consistency by adding sand or peat moss or any of the other inert materials, you will improve the soil structure, but you will upset the original balance of food elements. These you can restore by adding a very old organic fertilizer, bone meal. Use the steamed product, not raw bone meal—there are some dangers in that which are overcome by the sterilization process. Bone meal is excellent, because it will not burn even the most fragile root hairs. It breaks down extremely slowly, giving up its nutrients and trace elements over a long period so that it keeps the soil in good heart for a very long time. Avoid using any quick-acting fertilizers in a soil mix for potted plants until you are reasonably experienced. Chemical products and that admirable stand-by, dried cow manure, are liable to do damage to new hair roots unless they are used very sparingly. I also would stay clear of any novelty fertilizers; plant pills are not for beginners. It's the rare novice who has a light enough hand for any fertilizer except bone meal.

Always put bone meal in the lower layer of soil in the pot. Buried below the root ball, it will drive the feeding roots downward in search of its goodness. If you mix it into the top layer of soil, feeding roots may rise up after it, which puts them in serious danger, and the earth itself will grow an unattractive moldy growth all over the top of the pot. That is really all there is to soil. A very easy process to grasp.

Perhaps you should be warned that once you decide to adapt your soil to specific plants, things are never going to be quite the same for you. Knowing what you should do, the chances are that you will feel you must do it. You will in fact give yourself much more trouble, but that's how our plants improve. There's nothing to this process you can't do easily at home, no matter how gardenless you may be, and all the material is available in any area. All you need is the inclination to experiment.

Pots

In recent years, a small revolution has taken place in the world of the indoor horticulturist as far as pots are concerned. There are new shapes even among familiar clay pots, pots made of plastic or some space-age material, and many different varieties of imported pots. All this is a little confusing to the average grower, who finds newly purchased plants encased in unknown substances or shapes that are highly annoying to the conservative horticulturist who longs only for the traditional clay pot. And there's more to this change in pot types than just liking or loathing their appearance. Plants in pots made of these new materials need a different sort of daily handling from identical plants in clay pots. And since each new kind of plant pot is normally advertised as possessing some particularly specialized advantage, it is small wonder that even the most resilient gardener greets the announcement of yet another revolutionary pot with a slight groan. At present three pots are in general use: clay (making a determined comeback after having nearly vanished from the market), plastic, and styrofoam. The shops and garden centers are also full of all kinds of containers in a series of remarkable colors and shapes. The majority of potted plants are now sold in plastic or styrofoam pots. For commercial growers these materials have great advantages. They are cheap to produce, light in weight, stack easily, and are hard to break. But they are not popular with many indoor gardeners. People complain about the hideous colors of plastic pots, but why not try a little consumer resistance? Don't buy a plant in a white or gaudily colored pot, and the retailer will soon get the message. Insist on dark gray or dark green, both of which are available.

Experienced indoor gardeners often lament that, apart from much preferring the appearance of clay, their plants also don't grow well in plastic pots. This I feel comes from not fully understanding how different the treatment should be where watering is concerned. In a clay pot, the side walls are porous; that means both air and water can pass through them. There is a constant cycle in which air passing into the pot earth through the side walls dries out the soil. Drying soil absorbs extra oxygen, which activates the feeding roots, and these roots by their activity keep the earth inside the pot open and in good condition. If you overwater a plant in a clay pot, the immediate surplus will run out through the central drainage hole in the base, which is usually a good-sized vent. If you consistently overwater it, the long-term surplus water that is absorbed by the soil will pass through, or leach out (which is the technical expression) of the pot walls. An overwatered clay pot is easily identifiable. It looks very dark in color and has a slimy feel. In plastic pots part of this cycle is broken. Plastic is not porous; neither air nor water can get through the pot sides, and the drying-out process that activates the roots and keeps the soil in good condition can only come through the top. An overwatered plastic pot cannot leach surplus moisture; it has to depend entirely upon the drainage holes at its base to get rid of it. Unfortunately, these are frequently very small and inadequate, compounding the problem.

BASIC CARE

To grow plants well in a plastic pot almost half the amount of water should be given, compared to clay pots. It is extremely important not to rewater plastic pots until the topsoil not only looks dry but feels dry a little way below the surface. If you treat a plant potted in plastic as though it were in clay, the soil inside will almost inevitably become sodden and root rot will follow. The two types of pot also should have different kinds of internal drainage. All pots must be crocked—that is, have some kind of dry well material over the drainage vents to prevent the earth from clogging them. In a clay pot you can crock, or cover the drainage hole, very simply, as I have explained, with a couple of overlapping shards, but plastic pots are a different story. In most of them not only are the drainage holes small but they are spread over the base of the pot and much more dry-well material is needed. Rare and admirable plastic pots have enormous bottom holes, and some are made with long slit drainage vents and additional holes where the side walls

of the pot join the base. We should make a point of asking for these particularly well-vented plastic pots, for plants do much better in them. Turning over any plastic pot you may be buying and giving your opinion of the drainage arrangements eventually will have an effect, particularly if enough of us do it. As a gardener you will have no trouble with internal drainage in plastic pots if you make sure that you have provided enough crocking to produce a really fast runoff.

Another problem arises in the feeding of plants. The usual practice is either to scratch plant food into the topsoil and water it in or dissolve the food in a water-soluble solution. Most of us overfeed our plants; we are inclined to feel that a little extra will do no harm and may do good —this is a great mistake. If you overfeed a plant in a clay pot, the surplus salts will leach through the pot sides together with the surplus water. The green scum which grows on clay pots is always a sign of overfeeding. It is a form of algae that grows on the unused fertilizer. By disposing of the surplus in this way, pot soil in clay does not get so overloaded with excess salts that the root hairs are burned. However, if the gardener persists in overwatering and overfeeding a plant even in a clay pot, the resulting scum does eventually block the access of air and water through the pot sides. Clay pots covered with green scum should always be cleaned, and the gardening habits of the owner should undergo an agonizing reappraisal.

In a plastic pot the soil cannot rescue itself in the same way. Because excess salts cannot leach out, they will build up to great potency within the pot—usually leading to a sudden unexpected collapse of the plant from which it will never recover, because its feeding roots have been destroyed. It is necessary to follow the directions for applying fertilizer extremely carefully, but during my years of indoor growing I have yet to see the recommended proportions varied according to the type of pot the plant is in. It is therefore good sense to give half the suggested amount, about half as often, to any plant that is not in a clay pot. This rough rule of thumb has worked well for me.

One great advantage of the fact that salts cannot work their way through plastic pot sides is the fact that the outside always stays clean, and the inside can be wiped clean with a single swipe of a sponge. This is a help to the harried indoor gardener when repotting is needed. Plants must not go into dirty pots and an encrusted clay pot that has been put aside and allowed to dry out is a menace to clean properly. It will be necessary to use hot water and steel wool before it is reasonably well scoured. When it is clean, it must be set aside and allowed to dry thoroughly. Soil put into a wet clay pot will cling to the sides, undoing all the previous work and setting up danger zones for the feeding roots. There is another advantage to the plastic pot. If it has been absent-mindedly put away dirty, not only will it wash clean without any scrubbing, but also it can be immediately dried with a cloth.

Once the problem of the new kind of handling is mastered there are a good many other advantages to plastic pots. They don't break as easily. They will, however, often get a hairline crack along the side if they are dropped when full of earth. This often goes unnoticed by the grower but not by the plant. With a hairline crack in the pot, water will run out without penetrating the bottom of the pot and cause poor growth. Another hazard of plastic pots is picking them up by the rim when they are full. This produces a sort of Mad Hatter's bite, and again the root ball will be left improperly watered. Any plant in a pot with this sort of broken rim must be repotted. Despite these problems the breakage loss with plastic is nothing compared with clay pots.

A further great advantage of plastic pots is that the soil remains evenly moist in them much longer than in clay. This makes them better able to survive absent-minded or absentee owners. Plants in plastic pots can survive weekends, for instance, without watering where those in clay pots might perish. The fact that they don't weigh so much is a great asset, particularly where large plants are concerned. The lighter weight of plastic bulb pans also makes a great difference in the process of forcing, which always calls for a great deal of carrying the pots around. Above all, plastic pots are best for plants that need a period of waterless dormancy. This is a subject that will be dealt with more fully later on; here suffice it to say that more plants will survive this resting period if they go through it in plastic rather than in clay pots.

Another new type of pot is the one made of styrofoam. It has not been on the market long enough for me to have had a varied experience with it, but some generalizations are possible. Styrofoam is feather-light and knocks over rather easily. The advertisements claim that it is sufficiently porous so that air can pass through as it does in clay, but that water cannot do so. This is stressed as an advantage, both because the pots will not grow "disfiguring" algae, but also because the pot will retain moisture better than a clay pot while stimulating the soil inside by the free passage of air through it. If this is indeed the case, then it will be necessary to learn yet another style of pot care. With free air passage but water retention inside the pot, the interaction of these two elements upon the feeding roots must follow a different pattern from either clay or plastic pots. For a pot that is not water-porous, the drainage holes in styrofoam pots are woefully inadequate. So far I have not been at all successful with plants I have grown in them. They have not died, but neither have they made any progress: the top growth has been curiously inhibited, and the roots have not developed. Furthermore, plants that were left for a couple of months in styro-foam before repotting took very much longer starting up into active growth than plants knocked out straightaway and grown under other-wise identical circumstances. It seems certain to me that there was some mismanagement on my part and that it will be necessary to understand the special treatment that styrofoam pots obviously require. Styrofoam does not readily break, but it does dent extremely easily. It also has the capacity, perhaps peculiar to me, of setting my teeth on edge when working with it. The pots and small seed boxes come in a rather glaring white, which may not grow algae but get very dirty and are impossible to clean. There are some that have been colored to look like clay pots, but I feel the less said about them the better.

Some of the advantages of styrofoam are obvious. The pot walls are very thick and provide good insulation against heat. The rim of the pot is also soft. This has been made a strong selling point because it cuts down the danger from petiole rot. This is a fungus disease that attacks a leafstalk that has been injured by resting on either a sharp pot rim, as with plastic, or the rim of a clay pot that is full of excess salts. It is a problem that is more serious with large-scale growers of plants than with most indoor gardeners. Petiole rot does occasionally attack African violet leaves or the leaves of primroses. A way to prevent this without using styrofoam pots is to dip the rim of any other type of pot into melted paraffin wax. Do this a couple of times, letting the wax harden between each dipping, and your rim will be most effectively cushioned.

Another pot that is now appearing with increasing frequency is one made of a kind of flexible plastic or rubberlike material. This type I find quite lethal. Home horticulturists would be well advised to repot any plant they might buy in such a pot. Flexible pot sides do enormous damage to the roots resting against them. Also, there seems to be something toxic to plants in the material from which these pots are made. I ran a test with what had been a flourishing pot of ivy. I never touched the pot, so there was no danger of mechanical damage, and the conditions were almost idyllic for ivy. The control plants in different pots grew like mad, but this particular plant deteriorated.

Imported terra-cotta pots from Italy are now quite a status symbol. They are magnificent objects, usually extremely expensive and also rather heavy. Some of them have molded rims and other embossed decorative features. If algae are allowed to accumulate within these moldings, the pot cannot be fully cleared of it. Be extremely careful not to overwater or overfeed plants in a decorated clay pot. There is also a new design in domestic clay pots. They now have a more vaselike shape and a very thin rim. This style looks nice but has some great drawbacks. The thin rim breaks so easily that the pots are almost impossible to stack and store. The new interior shape is also so distinctive that transferring a pot-bound plant from one of these vase-shaped pots into a more conventional-shaped pot is impossible without doing serious damage by compression. This calls for quite an investment, if it is always necessary to have the special shape on hand every time a change of pot size is needed. It is also highly inconvenient!

Some plants need exceptionally fast drainage, orchids for instance, and there are clay pots especially designed for them. In an emergency it is possible to increase the size of the original drainage hole in a clay pot. To do this you need that almost prehistoric tool, an ice pick. Turn the pot over and set the pick at a sloping angle against the edge of the hole; give the handle a series of cautious little taps with a hammer and small chips will break away. You can twist the pot slowly around, enlarging the whole drainage area as you go. Very often you will end up with a mess of additional potting shards, but it is perfectly possible, with care, to open up clay pots this way. You can enlarge the drainage vents in plastic pots with a red-hot screwdriver, but this is a very smelly operation and usually not very successful.

No doubt still more pot novelties will be on the market within a few years. Whether they will do a better job than those now available, there is no way of telling. But whatever appears in the pot world, the good grower will use it experimentally and not assume that it can be treated exactly like the ones that have gone before. In this way there will always be plenty of pots to suit everyone's taste and particular skills.

Potting On

Flourishing houseplants are always an extremely pleasant sight, particularly if we have grown them ourselves. But to keep plants remaining in excellent condition over a long period, you have to look ahead and make certain that their root systems have enough space and nourishment to support the good top growth. Any thriving houseplant, whether it's being grown for foliage or flowers, eventually will need potting on—that is, being given a larger pot and fresh soil—if it is to continue to be your pride and delight.

Once you have mastered the art of watering plants and adjusting pot soil to their individual requirements, you will be rewarded by great thrusts of growth. But horticultural success, like any other kind of success, brings its own problems and the one that will now confront you is how to prevent your plants from becoming pot-bound. In nature, plants expand their root systems in proportion to the foliage spread. You may have noticed that men feeding trees insert the food along the outer perimeter of the branch spread, for that is where the feeding roots lie. Potted plants have a very difficult time, particularly if there is full top growth. Roots are exceptionally determined things and can

Pot-bound plant

force their way through cracks in cement or rock, but they cannot penetrate an entirely solid surface. In a pot they will grow outward until they reach the rigid limits of their prison. Prevented from going farther, they don't give up but instead turn inward and twist around inside their own root ball until they have taken up all the available space and driven the soil itself out of the pot. A badly pot-bound plant has roots that are a matted, tangled mass which fills the entire pot.

BASIC CARE

Unless a plant in this condition is moved to a larger pot it will suffer irreparable damage and will become a caricature of its former self. A serious pot-bound condition of this sort obviously does not occur overnight. Indoor horticulturists should be watchful of any plant that is growing particularly well and try to anticipate the increase in root growth and do something about it in good time.

That rare bird, the perfect gardener, knocks out his growing plants at regular intervals to see how they are getting on. Most of us have not reached that plateau of excellence, and we are reminded that we ought to do something about pot roots when the plant sends us out some rather strong signals. These, by the way, are not by any means early warning signals, but rather urgent cries for help! One such sign is a spread of feeding roots through the drainage holes in the pot as the roots thrust out fiercely in search of additional food. This practice is very dangerous to the plant. Wandering roots carry the vital hair roots at their tips and these, unprotected by pot or soil, are liable to desperate damage. A plant that is pot-bound will also wilt in spite of normal watering. You treat it as usual in the morning and by midafternoon it suddenly collapses. This is because there is no soil left inside the pot to absorb water, so the daily drink just rushes through the pot without doing much good.

A pot-bound plant will also shed its lower leaves; they turn yellow and die. Plants show amazing tenacity in staying alive, but in order to survive, the growing point, which is the tip end of each stem, must be kept adequately supplied with nourishment. Plants will sacrifice all other leaves so that they can sustain the vitality of the growing tip.

Growing point

Leaves that have died because the moisture they needed has been diverted into the all-important tip will never grow in again. So if your plant has become so badly pot-bound that it has had to make the choice between keeping itself alive by sending all the nutrients into the top or

losing its lower leaves, it will always choose to save the tip. In consequence the over-all appearance will be ruined even after you have got
around to potting it on.

Another bad sign is a deterioration in the size of the leaves. The
plant uses this trick to try to conserve limited nourishment. Bonsai, or
the miniaturizing of trees, works on this principle. New leaves are
always small but, like babies, they ought to grow. If leaves in a plant
fail to develop to their normal size, the roots are almost certainly
getting dangerously pot-bound.

It will take you a little time to recognize these various signals
correctly. Occasionally you will knock out a plant and find there was no
need. Only experience will teach you when the identical symptoms
really come from some other cause. But if there is no sign of overexuberant root growth, just put the pot back over the root ball like a hat,
turn it over and give the pot a rap to settle it into place, and the plant
will never know the difference. But don't wait until the root ball is
hopelessly tangled before repotting. If white root tips are showing all
around the compressed potting soil, the right moment is at hand. If you
wait too long, not only will the plant lose needed nourishment but also
the roots will overwhelm the crocks that covered the drainage holes.
Disentangling crocks, which has to be done, invariably damages the
roots, and, if the roots have worked out through the drainage holes,
drawing them back in again as you depot the plant will do yet more
injury. None of us can go on potting up plants indefinitely; we haven't
the room. But a valuable plant is usually worth at least one and
sometimes two moves up.

Well-grown foliage plants should go into new pots that have about
one inch of clear space around the whole circumference of the root ball.
Don't try and save yourself later trouble by putting your plant into a
pot very much larger than the one it is now occupying. This is a
technique known professionally as "jumping" a plant, and it takes a
professional grower to bring it off successfully. One reason for not
doing this is that a little plant in a large pot looks both silly and
pathetic; furthermore, it will not thrive. Pot soil remains in good
condition only when it has active roots at work inside. As has been
explained, foraging roots take up moisture and aerate the soil. In a
"jumped" plant, the working roots extend into only a small part of the
pot soil. In consequence, no matter how carefully you water, the outer

part of the earth inside the large pot will gradually become sodden and sour and your plant will first "pingle"—a family term for slow deterioration—and then die. So don't use a new pot that is more than two sizes larger than the one the plant is in. Pots, by the way, are measured across the diameter of the top, and they increase by ½-inch sizes. What will happen to me and many others when the metric system becomes universal in this particular matter, I cannot imagine!

Always be sure the fresh pot is clean and properly crocked. Unless the plant has been having watering problems, which might be solved by changing the type of pot, it is best to use the same material it has been in before. Like most of us, plants dislike any fundamental change in their style of life. Another reason for not changing from clay to plastic, or vice versa, is the difference in the inside of the two types of pots. Clay has an entirely smooth interior and the knocked-out root ball conforms exactly to the smooth contour. Plastic pots are molded with an inside rim, and if a plant gets pot-bound in a plastic pot you will have roots tangled along the rim as well as inside the pot itself. To transfer a pot-bound plant from a plastic pot into a clay pot, you will have to "jump" several sizes in order to accommodate the matted rim roots. It is also extremely difficult to work soil underneath this rim when you are repotting in a differently shaped pot. Nevertheless, if you are moving up a very large plant that has been in a clay pot, a change of pot type is obviously better for reasons of weight.

For potting on, you should prepare your appropriate soil mix beforehand. If you don't know what kind of soil the plant prefers, it is well worth while to look up its requirements in a simple plant dictionary. Appropriate soil, as has been stressed earlier, can make an enormous difference to plant health. Prepare a lot more soil than you think necessary; you can always store any surplus in a plastic bag, tightly sealed to keep the moisture in. There is nothing more exasperating, or nothing that happens with greater regularity, than finding yourself running out of soil halfway through a repotting job. It does your temper no good, and it may do the plant permanent harm if the root ball dries out while you whip up a second batch of soil. In an emergency of this sort, either use wet paper toweling or slip the root ball of the plant into one of those invaluable plastic bags. Your aim in either case is, of course, to keep the feeding roots damp.

Put the coarsest material you can find over the crocks at the bottom of the pot. Half-decayed leaves from the garden are good, while the gardenless gardener can use ½ inch of perlite. Next should come a pad of fresh soil. You will have to make a rough judgment about the proper amount to put in. You want your repotted plant to stand about half an inch below the rim of the pot for proper watering. Be careful not to

½"
below
rim
don't bury the
original surface
of the soil.

bury the original surface of the soil. Everyone, including land developers, needs to be reminded that a change in soil level is usually fatal to a tree or plants. A good plan is to knock out the plant so as to make a rough judgment. But as you are not yet quite ready to repot, cover the root ball with wet toweling. The main problem in potting is to make sure that the new soil is properly pressed against the old root ball throughout the pot. Roots will not stir into new growth unless they feel the pressure of earth against them. For the novice it is often quite hard to make sure the earth is really settled against the roots in the narrow area at the bottom of the pot. It helps this problem if you will make a kind of graham-cracker crust with fresh soil as a paste to line the sides of the pot. Then, after you have decided upon the necessary amount of the fresh bottom soil, scoop out a kind of earthen bird's nest and drop the old root ball into the center. If you next give the pot a slight rap, by banging the base on a table, the plastered earth will fall in around the bottom roots.

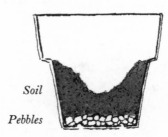

Soil

Pebbles

You should also have some implement with which you can press the new soil into place. A paint stirrer does a good job. You can get it into the narrow space between the sides of the pot and the old root mass, and, as it has a flat base, it will do a good job of compressing the new soil without injuring the old roots. Twist the pot around as you work and dribble the new soil in on all sides. Always try to make certain you have centered the plant. Put in off-center, it is always going to look like what it is—an amateur job badly done. All the time you are dribbling in the new soil, you should thump the pot every so often on the table. This action is not just horticultural totemism, it has a point. By banging the pot, the earth settles in securely without leaving air pockets. These can easily form if a piece of roughage sticks between the sides of the pot and roots will not pass through an air space. This banging is the spring signal call of all the neighborhood horticulturists as they repot their plants.

Once the soil level rises so that you can reach it with your fingers, press the new soil into position with your thumbs. There are excellent gardeners who work in gloves; I don't happen to be one of them. But gloved or naked, your hands are one of your most important gardening tools. Don't make the mistake of using your thumbs close to the stem of the plant in order to force the old root ball down. This can cause great damage; pressure on the soil should only be applied around the rim of the pot.

Some plants need what is called "hard potting." Geraniums and azaleas are two examples. In their case, the new soil encircling the old root ball needs to be rammed down. This you can do with any implement that fits the space and has a round end. I normally use a hammer handle, but most gardeners are ingenious enough to devise something that suits them. Hard potting is accompanied by even noisier thumping than regular potting, for the pot soil needs very tight packing. While you work, earth will spill over the table and over all the newspapers you have set out. When you bang your pot up and down, you very often bang it onto some of this spilled earth, and, as a result, soil gets clogged into the drainage hole. Once the plant is reset, your first action should be to turn it over, which, incidentally, will also show you whether you have planted it in firmly enough, and clean out the drainage holes with a small stick. After that, water the plant thoroughly until the excess runs out. Then set it aside, out of the sunlight, whether you have done the job outdoors or inside. The pot should stand on a dry well of pebbles, which can be kept moist, but water should not be allowed to rise over the bottom of the pot. Probably the plant will show not the slightest sign of distress, but, if it should wilt, spray the foliage with a mister. But keep your hands off the watering can until the topsoil looks dry again. Released from its strait jacket, the plant soon will start to grow and can usually be returned to its normal position within a week.

But the job is not finished until you have washed the pot from which you took the plant in the first place. There's a sort of Parkinson's law in horticulture which says that the pot you need most in an emergency is always a dirty pot. If you keep all your stored pots clean you can for once avert the Fates!

2 ❧ DISPLAY

Window Displays

People put plants in a window to give them the best possible light. But two or three different kinds of potted plants standing forlornly in individual saucers on a window sill do not do much either for the room or the grower's self-confidence; the effect is puny and uninteresting, and plants arranged this way are a nuisance to water.

The effect will be much better if you group your plants. For a start, try putting a tray on the window sill and filling it with small stones; roofing pebbles are the best color, if you can get them, but an excellent aggregate is also available. Avoid those glaring white or, worse still, parti-colored pebbles that are sold in florists' shops; these discolor very quickly and detract from the plants. All plants look more important set together on stones on a tray. It is worth reiterating that after watering, the runoff of the surplus through the drainage holes will evaporate from the stones and surround the plants with that pleasant humid atmosphere so essential to good growth.

Trays can be made of a great many materials, and any one of them will serve the purpose, as long as they are waterproof and have enough depth and lip to hold at least an inch of pebbles. For modern windows with no sill, you can add a hinged shelf that can be let down when the plant area is not in use. There are good plastic growing trays that come in just the correct depth but usually in rather poor colors. If you shop around a little, you can find these plastic trays in colors that look more attractive in most people's rooms—there is no need to settle for that hideous poison green. Make sure that you are buying a tray without bottom drainage holes, for some plastic plant trays are sold with open spaces at the bottom. Inexpensive tin and enamel trays can be used, but it is as well to treat these with a rust inhibitor before putting them into use—or one morning the entire base may horrify you by quietly disintegrating. A tray that fits the window area exactly looks best and can be custom-made by any sheet-metal supplier. These are usually constructed in rustproof galvanized iron, but they also can be made of aluminum or copper. Copper sheeting, which takes on a beautiful patina and always fits any room style, is expensive, but it is the easiest material for the home handyman to handle and it will last fore er. It and aluminum can be cut and held together with the new Epoxy adhesives. You will be well advised to put a very thick sheet of plastic between any tray and the woodwork, if you cherish your paint.

Having decided to change the way in which you show your plants, the next matter to be considered is the kind of window you have. Is it warm or do you always feel a draught near it? Is it sunless but very bright? Very sunny? Betwixt and between? Or has it a dull exposure onto an inner courtyard? Whatever kind you have available, the determined indoor gardener can find something that will grow. But when you are matching your plants to your exposure, you must also consider the temperature of your window—not only by day but also at night. It is not stressed enough that the temperature a plant collection is exposed to by night, as well as the exposure by day, makes an enormous difference not only to its general health but also to the kinds of plants that can be grown. To discover what goes on in your window by night, install a maximum/minimum thermometer. This, as long as you reset it each day, will tell you how high the window heat rose during daylight hours and how low it fell by night. Maximum/minimum thermometers are quite expensive, but they make a wonderful present and never wear out. For the beginning gardener they are the only slightly costly piece of equipment which I feel is really essential. They make all the difference in choosing suitable plants for available positions and can save you endless replacement of ruined and equally expensive plant material.

Flowering plants, for instance, need a drop by night of from 5 to 8 degrees if they are to continue opening their buds, and most foliage plants will thrive better with an equally marked change. In our grandparents' houses there were coal furnaces that were damped down at night for economy's sake. This cooled off the entire house and the plants loved it. For that reason we, with all our modern aids, cannot always grow some varieties of plants as well as our great aunts! House owners who care about their plants should always lower the thermostat at night, and so, of course, should people living in apartments who have some control over the heat. Indoor gardening is the most difficult for apartment dwellers who have no individual thermostats but are forced to live in that modern Utopia, a place with "even heat by day and night." Opening your bedroom window at night may solve the problem slightly for you, but it's going to do the plants in the living room no good at all. If you are faced with a heating situation of this sort, you should concentrate largely upon tropical plants that grow naturally without very much variation in temperature levels.

If the only available plant window remains 68 to 70 degrees by night, it should be considered a warm window. If it also gets little or no sun, this is the place where foliage plants will do best. It is possible to make a very pleasant arrangement by grouping inexpensive leafy plants. Such a position would also be excellent for ferns, bromeliads, and the Christmas cactus. At this stage I am not discussing the actual handling of such plants; that will come later. Instead, I only want to generalize about which group does best in certain conditions.

All windows look better if the surrounding framework is softened with hanging plants. But always keep your trailing plants under control; there's no need to have them dripping drearily in a tangle of thin stalks. Hanging plants need more water than those standing on pebbles. To avoid a daily cascade of water down your sleeve, from holding a watering can overhead, try using ice cubes straight from the icebucket. Put them like a diamond necklace around the rim of the pot. They will dissolve slowly and the soil will absorb the moisture evenly, and those maddening drips will be avoided. Also, no matter what you fear, the ice cubes will not hurt the plants.

A bright but sunless window is the best possible exposure for summering houseplants that can't be placed out-of-doors. So never feel ill-treated if that is your only growing area; you may, in the long run, do better with your plants than the neighbor with the sunny window.

Indoor horticulturists who possess a warm, sunny window can make more use of flowering plants. Any plant you want to make bloom or keep in bloom enjoys winter sunlight, even those usually classed as shade-lovers, such as the African violet and the various begonias. Despite frequent grim warnings, leave them in the sun without a qualm from October until late spring. After that, the light may be too strong and the shade-lovers should be pulled back. It is usually lack of sunlight that causes all those numerous complaints about non-blossoming African violets. A warm, sunny window is excellent for seasonal displays of poinsettias and lilies and it is a good position for a collection of succulents or cacti. Foliage plants with strong leaf coloring, such as crotons or tradescantias, also need warmth and sunlight to hold their interesting markings and to keep the color intense.

The only blossoming plants that will not have a very long life in a warm, sunny window are the magnificent flowering plants that appear in midwinter—the azaleas, cyclamen, and primulas. These plants need a cool location even by day. Conscientious dealers label them as needing very cool living conditions. At night they must be where the temperature falls as low as 60 degrees if they are to continue long in flower. It is possible for the home grower with a little ingenuity to produce such an area, and I will describe how to do so further on. But unless you can meet these rather specialized requirements, don't expect all the buds that come on those plants to open out or the foliage to remain long in good condition.

Most windows are not large enough to take many plants without overcrowding. You'll get more plants in, and improve the general effect, if you produce a variation in the levels at which the plants are displayed by lifting some of them up above the others. Showing plants off at different levels is called "staging." The term comes from the days when people had gardeners to grow the plants into peak perfection in a detached greenhouse. When they reached full bloom they were brought to the house and displayed or staged in a conservatory attached to one of the living rooms. I grew up with such a system, and I well remember the great seasonal changes: autumn when the chrysanthemums came in, remaining there through Christmas, as we then did not use poinsettias; midwinter when azaleas, cyclamen, and cinerarias took over the picture; spring brought bulbs and primulas; and summer, the heavy scent of lilies. The pots were staged on stepped wooden benches, not unlike modern bleacher seats, and they stood in their magnificence, each able to be shown off without hiding the one behind it.

This kind of plant display has gone almost as completely as the dinosaur, but the art of staging on a much smaller scale should not be allowed to be forgotten. Staging gives any grower much more space for his plants either in a window or in a small greenhouse; it makes it possible to use more plants and show them off highly dramatically, and

DISPLAY

it can be done quite simply. To lift up plants in a window, use something transparent. This prevents the light being blocked from the plants near to the room and also gives a rather entrancing floating effect. You can use inverted Mason jars, glass bricks one on top of the other, or narrow hollow plastic tubes with rigid sides. These can be obtained from manufacturers of chemical supplies and are expensive. Their great advantage is that, being narrow, they take up much less room and they can be cut to any size you wish. If you can possibly

Use of transparent jars, bricks, and tubes for staging

afford them, two or three of these tubes used in a window to raise your plants will transform an ordinary plant collection into a scene of high drama! Admittedly you will have to master the art of getting the plants balanced on the tubes and this will not be achieved without a few noisy calamities, but with practice you get the trick.

If you decide to try to stage, your window will look more effective if you will treat it just like a conservatory, using it only as a showplace and not somewhere to grow plants. For growing purposes you will need yet another window. Bushy plants with thick leaves, like chrysanthemums, poinsettias, or cyclamen, stage beautifully, and, if you will buy them in bud and not full bloom, they will last a long time. Small plants like African violets, or plants with thin leaves and long, skinny blossom stalks like marguerites, do not mass so well. A staged window also always looks better if you will use only one kind of plant. I personally also prefer a single color, but white can always be used as a blend for mixed colors. An obvious disadvantage is the cost of buying enough plants to make such a display and the fact that, bought at the same time, they will all also fade at the same time. In most windows there probably will not be room for more than three or four big flowering plants. Grouped together these will last much longer than they would if you placed them here and there around the room. They also hide each other's deficiencies when they are massed. If you set the initial cost of such a display against the cost of quick-dying cut flowers, the massed window will seem much less of an extravagance, for it makes such an effect that usually no other flowers are needed anywhere else in the room.

Any staged window looks best framed with long-lasting tall plants. In a warm window a pair of dracaenas, one elevated behind the other on each side, will last the entire season and point up the display. Evergreen plants of this sort also cut down the number of flowering plants that have to be bought. It is also possible to make a highly effective staged window using only one kind of foliage plant. I have occasionally done this when I have had nothing in bloom, but the general effect is sometimes a little somber because it darkens the room even though it looks well. Elevated massed foliage plants absorb a great deal of light.

With a staged window it is sometimes an improvement to put small plants along the room side of the base of the tray—a process called "facing down." This gives a very pleasant effect as long as it is not overdone in an attempt to hide the mechanics of staging. An all-out attempt to conceal the way the plants have been lifted up would mean crowding the facing-down plants very closely together. This never works; crowded plants deteriorate and ruin the very effect they are supposed to enhance.

Plants in full bloom will last longer if they are not given lavish watering. Budded plants need a great deal of water, but as the flowers open the amount should be tapered off. If the staged plants are in plastic pots, saucers will not be needed underneath them, but in that case the pebbled tray often becomes a watery swamp. Should that happen, put saucers turned the wrong way up onto the pebbles and stand the plants that are at ground level on them. In this way they will stay clear of possible root rot at their base, and all the plants in the window will get the advantage of heavy atmospheric evaporation from the wet tray. Obviously if you overwater to the extent that you could have goldfish in your tray, you must bail out some of the water and be a little more sparing in the future!

The plants that come to us labeled "warm conditions" dislike drafts more than anything else. I therefore do not follow the advice that I constantly see repeated that it helps plants to open a window near them in the room. If I leave the door open, the house heat is triggered off and, if I shut the door, the room itself becomes too quickly chilled off in cold weather to suit delicate plants. Turning down the thermostat if you are going to be out all day is far better for the plants, and usually they can get enough fresh air from leaking windows to keep them going. It has been my experience that most plants that want warm conditions can take much cooler living quarters, if that is all that is available, so long as they are accustomed to them gradually. You cannot take a plant that has been raised in a hot, humid greenhouse and put it, safely, into a very cold plant window. But often that same plant will do perfectly well in the cold window if you are able to condition it slowly to the change in temperature. Most plant windows are improved if it is possible to have some small ventilating pane that opens within the window area itself. This can be used to control the inside heat and a crack open all day will often provide the necessary cool conditions for plants that must be so treated, without freezing the rest of the house.

Those midwinter spectacular flowering plants that demand cold conditions at night will do even better if you are ingenious enough to provide them with living quarters in which they are protected not only from the freezing weather out-of-doors but also from the house heat inside. Plants needing this additional cold will do well in a bay window or window seat where the temperature is always a little lower than the rest of the room. Azaleas, cyclamen, and all the members of the primula family like bright light, though not necessarily sunshine, once they have been brought into bloom, and they will continue opening

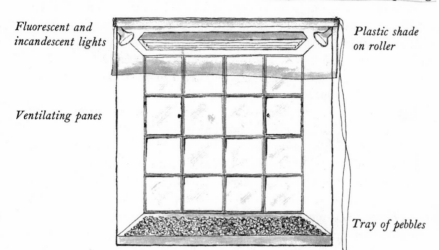

Fluorescent and incandescent lights

Plastic shade on roller

Ventilating panes

Tray of pebbles

their buds so long as they can have a drop of at least 10 degrees by night. I stumbled by chance on an easy way to provide these plants, which are the backbone of any midwinter flowering display, with this kind of growing condition. During the World War II blackouts, our plant window had to have heavy curtains rigged up that could be drawn in front of it after dark. Up till then I had always faithfully believed the advice I read everywhere that shutting out the house heat by the use of thick curtains would freeze the plants left isolated behind them. This proved totally incorrect because the azaleas, which were then on show not only survived but improved. In a few weeks it was obvious that they were doing much better than usual; not only were the flowers lasting longer but the foliage looked healthier. Later, when flexible plastic appeared on the market, I installed a plastic blind that allowed me to see the plants at night but still shut out a great deal of the house heat. I then found that plants that needed warm growing conditions did not do particularly well if I left the blind down by day and by night; this kept them too long at too cool a temperature. The cool-loving plants, on the other hand, reveled in an arrangement in which the plastic blind always stayed down, all the time, for this held the house heat at bay by day and still allowed the heavy drop by night, with the window temperature occasionally falling as low as the high forties. In very cold weather I raise the blind slightly at the bottom so that some house heat can get in and prevent cold, stagnant air which can damage even the hardiest plant. This very simple arrangement has worked like a charm for me for years. I have also seen some very good variations on the same theme in which the plastic curtain is replaced by sliding glass doors. With my plastic blind I created the equivalent of a cold conservatory in my room—a place where even camellias will open all their buds, and anyone who has ever tried to grow camellias indoors knows what a problem bud drop normally can be.

Before embarking on something like this, you can test out the idea by tacking a sheet of wide transparent plastic in front of a window: thumbtacks will hold the sheeting in place at the top while the lower end can be held taut by rolling the sheet around one of those bamboo poles and thumbtacking it in place. A makeshift arrangement of this kind is a little harder to get behind when it is necessary to water, but it has exactly the same effect of lowering the interior temperature and providing a wonderful place for expensive plants like cyclamen to live for months on end. I possess both a roller-blind window and a home-made job, and they both have functioned flawlessly. I heartily recommend experimenting with them.

But even when the plants and window exposure have been well matched and you have arranged a fine staged display, there is still another dimension available—the effect given by night lighting. You will get a bigger bonus for your trouble, if you show off the plants with lights. A lighted window brings pleasure to you and to any passer-by, and it also does the plants a great deal of good. With such a combination, how could anyone fail to make light available? You can light any plant window extremely simply by means of two 100-watt lamps placed in the corners of the window frame. Some kind of arrangement should be made so that the bulbs are hidden on the room side, a very simple panel of wood or small valance will do the job. Extra light hours always help plants, particularly during the very short winter daylight hours. Your plants will enjoy the three or four hours of extra light that comes from illuminating them by night. But if you want to use lighting in your window to produce real improvement in the life of a plant, it is worth considering installing long fluorescent light tubes under a reflector. These lights have the effect of daylight upon the plants in some respects, and they produce extremely powerful light without the heat that would come from an equal intensity of incandescent light. I use fluorescent lighting in my bay window by having it set into the ceiling above the plants, but it could also be installed along the side of the window frame—just so long as there were a reflector behind to keep the glare off the room side. These lights will not bring a plant to bud and bloom (this is a matter which will be considered in Chapter 10), but they will help a well-budded plant open into full flower and provide the needed light for active formation of plant energy. They also have

Cold window display of cyclamen and English ivy

an additional advantage in that they prevent the plants from all turning toward the natural daylight and presenting their worst side to their owners.

Fluorescent lighting is rather harsh, and I dislike it at night. That cold gleam reminds me too much of a filling station. Plants don't care when they get extra light so long as they get a fixed ration every twenty-four hours. I therefore have my fluorescent lights set into an inexpensive timer that turns them on very early in the morning and shuts them off at dusk. When I want to enjoy the window in the evening, I turn on the pair of incandescent lamps that are also installed in the two corners. Don't overdo the matter of artificial light by putting the lamps onto one of those photoelectric cells that turns on at dusk and off a dawn. That way the plants will get no darkness, which they must have for some period every day. Deprived entirely of their rest, plants will slowly die from exhaustion.

I use lights to supplement daylight not only in my winter windows but even on my summer porch. I find them invaluable at any season for the health of my plants and for my own pleasure.

Accent Plants and Floor Arrangements

Not everybody has a plant window where he can grow plants. Indeed, not all indoor horticulturists want to use their window areas for displaying plants. Some people prefer to show big individual plants as accents within the room area itself, which is a dramatic and exciting way to handle them. The most outstanding examples of using large-scale potted plants can be seen nowadays in many public buildings where the emphasis is very much on living material and the effect is often breath-taking. Something on a slightly smaller scale can also be produced at home, though at quite a cost, for large and dramatic plants are often dramatically expensive. But if the right plant is chosen for the right place, it can be extremely long-lasting and well worth the initial outlay.

The use indoors of single big plants is, in fact, a revival of a previous fashion. Some of us can recall large rubber trees blocking the front-room window; other families made it a practice to board their stupendous palms at the local greenhouse before they went on their annual holiday. And everywhere, huge Boston ferns cascading proudly from bamboo plant stands were as much part of the furnishings of an average house as the hat rack in the hall. When a fashion revives it generally does so in a modified form, and this has been the case in our present-day interest in specimen plants. Our tastes and how we use the plants have changed. Nowadays they are an integral part of the whole decor of a room instead of being in the middle of a window, blocking out the light. Whereas our grandparents could not do this, we are able to because of the greater variety of plants now available. Among them are those suited to the very bright light of modern glass-fronted offices and window walls, as well as those that prefer more filtered light farther back in the room.

Because modern houses are so warm, most of the large specimen plants considered best for the indoor horticulturists are tropical plants. Some of these are old friends that were popular in the old heyday of big plants. Others have very recently been made available in large quantity to the ordinary grower. But even familiar plants come to us today in new and interesting forms and with a greater built-in tolerance for difficult growing conditions. We also have horticultural advantages that our forebears did not have. We no longer have to struggle against the death-dealing fumes of manufactured gas. We have lightweight pots, packaged soil, and substitute soil mixes. There are modern insect repellents to kill the pests that no good grower ought to have but which most horticulturists find sooner or later on their plants! We have new fertilizers that can be used indoors without driving the owner out-of-doors and, above all, we now understand that artificial light can be used to encourage plants. But everything is not coming up roses. We also have to contend with some difficulties that our ancestors did not. The atmosphere of our rooms is too hot and dry for most plants and, unless we can make some special provisions, we have to rely very largely on plants from tropical areas that are largely foliage, not flowering, plants. These tropical plants are best able to adjust to modern man's idea of a suitable indoor temperature, but, during the process of living by night and day in heat of around 70 degrees or over, these plants lose a great deal of moisture through their leaves in a process called transpiration. This they must replace daily, not only through water drawn up by the root system but also from the humidity of the atmosphere.

DISPLAY

The process of transpiration, and its replacement from atmospheric humidity, is carried out by a series of minute openings called stomata, which exist both on and under all leaves. Big plants, by their very size, lose an enormous amount of water through the leaves and will do badly unless you compensate with additional humidity. When the house air is too dry, the edges of the leaves turn brown and unsightly, or the lower leaves yellow and fall off. It should be constantly reiterated that leaves lost in this way will never be replaced.

Big plants, used individually, should always be put in plastic pots, which hold moisture better around the roots. They also should stand on as wide a saucer as possible, with a deep spread of pebbles at their base. They urgently need the moisture that will evaporate from this area. A large plant may need daily water if it is in full sunlight. If it stands in filtered light, watch the topsoil and water it only when dry. Misting large specimen plants on and below the leaf surface is essential. If all this seems a lot of trouble, think back to the initial cost of the plant!

The problem of providing enough humidity for big houseplants is often solved in public buildings by the use of a planter. These are the large boxes, sometimes lit with fluorescent lights, that are used as space dividers in offices, banks, and restaurants. Enormous planters are not possible for ordinary indoor horticulturists, but, whenever you grow plants together, they help each other by transpiring around each other's foliage and in that way creating among themselves extra humidity and forming what horticulturists call a microclimate. Planters serve this need excellently. If you want to attempt a home-size planter, try to find or have made a sturdy box deeper than your largest pot and about 18 inches across. It will be easier to handle and give you greater flexibility in its use if it is on casters. A first attempt with a planter box can be very simple. Paint the outside a color that suits the room, and line the inside with strong plastic (like that used for shower-curtain liners) which you can staple in place. Next fill the box to a considerable depth with pebbles or aggregate to form a good dry well. Put some upturned pots on the pebbles and stand your plants on the pots. You may have to change the size of the upturned pots to accommodate them to the size of the planted pots, for, as you make your arrangement with the tall potted plants at the back of the box and the smaller ones in front, the various pot rims should all rise to the same level. Put damp peat moss around the pots and about halfway up—this will provide for a steady evaporation of moisture around the plants. The wet peat moss also cuts down on the amount of watering they will need. By standing the plants on pots on the pebble base, you are still providing good drainage. It is a good idea to bore a bung or drain hole into the bottom of the box, which you can keep closed with a cork. This enables you to empty the dry well of surplus water. If you don't have a vent of this kind, the peat moss will very soon become a swamp.

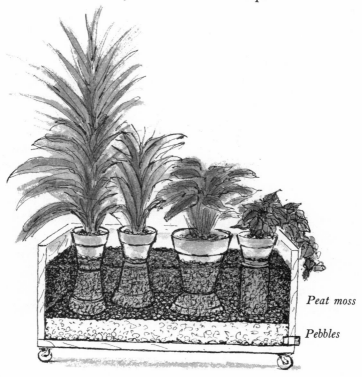

Peat moss

Pebbles

Arranged in this way, large plants blend together and turn toward the light. They can also be easily, and very dramatically, spotlighted by night with a small Tensor light arranged either to shine down upon them or up among the leaves. If you put your planter box where the light is very poor, you should choose shade-loving plants and try to provide them with regular artificial light. As I noted before, fluorescent lighting is harsh and most of us dislike using it at night. But I would like to stress again that plants don't mind when they get extra light as long as they have a regular amount. If you can arrange extra lighting so that it turns on in the small hours when no one is around, it will help the plants without annoying you. Don't move your planter box too much in and out of shady and sunny places. Choose plants that either want sun or shade; don't try to combine the two.

A more elaborate planter can be lined with metal and have a small spigot at the base. Simple or expensive, the principle is the same—but you must understand that this is not a box in which the plants are expected to grow with free root run. It is intended only as a moisture-producing display area. Never take the plants out of their pots.

If a planter seems far too ambitious an undertaking, you can make a microclimate or miniclimate by using a wide and rather deep pebbled tray on the floor. This obviously will not be movable, but it can be positioned to make a very attractive area of grouped plants. For the sake of your floor or carpet, always put waterproof sheeting under the tray and regularly check to see that moisture is not seeping through. A good Oriental carpet in our family rotted away unobserved under just such an arrangement! A group of plants on a floor tray can be very spectacular, particularly if some of them are chosen to have a billowing outline and others to point up the effect with Gothic spires. The much-scorned sansevieria produces just the right effect of a Manhattan skyline. Don't let the plants spread outside the perimeter of the tray or they will be constantly damaged.

This floor tray, set where strong light from a window falls on it, is an excellent place to grow some of the small citrus trees, which will carry sweetly scented flowers and rather sour fruit simultaneously. These are more tolerant of indoor growing conditions than most of the other blossoming foliage plants and are well worth the trouble of misting and searching for pests, which are almost always present. In Chapter 13 I will explain how to treat them. Here I want only to mention that wildlife is one of the inevitable features of indoor gardening!

A floor display is also a wonderful way to show off a single flowering plant, a big chrysanthemum or gloxinia. These, seen at eye level, often look all pot and stems; but seen from above, and surrounded by a little green frill of small, inexpensive foliage plants, they are strikingly effective. If you are putting together plants on a tray that require different watering conditions, always raise up the one that needs less water. Baby-food jars, transparent sandwich boxes, or glass bricks serve equally well—anything, in fact, that takes the base of the pot out of possible wetlands. Again, the humidity evaporating around this arrangement will give it much longer life. Both for permanent foliage displays and as a temporary arrangement to dramatize heavy-headed flowering plants, a pebbled tray on the floor with the light of the window slanting down on it can hardly be bettered.

When I first started indoor gardening in America, I lived in an apartment where there seemed to be absolutely no viable living space for plants. Every window, except a minute one in the bathroom, faced north or onto a dimly lit inside well, and they all had enormous red-hot steam radiators in front of them. There was also no way of diminishing the heat without shutting it off entirely, and we had either to freeze or live perpetually in the desert atmosphere enjoyed by the janitor. I had grown up with plants indoors and outside in a very different climate, and, as the endless winter dragged on, I felt a desperate need for growing things around me. So urgent was this plant homesickness that I longed to have plants even in these unsuitable conditions and eventually managed to grow a small collection of plants without using any window space. In retrospect, I think, this was rather a spectacular achievement. The plants that accommodated themselves to these almost intolerable growing conditions were some rather somber foliage specimens with a built-in, cast-iron constitution that allowed them to survive. They were all plants that in nature come from tropical-forest floors. This rather dingy group stayed with me—they didn't die nor did they flourish, but at least they continued to exist and made me feel a little in touch with the soil. I still possess two members of this group, a pair of vining monsteras from which innumerable young plants have since been given away. Knowing, after all these years, that these two plants can take it, I continue to grow them even today in very poor lighting conditions where I need large and striking plants. Their leaves have over the years reduced in size and during the winter grow very far apart from each other, which is always a sign of inadequate light. The reason for their tenacity under continued ill-treatment is that they always have been taken outside during the summer to recover from their winter woes. This is a matter that should also be taken into account if you have to grow plants in poor light. Do not expect a very long life from them, unless they can be given a summer of rest and recreation outdoors in deep shade.

If I had to grow plants in that same apartment today, the situation might be a little simpler. To begin with, it is now usually possible to have some control over the heat in your apartment, and I could also use artificial light to help the cycle of plant growth. The effect of lamplight on plants was then just coming under discussion. The collection of plants nowadays would not need to be quite so limited or quite so dull, for horticultural research in recent years has made available many other interesting plants that can also take reduced light. Outstanding examples are the spathiphyllum and the clivia, both of which perform excellently as foliage plants.

Another help for the horticulturist with poorly lit areas is the increased number of familiar long-lived plants now available in variegated forms and the introduction of new lively leaved plants, like the aphelandra and bromeliads, into the market. Even the aglaonema, the Chinese evergreen—normally the world's dullest plant—has moved with the times and now comes with striped, flecked, and multicolored leaves. Out-of-doors I am not usually very enthusiastic about variegated plants; they always look a little as if they had leprosy, but indoors they liven up any grouping. The only problem is that variegated plants need strong light to keep their marbling, and it is as well to buy more than one of the inexpensive kind and rotate them, keeping the alternative in a bright window so as to sustain the color—almost everyone has some area with strong light. Giving these plants an occasional change of location will prevent the new leaves coming in a dreary green. Again, don't expect any very long-term success. One good show for a whole winter is quite a triumph for the owner of plants in impossible places.

You must be even more careful than usual about watering and the atmospheric humidity if your plant has poor growing conditions. Plants in poor light never flourish because photosynthesis, which produces both leaf and root activity, cannot be properly stimulated, and the general energy level is extremely low. This is quite obvious where the top growth is concerned, because no new leaves appear, or, if they do, they are diminished in size and, in variegated plants, weak in color. But equally sluggish action is also at work in the root system, and this often is not realized until it is too late. It is vitally important that an inactive plant is not overwatered. Feeble root systems cannot handle much water in the pot soil; the moisture remains unabsorbed and the earth becomes sodden. Allow the topsoil to dry out quite markedly before rewatering unless the plant protests violently by wilting heavily, which will happen with the spathiphyllum.

Try to make sure that any new plant you are buying has a good root system, particularly if your growing conditions are less than ideal. It's a rare store manager who will allow us to knock a plant out of its pot to look, though this is really not such an unreasonable request if you are getting an expensive plant. But because some foliage plants root very easily from cuttings, they are sometimes offered for sale with a quite big top growth but an immature root system that will not survive in poor light. Try to judge how well the plant has rooted before you buy it. It should not have a great deal of top growth and still be planted in a very small pot, nor should it be a small shoot in a huge pot. Check to make sure that all the lower leaves are still there. A plant that has a poor root system, or has been left too long in a pot, will have shed the lower leaves. A well-grown, well-rooted plant is elegantly clothed in leaves right down to the lowest level.

DISPLAY

In locations of poor light, good humidity remains extremely important. You can use a large tray with a deeper dry well of pebbles than usual, or you can make a modified use of wet peat moss, which is so effective in a planter box. Plants in poor light would not be able to exist with peat moss rising up the pot sides in the manner suggested for a planter box, for this would keep the soil within the pots much too saturated for the inactive root system. Instead, stand the pots on the usual dry well, but spread a thick layer of peat moss around the outer edge of the tray on top of the pebbles and under the foliage spread. This, kept damp, provides excellent humidity. But do not stand the pots themselves on the wet peat moss.

Plants in poor light also enjoy a daily misting. Don't do this if the foliage is still wet by night. Allow the leaves to dry out before repeating the shower.

A very usual mistake made by the novice horticulturist is to suppose that plants living in poor light can be helped by extra food. This is usually a fatal mistake. The last thing a sluggish root system needs is fertilizer. It's a little like giving a convalescent patient broiled lobster. Keep all food out of the pot soil. If new leaves show up, proving how well you are managing your plants, give them a very light misting with a very weak dose of water-soluble plant food. Foliar feeding, which is the technical term, should be given only when plants show signs of active growth. Fertilizing any large plant calls for rather careful thought. For plants in good light, extra food will produce a spurt of growth, and you have to decide whether you have room for an even bigger plant. If your accent plants are already super-scaled, it may be better to try to hold them to their present size by giving them little or no fertilizer and not too much water. Feeding is advisable only if you want the plant larger.

Most big plants remain comfortable in their pots for several years if you will top dress them regularly. Top dressing consists of removing —scratching out, that is—the upper two inches of soil in the pot and replacing it with the appropriate home-improved mix. This process, faithfully repreated, will put off the horrible job of repotting a large plant. When roots take up all the interior space in the pot and compel you to reluctant action, you have two choices: to move the plant into a larger pot, or to root prune, which is discussed in Chapter 3. Root pruning calls for a certain amount of strong-mindedness on the part of the grower, but it does have the great advantage of keeping the pot size unchanged.

If you love big accent plants but can't afford one, make your own; it's not at all hard. Get a large plastic pot (8 to 9 inches across the top); crock it well and fill it three quarters deep with a good, rich soil. Have ready three small identical plants. If you have bought varieties such as the *Dracaena warnecki*, which eventually grow very tall, make sure that your pot is a deep one, not a shallow pan. Knock out your plants and set all three root balls on the soil in the big pot. When the root systems are in place there should be no crowding but a little space between them and the outer edge of the pot. Fill in with extra soil so that the new triple planting stands at the same soil level the small

*Making your own
accent plant*

plants were at originally. Your new accent plant will at first look rather out of proportion, but don't flood the pot in an attempt to hurry it on until new growth begins. When the plants really start to grow, give the leaves regular light foliar feeding. You will have a striking plant in an amazingly short time.

These are the possibilities open to you, if you cannot or do not want

DISPLAY

to use window areas for plants. Lack of window space is no excuse for not having plants. There are still plenty of places in every house where people can have an exciting show of plants without cluttering up their windows—the decision is yours.

*Completed
accent plant*

3 ❧ CONTROL

Pruning and Pinching

Well-managed houseplants usually respond with a mighty surge of growth. This immediately presents their proud owners with a host of new problems engendered by their very success. It rapidly becomes essential to institute some form of control. The speed at which a thriving, thrifty collection of houseplants can deteriorate into an over-crowded jungle can be an unpleasant surprise. Previously docile plants climb onto the curtains or walk out of their pots, and it is hardly possible to pass the plant stand without being snagged by a wandering branch. Rampaging, uncontrolled plants crowding up against each other lose not only their style and form but also suffer in health. This is because air can no longer circulate freely around each plant, and this in turn affects the vital process of transpiration. Furthermore, branches that are entangled in each other invariably lose their leaves or get brown and ragged-looking. Action should be taken before matters reach this pass. But rather than trying to find even more space to accommodate plants, it is better to learn to control them through pruning before you have to resort to desperate measures like throwing them away!

The most common method of dealing with overenthusiastic growth is to take a pair of clippers and cut it back. Climbing or vining plants can be treated in this summary fashion and so can any plant that carries many individual branches each with growing points above a single stem—an azalea or a citrus plant would respond to such treatment. However, not every type of houseplant can be treated in this way and still look well. Succulent plants, for instance, will always show a scar where they were cut, and plants that grow with a single stem, like a palm or a dracaena, have their appearance ruined for so long as to make the process impracticable. It is also impossible to prune the foliage of plants like ferns and spathiphyllum, which spring directly from the soil level; the best that can be done here is to cut out the leaves below the pot surface, which produces a very ugly effect.

So what to do? How are overlarge plants to be handled if they cannot be cut back? Two solutions exist; one is beheading the plant thus forcing it to make new shoots along the stem by a process described in Chapter 11. The other is root pruning, which can be repeated on most houseplants several times before they get too large to handle. This is a horticultural skill that is not suggested to the new grower often enough. It seems rather dramatic and destructive and therefore frightens the beginning gardener, but it is, in fact, the simplest way to enjoy some of the best indoor plants without having them take over your house.

Almost any plant that is likely to turn up in the average plant collection can be root-pruned, which is more than can be said for foliage pruning. If you have turned into such a good indoor gardener that your plants are overwhelming you, you will have no difficulty in learning how to reduce the root ball so that growth is temporarily checked and the plant can remain in the same size pot. Root pruning is almost always a success if it is done at the proper time in the life of the plant. With most houseplants the right time is spring, for then growth is the most active and root wounds will heal quickly. You will need a sharp knife—a flat-backed butcher's knife is very good. But do get one specially for the purpose. If you take a knife from the kitchen, it will always be among the tools when you need it for cooking, and in the kitchen drawer when the essential crunch of dividing is at hand. Plant diseases are extremely easily carried by contaminated tools, so an invaluable adjunct to the proceedings is a bottle of rubbing alcohol with which you can give your knife an occasional sterilizing swipe.

To do the job, knock out the plant, put the root ball on a hard surface, and trim off portions all around. Use a sharp knife and shave down the sides of the root mass in an action not unlike slicing coleslaw. Avoid using clippers on roots; the compressing action by which they operate is harmful. Plants that are a little pot-bound and have a tight, fibrous root system are the easiest to manage. A fern root ball, for example, can be carved into any shape you wish. Don't have the pot soil too dry before getting to work or it will fall away and make the whole affair more difficult. Plants with a big, fleshy root mass, such as an agapanthus, may not hold together so well, and here the roots sometimes have to be cut individually with a knife. Try and reshape the root mass to the form of the pot sides, wider at the top than the bottom. Cut around the whole root ball, not only on one side. A plant that has been root-pruned will probably recover faster if the heart of the root ball is not disturbed, but it is important to try and extract the old crocks at the base, which are probably overgrown with roots. Pick these out with a sharp stick and then trim off the loose roots that once covered them. Your aim should be to reduce the root mass enough so

Slice off portions all around the root ball

that there will be a clear inch between it and the sides of a pot of the same size it was in before. Don't overdo the pruning. A plant left with too little root system will be very slow to recover. Repotting should be done in the usual manner.

Root-pruned plants will recover faster and wilt less if they are given what old-fashioned gardeners used to call a "close atmosphere" after they are repotted. In the days when everyone had a special growing area, a close atmosphere was produced by putting the plant into an outdoor frame and keeping that tightly shut. Inside, there built up a warm humid atmosphere that enabled the plant to survive the initial shock by taking in moisture through the leaves to compensate for the injury to the hair roots. Today most gardenless gardeners hardly know what an outdoor or cold frame is—let alone have access to one. But they can still provide the necessary close atmosphere by setting the plant into a closed plastic bag and keeping the shrouded plant out of the sunlight. Atmospheric humidity provided by the enclosure and the house heat will keep foliage in good condition until new feeding roots start to form.

If you have root-pruned a plant that also can have the foliage trimmed, it will speed the recovery period if you cut off a compensating amount of top growth. With less foliage, the shocked roots will have less work to do. When trimming off excess foliage after root pruning or just for everyday control, don't cut away all the new growth. Some new stems and leaves will be needed, because every plant must eventually shed old leaves; there is only a fixed period of time in which any one leaf can remain in active use. When that time ends, the old leaf will fall and its work be taken up by a new one. If all new shoots are consistently cut out, the plant will fairly soon become a skeleton requiring absolutely no pruning!

It has already been stressed that only certain plants profit from having the foliage trimmed back. For those plants with which it is possible, top pruning can take place in three intensities. The most severe is called hard pruning, or cutting back into the old wood. Wood is the term that is always applied to the stem of a plant. In hard pruning, portions of the stems that carry leaves are cut out and only leafless portions retained. Hard pruning is usually a sign of desperation. No indoor plant is going to look anything but frightful for a considerable time after this treatment and should not in fact ever be allowed to get into a state in which such drastic action is needed. But we all put things off and occasionally a fast-growing prunable plant, like an azalea or a pittosporum, gets away from us and must be hard-pruned. Take your clippers and cut back into the brown, leafless stem to a point where you want the plant to branch out again. Remember, however, that plants live by light falling upon their leaves, and it is unwise to cut out all the leaves at once. An overgrown plant that needs hard pruning is more likely to survive what amounts to a considerable ordeal if it is rejuvenated piece by piece. Cutting only two or three stems at a time will give the plant a chance to rescue itself by sending out new shoots.

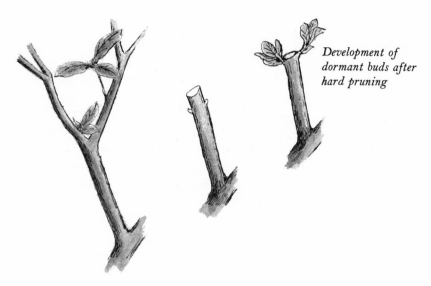

Development of dormant buds after hard pruning

These new shoots appear because all plants are provided with a series of dormant leaf buds that never stir into life unless some emergency strips the plant of all its leaves. The first set of these dormant buds lies in the axils of the leaves themselves where the leafstalk is connected to the woody stem. If a violent rainstorm or freak wind tears all the leaves from a tree or bush, the previously inactive axil buds will develop and take over the process of photosynthesis. If, in the same kind of storm, the entire branch carrying the leaves should be broken off and all the axil buds are destroyed with it, there still exists another back-up rescue system. These are the dormant stem or eye buds that lie underneath the bark of all plants. Axil buds can often be seen; stem buds are entirely invisible to the naked eye, though it is sometimes possible to see the slight outline of their position through a magnifying glass. Stem buds will break through the hard, woody bark of an old tree in an emergency rescue operation. They can be observed doing this in trees that have been defoliated by hurricanes or by disease.

In hard pruning we take advantage of this built-in system of plant protection, for by removing all the leaves from a stem we force the

CONTROL

dormant stem buds into action and induce the plant to leaf out where we cut it. But this is hard work for the plant, particularly if the place where the cut has been made is surrounded by very old, very hard bark. It will both help and speed up the process if you mist the area regularly. And, if you have an unobtrusive place where the plant can languish unobserved, you can tie a plastic bag over the cut-back branch, an action that will also help to soften the bark with enveloping humidity.

The second, less drastic, form of action is called softwood pruning. This takes advantage of the presence of the axil leaf buds and sets them to work by removing all the soft, green, leaf-carrying stems above a pair of leaves. Softwood pruning is used to promote thick, bushy plants, because two new shoots will grow from the pair of axil buds where one single stem existed before. It is practiced on plants that flower on new wood—that is, form flowering buds on the growth that appears fresh each year. Fuchsias and lantanas are examples; with such plants the more new wood that can be forced to grow, the greater the number of flowers. Softwood pruning is used to prevent foliage plants from stretching out with thin, spindly stems and to hold them in a bushy form. The trimmings from this process are often used to create new plants by a method discussed in Chapter 11.

Before pruning

After pruning

The mildest kind of pruning is done with the fingertips and is called a pinch. Pinching consists of removing the growing point of a plant. This checks the growth and often causes dormant stem buds to break in order to replace the vital growing point. Flowering annuals are treated in this way to force extra bushiness and prevent elongation into a single-stemmed plant. A variation of pinching is a process called a soft pinch. To do this, you wait until a flower bud can be seen just below the growing point. This bud is allowed to develop slightly and then the tip beyond it is taken out. The bud takes all the nourishment that otherwise would have gone into the growing tip and turns into a larger and longer-lasting flower than buds formed in the usual way.

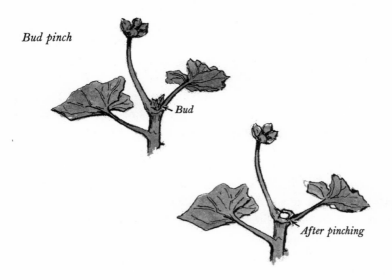

Bud pinch

Bud

After pinching

Show exhibitors produce immense blossoms in dahlias, geraniums, and begonias by this treatment. It is also a very useful piece of horticultural expertise for the complete beginner. My only difficulty with the soft pinch is the fact that, like all gardeners, I have very short fingernails. Good soft pinching can be done best by a sharp nip between the nails of the thumb and first or second finger.

A good gardener can always be recognized by the manner in which his collection is controlled. New growers sometimes feel that a kind of boom-town appearance in their plant collection spells triumph. To the accomplished horticulturist, unpruned, wandering plants merely represent sloppy growing.

Most pruning involves a stitch in time . . . and that's all there is to it, but do take that stitch, or your plants will overwhelm you both ruthlessly and very untidily.

Dividing

Even if you have been regular and thorough with your pruning, some houseplants have to be given away when they grow extra large and flourishing. They can't be reduced in size forever without mutilation, and no house can expand enough to allow us to go on potting them up indefinitely. Other indoor plants grow equally large but can be broken up into smaller replicas of themselves. This is the process known as dividing, and it usually brings to its possessor the reputation of being a very generous donor of surplus plants. Dividing is not hard to learn, and once you have got the knack, like swimming or riding a bicycle, you will always understand the method. To be able to divide is an essential piece of knowledge for every indoor horticulturist.

Before you can learn to divide a plant, you obviously must be able to distinguish between those that can be salvaged in this manner and those that will be killed in the attempt. Fundamentally, this is a complicated subject, but some quite straightforward guidelines exist about most of the plants likely to be used by the home horticulturist.

For instance, any plant that increases in size by sending up a dense thicket of soft, green stem growth within the pot at soil level can be divided. The spathiphyllum is an excellent example and so are the numerous hybrids of the old, familiar Boston fern. You can also divide plants that produce miniature plantlets around a mother plant. African violets belong to this type. We have all seen pots in which the original plant has almost been crowded out by numerous identical offspring that have grown up around it. The familiar chrysanthemum belongs in this category.

Plants that form offsets are also dividable. Technical terms such as offsets often frighten beginning gardeners. But it's better to learn them from the very start—then they don't have to be re-explained every time. An offset is a small, complete plant that grows either obviously fastened to the roots of the parent plant, as in the clivia, or springs up in the pot some distance away, as occurs with the sansevieria. The offsets that appear a little distance away from the main plant are, in fact, still attached to it by underground runners while they continue to develop an independent root system for themselves.

Plants that form double- or even triple-headed growth side by side within the pot, like the self-heading monsteras, are also dividable. (I have not forgotten orchids, all of which need regular division, but this is a specialized subject not under discussion here.) In brief, for home horticultural purposes, you can safely divide any plant that has soft multiple growth crowding the soil surface or one that has formed junior editions of itself.

Dividable plants

Plants you cannot divide are those that carry their foliage above or upon a single stem. Nor can you divide any plant that has woody or hard bark. It is easier to be deceived here than might be expected. A well-grown marguerite, fuchsia, or impatiens plant may have been cut back at a very early stage so as to produce numerous bushy side shoots.

CONTROL

On first sight, these might look like one of those plants with multiple-top soft growth. Careful examination will always show you the original single stem from which all the additional growth has come. Any attempt to divide a single-stemmed plant must end in disaster. To survive, a plant must have a crown or main growing area. Single-stemmed plants have only one crown no matter how many side shoots they may throw out. You also cannot divide plants in which the leaves wrap themselves around the base to form a single stem. Many people grow small palms that are examples of this kind of growth, and so are the various dracaenas now extremely fashionable. Vining, trailing, or climbing plants cannot be divided. There is, however, no need to allow any of these to drive you out of the house. All climbers can be cut back to any point that suits your taste. You also cannot divide the succulent plants that store water in their leaf or stem tissues, such as the Christmas cactus and the crassula, or jade tree. Bulbs, corms, and tubers can be divided, but this is expert work and should not be attempted by the complete novice. In scholarly horticulture there are,

Plants that cannot be divided

of course, many shadings within these categories, but this sketchy outline should serve the purpose of the average home horticulturist.

Dividing is major plant surgery; it gives both the original plant and the severed portion a severe shock. It should only be undertaken when it is absolutely essential and, as with all operations, with all the necessary tools collected beforehand. The plant itself must be in good health; you cannot divide a sick plant in order to improve it—this simply will not work. The timing of the action is also important. Unless there is some kind of emergency, such as the familiar one of knocking down and breaking a pot, you should make sure that the plant is at the best stage of growth to recover quickly from the division. A flowering plant is best treated soon after it has finished blossoming and just as the new foliage growth is starting, for this is a very strong period of growth. Evergreen foliage plants should also be divided when the new growth appears. With most of them, this is in the spring, and, by and large, spring is far the best time for almost all dividing. The heat of the summer is a very bad time. When you divide, you inevitably ruin some of the root structure. This, in turn, deprives the foliage of much-needed moisture, and the whole essential problem of keeping the top growth alive while the roots recover is much harder in hot weather. Midwinter is also a poor time. During the period of short daylight hours most plants rest; they relapse into a form of dormancy in which very little internal activity takes place. A root ball that is cut during a plant's dormant period receives very little energy to promote healing. In consequence the callus, or covering, that must form to seal off the wound often fails to form. When this happens the injured roots rot and die. So, if there's a choice, add plant dividing to your already overloaded list of things to do in the spring!

Dividing is a messy job and there's no point in pretending otherwise. If you can get out of doors, divide your plants standing at a table. Squatting down on the ground working over a plant is only for the very young. If you must work indoors, spread a great deal of newspaper around and do so before you start! Again I would suggest working at a table or a counter. You will also need something hard to cut on: an old breadboard will do extremely well. You will need extra soil, which you should prepare according to the requirements of the plant you are working on, and, as usual, make up a batch of soil ahead of time in a plastic bowl. Remember that no fertilizer, other than a dusting of steamed bone meal, should ever be added to soil that is going to be put against injured roots. I am well aware of the fact that I am constantly repeating the same advice, but until these actions come naturally to you, which will soon happen, you will need this rather boring, reiterated advice.

Bring out your sharp gardening knife, and, if you are going to tackle an enormous plant, it may also be wise to provide yourself in advance with a small narrow-blade saw. Don't forget alcohol or even a jar of boiling water for sterilizing these implements: clean tools are equally important in this process. You will need a collection of clean pots and a supply of broken shards of the same kind used for potting up. Most of us don't bother, but, if you are using very old and very dirty shards, drop them first into the boiling water in case they harbor old plant diseases.

As you have only one pair of hands, there is another extremely important piece of equipment that is often overlooked but should always be available—plenty of wet paper toweling. This is important because some of your divisions must inevitably wait around while you pot up the others. This is a very critical moment for the survival of the plant. Cut, exposed roots are very vulnerable, and their chances of recovery are greatly increased if they are not allowed to dry out even for as short a period as a few minutes. Plants often fail after an otherwise excellent piece of dividing because the severed root sections were left exposed to dry air indoors or hot sunshine outside. If the telephone rings, take the extra precaution of dropping the wrapped root ball into a plastic bag. You never know how long your friend may talk, and what may seem like a short period to you may spell lingering death for the plant. Plastic bags are therefore also a wise addition to your tool kit.

When you are planning to divide a plant, cut down the water you give it for several days before taking action. This has the effect of slightly hardening—or toughening—the top growth and making it a little less lush and vulnerable. But don't, of course, carry this action to the extreme of setting in foliage collapse. Limiting the water supply also makes the old soil easier to shake off.

For a start, try a plant that has formed numerous small plantlets inside the pot, perhaps an overgrown African violet. Knock it out of the pot in the usual way, and then, holding it carefully by the leaves, shake off as much earth as possible. Experts sometimes suggest that you wash off the soil. I find this whole proceeding messy enough without that. Also, a dry root ball is much easier to work on. A plant that grows miniature replicas within the pot usually falls apart into natural divisions. All that is needed is to separate the strands or roots that still hold it to the mother plant. Use a sharp knife, never clippers, for, as was mentioned earlier, the squeezing action bruises the root tissue, although the damage is not visible to the naked eye. Clippers should only be used to trim off broken foliage. Try not to make the new divisions too small. The process is hard on the plant and it will not recover quickly if it is broken into such a small section that it has to be put into a very small pot. Little pots are very hard to keep properly watered, and, though a minute division will die in a large pot, because the soil ball will go sour, a minute division in a tiny pot may equally well die because the soil within constantly dries out too fast. Repot the divided material in the manner described in Chapter 2.

Once the divisions are in place, they are going to look pretty sad. Water them well at once and keep them in a sunless position—strong shade is the best, with no more water until the top soil looks and feels slightly dry to the touch. If the foliage continues to look extremely miserable, give the leaves an occasional light misting but do not rewater the earth in the pot. Overwatering is one of the main reasons for failure for the novice divider of plants.

Plants that throw up a thicket of growth within the pot are a little harder to handle. The basic procedure is the same: knock out the plant, and, after shaking off as much old earth as possible, set it on the cutting board. This kind of plant will not separate naturally into individual plants; this time you have to operate by cutting to make new plants. Try always to match the amount of top growth and the proportion of remaining root ball. A plant will be unlikely to survive if it is given an immense tuft of leaves and almost no roots. Most spathiphyllums, for instance, recover best if they are divided in half, and this also applies to the ferns. Smaller divisions always have a rather pathetic, not to mention tatty, look, and they take forever to round out again. Above all, act with precision and decision. Plants that have to be treated rather severely seem to respond better if they are handled quickly and with self-confidence. Never mind if you don't feel at all confident—but do put on an act. To speak more plainly, don't dither. The greater your anxiety, the more you will hesitate. And if you hesitate, you not only won't make the sharp, clean cut which is the key to success, but you will also prolong the time in which you are exposing the root ball to the drying effects of the air. If, in spite of all this advice—or perhaps even because of it—you make a poor cut that ends with a great deal of foliage and very little root, trim off enough leaves so as to make a rough match of the two sections.

Divided plants with tall foliage often wilt extremely badly. If the leaves topple right over and are left that way too long, the inner capillary tubes, which pull up the moisture from the soil, may become permanently kinked and unable ever to recover. To prevent this, put small bamboo stakes around the rim of the pot and make a light picket fence of yarn. This will hold the foliage upright long enough for the sap to begin to rise naturally again and hold the leaves upright unsupported. With all dividing, no matter how expertly done, there will always be some leaf loss. This usually occurs on the outer edge of the plant, and yellowed leaves can be easily cut off without any noticeable effect. Large single-leaved plants, such as the self-heading monstera, which are divided in exactly the same way, should have each long leafstalk tied to an individual stake. This is particularly important with these plants because new leaf growth is slow and comes only from the center. The loss of an outer leaf, therefore, has a damaging, long-lasting effect on the look of the plant.

Plants that throw offsets a little distance from the mother plant are very easily divided. After knocking the plant out and shaking off the soil, all that is needed is to sever the attaching runners. But wait to do this until the new plant is quite a good size. Offsets do not grow well unless they already possess a considerable root system of their own, and the top foliage growth frequently develops in size much faster than the capacity of its own roots to sustain it. There is a short-cut method of getting out these detached offsets. Cut into the pot with a sharp knife beside the infant plant and between it and the parent. Then turn the blade of the knife so that the edge faces toward the outer rim and cut underneath the offset. You can then lift out the division by pulling lightly on the foliage. In a plastic pot there is always the danger that if your knife is sufficiently sharp you may also cut through the pot, but horticulture is so full of unpredictable hazards that one more hardly matters!

Dividing the huge plants that grow offsets on top of the established root system is more of an undertaking. Clivias, for instance, cannot be allowed to continue indefinitely throwing enormous offsets within a single pot. Unless you have space to grow them in old half barrels, sooner or later you must brace yourself for the tremendous job of cutting one up. No one who grows clivias looks forward to this. The mess is stupendous, and most novices are terrified even to try because clivias are so expensive. They are excellent indoor plants that can be used as foliage accents or shown off for their lovely flowers, but, unless they are divided, clivias will deteriorate quite rapidly. So, frightened or not, this is a job that must be done. Clivias belong to the amaryllis family, and all members of that group resent having their roots disturbed. It would be the understatement of the age to pretend that you are not going to shake them up tremendously when you cut out an offset. If you grow them for bloom, you must resign yourself to the

Clivia as a foliage plant

possibility that the plant will sulk the year after division and not blossom. Getting a big pot-bound clivia out of its pot is quite an effort; sometimes it is almost a two-man job. If you simply cannot make it come out, break or cut up the pot in which it is growing. Once out of the pot, you will find an enormous mass of huge, white, fleshy roots that have displaced all the original soil and a quantity of old, withered root debris on top. Clivias originate their offsets very close to the mother plant—so much so that, although the new growth may be quite large, it is impossible to get a knife or saw between the two growths. Don't try to divide these plants until the offset has grown enough away from the parent to make a division possible. A well-grown clivia is usually rather lavish with its offspring; a single pot often contains three well-separated offsets as well as smaller ones still huddled close to their parent. Once the plant is on the cutting board, the possibility of reasonable division is usually perfectly obvious. You are going to make new plants from mature offsets, and you are going to cut through the main heart of the plant to do so. There will follow the most frightful mess, because it is quite impossible to divide a plant like this without damaging a great deal of root that is extremely brittle. If you are unlucky, you may also find yourself thwarted, as you saw through the heart, by coming upon old crocks that the plant has drawn up into the root mass. If this occurs, stop cutting, pull out the knife, and try to work the shards away with your fingers. In spite of the fearful massacre of roots, the big divisions you make will recover extremely fast. Put them into pots the same size as the original one. You will not need to support the leaves, but you must expect some loss of the outer leaves of the fan-shaped foliage. Once again, clivia divisions do badly if the offsets are too small; a very immature offset will take years to recover. The one problem is in the repotting. It is absolutely essential to get new soil thoroughly worked in among the fleshy roots. Put a pad of soil at the bottom of your new pot and then hold the clivia in the pot with your left hand, with the roots dangling. Pour the new soil mix in and around the roots, working it in with your fingers, poking and pressing it down. Clivia roots eventually always rise above the pot but begin by having the neck of the plant just below the rim. A good deal of thumping and banging will be needed to settle in the earth, and the pot will probably be at least three quarters full of earth before the plant begins to stand alone. As you work the soil in, make sure that every layer is being firmly pressed down and against the roots. By the time the upper layer of new earth is in place, the plant should be firmly anchored and able to stand upright. The soil should be rich and have particularly good water-retaining ability. Add a little more wet peat moss than usual, but be sure also to put a handful of sharp sand or perlite into the soil, and give the pot plenty of drainage shards. Clivias grow in nature hanging above streams, so they like soil that gets thoroughly wet but that also drains through very rapidly. After repotting, the treatment is as usual —one thorough watering and then only light misting of the foliage until the topsoil locks and feels dry to the touch.

Convalescing plants do best in the open air in fairly heavy shade if you can manage it. If you must keep them indoors, choose an airy, sunless window and make sure that all repotted plants stand on a good dry well of stones in the saucers so that there is no likelihood of the injured root mass having the soil inside the pot become saturated.

When you successfully divide plants, you have taken a giant step in horticulture. You will have learned to identify which kinds can take the treatment and which you will kill, and you will have added a new dimension to your two best gardening tools, your eye and your hands, by training them to work together. In risking the life of a plant to improve it, you will bolster your self-confidence and that, after all, is how a good gardener slowly evolves.

Dormancy

Growing successful houseplants is a challenge in three stages. At first, the novice is pleased if he can just keep his plants alive over one season. The next stage begins when some particular plant does more than just exist: it expands and improves in appearance, and the owner realizes, with a mixture of delight and anticipatory terror, that it is also outgrowing its pot. After dealing successfully with that problem, the final stage is achieved when the now seasoned indoor horticulturist decides to carry the collection over from year to year, anticipating even lusher foliage and yet more abundant bloom. This is perfectly possible to achieve so long as one intermediate period in the growth cycle of every plant is recognized and accepted as inevitable. This is the period of rest or dormancy that every plant has to be allowed to take at least

CONTROL

once, and occasionally several times, in the course of the cycle of a single year's growth.

For sustained good health, human beings and animals must sleep sometime during each twenty-four hours. The point has already been made that the plants we use indoors also need a period of darkness once every twenty-four hours. But, in addition, most plants also want a period of inactivity that may be partial or complete, during which they remain alive but do not grow, and when their root system comes either almost to a stop or else withers completely away. This is the dormant period. Unless it is recognized and accepted by handling the plants in a different manner, they will eventually deteriorate, no matter how excellent the rest of the care may be.

One of the first problems with dormancy is how to discover when the process is underway and what triggers it off. In nature, dormancy is preceded by a slowing down of the whole process of growth, either because the temperature is rapidly cooling off, or because the daylight hours are shortening markedly, or because a period of reduced rainfall has set in. In northern climates, for instance, deciduous trees drop their leaves, and evergreen trees and bushes cease any active growth as soon as the first frosts hit. In the desert and some tropical areas, plants diminish their root activities in order to accommodate themselves to an ever-decreasing supply of water. In countries where there are periods of blazing heat, plants either lose all their top growth and go underground to wait for cooler weather, or they slow down all active growth in order not to lose too much moisture through transpiration in the great heat. In Arctic regions, the sudden diminution of the light hours rushes the plants into retreat so that they can withstand the oncoming bitter weather.

All these ways are provided by the elements to make sure that plants will survive and carry on the species. They regain strength by this period of inaction during which they do not die but exist in a state of suspended animation. Understanding dormancy and its importance to successful home horticulture is not stressed sufficiently to most novice growers.

We grow plants from most parts of the world indoors, but since they are no longer exposed to the natural weather patterns that force the resting period on them, some show only very limited periods of dormancy. Others fail to rest at all unless we force them to do so.

Growing indoor plants very successfully calls, therefore, for two additional skills that are not always understood. The first is the ability to recognize when a plant is at rest and only wants to be left alone, and the second is learning how and when and for how long to impose a resting period upon a recalcitrant plant in order to get either better bloom or longer life from it. This may seem rather unnecessary if the plant seems perfectly willing to continue growing indefinitely. Why force dormancy upon it? The answer lies in the fact that all house-plants, even though they may be generations removed from their wild forebears, still will do better if they are made to follow their hereditary growing pattern.

There are some plants, mainly those with bulbs, corms, or tubers, that make it crystal clear when they intend to rest by discarding all their foliage. Cyclamens, for instance, simply refuse to continue sending up new leaves after a certain length of time no matter how well they are being grown and rapidly deteriorate into a singularly depressing mess. If you can steel yourself to look under all the decaying foliage, you will see that the corm is still plump and fleshy. The plant is not dead; it has merely retreated into its annual resting period. Other familiar houseplants that stick firmly to their ancestral pattern are some of the begonias, gloxinias, caladiums, and achimenes. Many new gardeners faced with a pot containing apparently nothing but a mass of withered foliage give up and throw the whole thing out. This is a pity, for all these plants can be stored safely in their pots in any out-of-the-way place and left without any more attention for a considerable time. They can be revived to bloom again a second year extremely easily.

Some of the summer-blossoming houseplants also proclaim their intention of relapsing into dormancy by shedding the leaves from their branches. Fuchsias and hydrangeas are examples of houseplants that will not continue without a complete period of rest. These present much more of a problem than the bulbous plants, for, though they lose their leaves, they still must be allowed to keep the unattractive skeleton of their branches, and they cannot be allowed to dry out completely in their pots. The branches have to be kept plump and alive. To achieve this, the root ball has to have an occasional dribble of water, but it is hard to gauge when and how much should be given. This is the main reason for many failures to carry these plants through their winter rest successfully. They also have to be allowed to take this period of dormancy in a cool place. Somewhere like a frost-free attic or cellar is excellent. All these requirements make such plants difficult for most

CONTROL

indoor gardeners. And if you add to the basic problem of keeping them both alive and yet dormant the long, slow period of regrowth, which has to be endured before they will bloom again, it is really not worth the effort they are going to demand of you. Treat them as expendable; enjoy the summer bloom and then throw them away.

For really determined horticulturists with cold cellars who do want to try and carry fuchsias and hydrangeas on into another year, I would suggest growing them only in plastic pots. Plastic, as we know, retains moisture much longer, and pot soil left unwatered in plastic pots is less likely to get completely dried out during dormancy. Do not try and by-pass this problem by watering leafless plants regularly. Dormancy has always to be equated with almost total inactivity of the feeding roots and regular watering will kill the plant by setting in root rot.

To recognize the need for dormancy in plants that flaunt it under our noses is obviously no problem; but other plants do not make it so simple for us. The plants that store water in their leaves or stems, such as the spiny and the spineless succulents, have done so in anticipation of the rainless period they once faced. They will grow better and are more likely to do well and set bloom in pots if they are given an artificial rainless period. The method is to stop watering entirely— usually during the fall—and when you do start rewatering give only a little and slowly increase the amount given. A month is the usual waterless period for plants that have not stored up very much of a reserve. Heavily succulent plants, with well-swollen tissues like many of the cacti, are exactly like the camel and its hump; the plant draws upon its own inner supply until that is exhausted. You can gauge roughly the length of time a succulent plant can live without any water from the state of the tissues. If they begin to show a slightly wrinkled quality, the inner supply is depleted and watering should start again. Most succulent plants set their buds during the last part of their waterless period, which in nature is also a time of very short daylight hours. If they are not given this rest they often refuse to bloom at all, though they will grow successfully as foliage plants without a dormant period. The Christmas cactus is a case in point. Many people have magnificent plants that bloom regularly no matter how they are treated. It is, however, a very common complaint among owners of this plant and its numerous hybrids that it sets no bloom. I struggled with some heirloom Christmas cactus plants for a great many years with never more than a few miserable blooms. I then discovered that if these plants were hung in a dimly lit place with absolutely no artificial light at night and kept entirely without water during October they set hundreds of buds. If you have one of the nonblossoming varieties of Christmas cactus, try this treatment. Be strong-minded and don't even look at the plant during its enforced misery. When you come to take it back into the light, tiny buds will probably already have formed.

Clivias are magnificent and rather expensive indoor plants that should be more used. They will grow in very poor light and produce a huge arching fan of green leaves. Given good light, they throw up an immense umbel of long-lasting, trumpet-shaped orange flowers. My difficulty was trying to discover when the buds were likely to appear. I had no trouble getting blossom; the problem was that I could not get any fixed time for flowers. It then occurred to me that, as they came from Natal in South Africa, they must in nature have undergone a period of considerable drought, and it followed that the bud set probably occurred once the waterless period was over. This proved entirely correct. Now I find it possible to time the period when clivias will bloom very closely, for a bud will appear through the side of the fan about a month after the plant is brought out of dormancy. I like my clivias to bloom in the spring so I withhold water from October until the New Year, and I have had only an occasional out-of-season flower since I established this routine. I have no doubt that a bud would follow three months of artificial drought at any time of year.

Dormancy is not only needed to produce flower buds, it is also needed by foliage plants for recuperation. Some that we grow fall naturally into a period of reduced activity during the dull, short days of midwinter. New leaves cease to appear and the whole plant takes on a monotonous single-color look. When this happens, don't panic and try to revive the plant with heavy misting and additional amounts of water or, perish the thought, by giving it additional food. The plant is behaving not only in a natural manner, but in a way that will lead to better growth later on. If you try to stimulate it by putting extra food into the pot or spraying water-soluble fertilizer onto the leaves, you may well be adding the kiss of death. The plant is half asleep and cannot possibly absorb the extra food. Far from trying to stimulate a dormant plant, reduce the amount of water you are giving it. Also, if you are using artificial light cut that amount down, too. When the plant is ready for more water it will stir into life and throw out new leaves.

CONTROL

If your foliage plants show no signs of going dormant, it is still a good plan to reduce the amount of water you are giving them, though never so much that the foliage wilts. A resting period can also be given to all plants by reducing the amount of light they receive. Even a moderate, artificially imposed rest of this kind does most foliage plants a great deal of good.

Short daylight hours are a factor that has considerable bearing on the growth pattern of many plants. Some will not set bud until the days grow shorter. Chrysanthemums, kalanchoes, and poinsettias are all plants that will not bloom when there is long daylight. We now have chrysanthemums in bloom the year-round because professional growers artificially shorten the hours of light the plants receive on a timed and exact schedule by covering the plants with black cloth. This brings the necessary buds both to them and to other plants with similar habits, all of which are called short-day plants. That exasperating Christmas cactus is a very determined short-day plant. On the opposite side are plants like gloxinias, which will only bloom freely when they have maximum hours of light. Professional growers can change the seasons on these long-day plants by giving them a huge extra dose of artificial light.

Many plants get thrown out every year under the mistaken idea that they are failing, when in fact all they are doing is taking their natural rest. Not only is dormancy impossible to prevent in a plant that means to rest, it should actually be welcomed as a sign of very good culture. If you will take a relaxed attitude and ride out the poor-looking period of some of your plants, the aftereffects will be amply rewarding.

4 ❦ NEGLECTABLE PLANTS

ONE OF THE PROBLEMS that besets the indoor gardener is how to go away—who is to water the plants? And this is a very real difficulty, for many of us dread having to abandon the results of months of anxious care. Plant sitters, let alone experienced plant sitters, are almost impossible to find. If you want to grow living plants but know you have to go away a lot, why don't you choose plants that can survive without water for quite long periods and may in fact even benefit from being occasionally left to themselves! For horticulturists who ski, or who own weekend cottages, or who don't want all their holiday plans to be dictated to them by the demands of their plants, there do exist quite a number of neglectable houseplants.

These admirable plants are those that have had to learn to survive in the wild for considerable periods without rain. Waterless periods exist for plants in very different climatic conditions all over the world—in deserts, on high rocky ledges, in tropical forests, in areas of great heat and intense cold—and plants have adapted themselves to dealing with the problem under these varying circumstances in many different ways. One of the most familiar is succulence, that is, having the ability to store water in the tissues that can be drawn upon when water is not available to the roots. All succulent plants also lose water through transpiration at a much slower rate than other plants.

Plants store a hoard of water in their leaves, stems, or understock to provide themselves with a form of insurance to carry them through the inevitable drought they suffer in the wild. They conserve moisture even further by falling into dormancy during the natural waterless period, and by that means slowing down all the vital processes of plant growth

NEGLECTABLE PLANTS

that might otherwise deplete their store. All these factors make succulent plants particularly useful to rather casual horticulturists, indeed our hot and dry house air presents almost as much of a challenge as their native environment! In this section I want only to discuss succulent plants that store water in their stems and leaves; plants with underground water-storing capacities are discussed in Chapter 10.

Succulence in plants comes in varying intensities, the amount of stored water being an indication of how long the plant can remain without attention. The crassula, for example, with its very thickly swollen leaves and stem, is heavily succulent and so to a lesser degree is the Christmas cactus, which has in fact modified or changed its leaf and stem growth so as to enable it to survive more easily in its

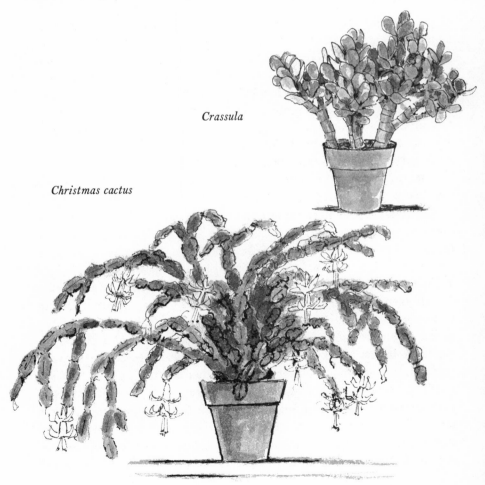

Crassula

Christmas cactus

particular environment. The Swedish ivy, an Australian plant that is obviously not Swedish, nor is it an ivy, is an example of minor succulence, though it, too, can survive quite a long siege. The zonal geranium, gloxinia, and, unexpectedly enough, the African violet are also succulent plants though much less obviously. So, also, is the hoya.

These diverse plants all have tissue-storing capacity in common and, in consequence, need slightly different treatment from other houseplants. A beginning gardener is far too likely to forget their individual requirements and water them regularly like the other plants.

Desert cactus

They are, however, delightfully easy to manage if the entire collection consists only of succulents, and this is a very good way for the casual gardener to start. Succulent collections also attract expert gardeners. Frequent use is made by them indoors of the most familiar of the succulent group, the spiny desert cactus in its many varied forms and astonishing flowers. Cacti, and their terrifyingly thorny cousins, the euphorbias, can be readily combined into spectacular displays by a complete novice, even without getting them to flower, if their simple requirements for indoor living—cool conditions and good light—are met. Among the other excellent qualities of a cactus collection is the additional bonus of very slow growth. A cactus collection does not demand a lot of repotting, which is perhaps just as well considering their fearful thorns. If you must handle these plants, equip yourself with very thick leather gloves and hold the plant in a pad of newspaper. Like the porcupine, the cactus is admirably equipped to defend

NEGLECTABLE PLANTS

itself from animals which, searching for water in otherwise arid country, would alternatively eat the plant for the reserve of moisture it contains. The aftereffects of a losing battle with an indignant cactus can be painful for several days.

It is those spines that make me dislike the plants; there is nothing lovable to me about something that has to be handled with tongs. I much prefer another huge clan of water-saving plants which come in an amazing variety of form and texture but without any spines. These plants are inaccurately but generally called "the succulents" and they are grown largely for their subtle foliage colors, which can range through the ivories, green-grays, mauves, soft purples, and marbled greens and yellows. Some of them do bloom, but in the main they are not grown for flowers. It is the foliage, angular or softly rounded, pointed or cup-shaped, shiny or soft-textured, that catches the attention. Most of these plants increase quite fast, so these attractive forms can be massed in quite large groups and allowed to boil and tumble dramatically over the rims of their pots. Most of the spineless succulents are not winter-hardy in the north, but, being a gigantic family, there are exceptions here as with every rule.

Kalanchoe

One succulent that is grown primarily for winter bloom is the kalanchoe. This family includes some delightful soft-leaved members that are used only as foliage plants, but the more usual blossoming variety, with thick, fleshy leaves, is the one offered us in bloom in the shops around Christmas. The flowering kalanchoe is a short-day plant that can be trapped into early bloom exactly like the other short-day plants by withholding light on an exact timetable. If you are growing your own flowering kalanchoe indoors, don't expect a midwinter display. Unless you are prepared to put the plant through a rather elaborate process, there will be no flowers until spring. Kalanchoes now come in a great many soft colors and are easily raised from seed, but the one we are most often offered is a short, multiflowered red variety with a solid head of ever-opening blooms. Those we can buy are usually extremely small plants and look much more effective potted two or three together in a bulb pan. Crock the pan well, work with dry soil, and keep the plants on the dry side. They will never turn a hair.

Sedums

Another extremely attractive group of succulents are the sedums. These are very fleshy plants with small, thick leaves set around sturdy stalks that slowly lengthen while fresh shoots spring up at the base. Sedums have the great advantage of retaining these fat little leaves as the stalks lengthen. The only problem is the intense brittleness of the plant as a whole. It is almost impossible even to change the position of a sedum without breaking something, a leaf, or piece of stem, or both. But as every single piece of leaf or stem will root without the slightest encouragement, sedums are slightly inclined to overwhelm you if you take any minor disaster with them too seriously. We all have a tendency to react a little sentimentally to any small shoot that can be discovered indomitably sending out small, thrusting roots from minute sections broken and left forgotten weeks earlier on the floor of the car. But if you allow yourself to be bullied by the tenacity of the sedum, you will soon have pots in every nook and cranny of the house. Throw or give away the broken pieces before they compel you to pot them up and adopt them. Sedums do bloom, but the flowers are unimportant. The magnificent donkey-tail sedum that hangs supreme in a plant window is the only member of the family that does not make a reproductive nuisance of itself. Donkey-tail sedums rather unexpectedly, considering the behavior of their relatives, are quite hard to grow well. They unfortunately have a tendency to shed their leaves, if they are knocked or even slightly overwatered, leaving a rather ungainly, stringlike stalk with a tuft of leaves at the end. The common name obviously came from this tiresome characteristic leaf drop, so if, or even when, it happens to you, there is some consolation that you are not alone in your failure. But don't give up the donkey-tail sedum; cut off the stalky stems and let it try again. This is a very long-lived and attractive plant and does much better if not overpowered with attention. Sedums all look well as hanging plants and, because of their brittleness, do much better displayed this way than crowded in among the general window-ledge clutter.

Echeverias

A succulent family that is a delight to look down upon are the many kinds of echeverias. They grow in cup-shaped forms designed to catch and carry every drop of rain or dew down to the roots of the plant. They come in magnificent pastel foliage colors, and the stronger the winter light they are given, the more intense the shading. Full summer sun, however, will darken or even scorch the leaves of some varieties. Echeverias and sedums are both shallow-rooted plants, and echeverias look particularly well in either the glazed or unglazed bowls and pots used for growing bonsai. Echeverias throw up an occasional very long stalk of bloom that will last well in water. Once an echeveria rosette has blossomed it will grow no larger. If you want big, foliage rosettes, always cut off the flower buds as they form. Most echeverias, and a rather similar succulent called an aeonium, slowly lose their lower leaves and become stalky. You can handle this situation by cutting off the rosette at whatever point you want new growth to form; the succulents are full of dormant buds. The cut stump is always obvious, however, so I usually trim it off right back to ground level where it will break in a less obviously multilated manner. If you want rather interestingly shaped plants, allow new buds to break and grow along the whole length of the beheaded stalk. A cut-off rosette roots almost as easily as a sedum: simply put the piece of stalk into a small pot and wait. There are other echeverias that throw outside offsets still attached to the mother plant and do not elongate at all. These make attractive massive groups in a pot, forming big, rounded mounds. They can also be very easily separated.

Aloe

Another delightful group of indoor succulents are members of the aloe family. These are angular in form with speckled and flushed foliage. They produce a jagged skyline in a pot giving the whole plant an unusual silhouette, apart from the pleasure given by the muted and mellow colors. Aloes increase by means of underground runners; young plants appear above ground some distance away from the parent. They grow slowly and with nothing like the tenacity of the sedums or echeverias about rooting, but a panful (for they too look best in shallow containers) is always a conversation piece. Aloes flower easily indoors but the blossoms add nothing to them. Like any succulent, they need a bright, cool condition with very careful watering.

Sempervivums

A group of hardy, rosette-shaped succulent plants that will tolerate tremendous neglect and very poor soil and can be left outside even in the north are the sempervivums, whose very name means "live forever." These plants are called, colloquially, hen and chickens, because they spread by means of little rosettes, over which the mother plant seems to brood protectively. Sempervivums exist in nature high on cold, rocky ledges off which the water shoots extremely rapidly, they hug the ground closely to get protection from the wind, and they can live with almost no soil. In Europe they often establish colonies on the tile roofs of old houses, so they are excellent also for very shallow pans and for containers without drainage. They need exactly the same treatment where water is concerned as all other succulents. Sempervivums will grow indoors in good light and in a cool location. A glazed bowl planted with either echeverias or sempervivums makes a wonderful ornament for a dining-room table, but don't try to grow them in any such location—let that be only a temporary display.

The handling of all these plants is not hard. During their active period, they show strong signs of growth, forming new rosettes and offsets, with inner leaves usually slightly lighter in color. During full growth, when they are watered, it needs to be a very thorough proceeding—lavish enough to pour out through the drainage holes. Because of their shallow roots and water-storing capacities, succulents can be grown quite successfully in undrained containers and look particularly well in colored pans. The proper watering technique for succulents in undrained containers consists of saturating the soil until it can absorb no more, and then allowing the free-standing water to drain out by setting the container on its side and leaving it there for a considerable period. After one of these treatments, no more water should be given until the soil feels hard and dry to the touch. All succulents should be grown in the coolest, lightest place you possess; they can even stand a bright window in an unheated attic, so long as it is frost-free. If they are in a very cold place they should have almost no water at all; just keep the foliage from shriveling.

Dormancy usually sets in when the light hours shorten and is noticeable because the plants cease to expand and their colors diminish in intensity. This is the period for no water while the tops and roots are resting. It has already been mentioned that watering the succulent Christmas cactus during its dormant period often prevents the formation of buds. The same holds true for the hoya, or wax plant, which blooms in the summer but needs a waterless rest during most of the winter. Overwatering is one of the principal causes of lack of bloom in this plant, though another is cutting off the long, thin, trailing shoots. Hoyas are some of the very few plants that have to be allowed to grow long, thin, and untidy. They will not bloom until the stalks have

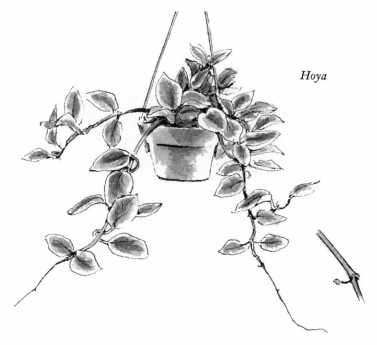

Hoya

NEGLECTABLE PLANTS

elongated to a considerable length. That is why hoyas, for all their sweet scented bloom, are not very attractive hanging plants and are usually better grown trained around a wire form and tied in. This gives a more attractive appearance than if the plant were allowed to trail untidily.

Succulent plants start into regrowth when the days become longer. Then the usual careful watering can be resumed. These spineless cacti are not desert plants like the thorny cactus and do not want the poor soil that suits the latter. Succulents want a soil that is rich in organic matter but has a great deal of gritty material in it to keep the soil open and allow for rapid and complete drainage. I use a fifty-fifty mixture of sharp sand and compost, and I add a little steamed bone meal for slow-acting nourishment—these plants, being fast growers, are also heavy feeders. It has already been stressed that succulents, being so shallow-rooted, do best in shallow pans. If you are forced to use ordinary-sized pots, make sure that at least a quarter of the interior is taken up with heavy crocking. Clay pots serve the plants best, and they will do even better in them if you will break rather larger holes in the bottom beside the drainage vents by chipping around them with an ice pick held at a slant, in the manner described in Chapter 1.

When repotting or potting up succulents, always have your soil mixture dry. Steer clear, for instance, of soaking wet peat moss if you are making a home-improved mix. Let the peat moss dry out for several days, after wetting it, before incorporating it. Though peat must never be bone dry, it must also never be saturated when used in a soil mix for these plants. Fill the crocked pot right up with the soil mix very nearly to the top—the whole process in repotting a succulent plant is, as you will see, different. Then, holding your plant in one hand, set the plant roots lightly on the surface of the soil. Do not press it down; merely trickle a little dry soil over the exposed roots. If the plant is tall and refuses to stand upright, anchor it into position between something like two flat plant labels which will balance it without forcing the roots downward. Never bury any fleshy portion of a succulent, for this inevitably will rot. Once you have induced a plant to stand steady, set it aside for a day or two without having given it any water. All this, as you can see, violates another of the usual canons of potting. Despite their tenacity as plants, succulent roots bruise easily, and they need a dry period after handling for the wounds to callous. Leave newly planted succulents without any attention for several days and then give the root area a light spraying. Do not use the normal method of heavy watering for at least two weeks after repotting. If you allow for these peculiarities, succulents will give you no trouble. Only if you ignore their slightly offbeat union rules will failure follow.

I still mourn a horticultural disaster that befell one of my plants, a twenty-five-year-old crassula full of sentimental associations, with tall, thick trunks like the redwoods and a wealth of white, sweetly scented bloom in the spring. When I was away for several months, it got knocked over and the pot broken. The horrified plant sitter immediately repotted it, but it was a huge plant and could not be made to stand upright in the same size pot it had been in before. To get better anchorage, it was thereupon put into very wet soil in a much bigger pot (and a plastic one, at that) and buried far more deeply than before, with some of the huge, fleshy stalks underneath the soil level to induce it to stand alone. Then, following what would have been proper horticultural practice with any other plant, the sitter gave it a thorough weekly watering. By the time I got back, it was too late: rot had spread through the entire system and the plant could not be saved.

Both echeverias and sempervivums can be used to make delightful wall panels for a balcony or any place where growing areas are limited. You will need the rather unpromising horticultural materials of a wooden plank, some lengths of small-meshed chicken wire, a stapler, and some tin snips. Staple wire down the whole length of the back of one side of the board. Trim the wire and fold it over both ends of the plank, leaving a loose fold but stapling the wire firmly into position. During the stapling process, wet down with hot water a considerable quantity of long-grained, that is, the unchopped, version of sphagnum moss (this is available at all garden centers). After fastening wire on both ends and on one side of the plank, stuff the wet sphagnum moss in a thick layer against the mesh so that it forms a sphagnum-covered bank. Fill up the moss-lined cavity between the wire and the plank with damp peat moss mixed with an equal quantity of perlite, the latter to provide proper aeration of this rather swamplike growing medium. Stretch the moss-covered wire over the inner fill so that the plank is entirely covered and the wire mesh is raised and rounded. This will call for the insertion of much more peat moss and perlite inside than you originally expected. You must put in enough inner material to have to strain the moss-covered wire over it to reach the far side of the plank. Bend the wire over the edge of the open side of the plank and

NEGLECTABLE PLANTS

staple that down under pressure on the back too. Cut off any surplus wire. You will scratch your hands doing all this and you may have to wear gloves. In spite of the rather complicated directions, the actual process is extremely easy and you will have created an ideal small-scale growing area that can be hung from a hook outdoors. In this plank many plants will thrive and none better than sedums, echeverias, and

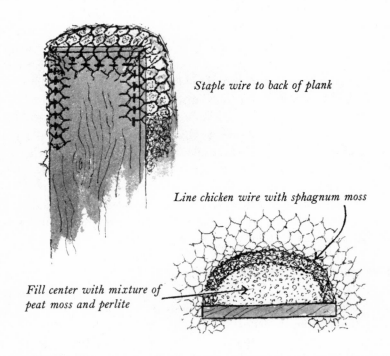

Staple wire to back of plank

Line chicken wire with sphagnum moss

Fill center with mixture of peat moss and perlite

sempervivums. To plant a plank, poke a hole through the mesh of the chicken wire, insert the cut stem of a succulent or the roots of a sempervivum, and press and hold them into place with some additional wet sphagnum moss. The rosettes look best grouped in specific patterns, and, as new growth starts or the stems elongate, they can be held in position with small hairpins. Planks dry out quickly and need regular watering and, as the rooting medium is sterile, the rosettes should also have an occasional foliar feed. Do not feed the actual growing medium itself when the plant is hanging up. If you do, the fertilizer will accumulate in the absorbent moss at the bottom, and growth in that area will become rank and unpleasant. When you want to give food to the growing medium, take the plank down and lay it on its back and water the food in. This will distribute fertilizer evenly throughout the interior. Echeverias and sedums on a plank can only be used outdoors in the summer; bring them into a cool place before

Plank planted with succulents

NEGLECTABLE PLANTS

frost and prune them right back to the wire mesh. This will produce new rosettes close to the wire, give you plenty of surplus material to root, and you can pull the sphagnum moss over the scar. Sempervivum planks can survive a winter out-of-doors.

Succulent rosettes can also be used in an unusual holiday decoration. For this you need to bend small mesh wire around the back of a box frame, which can be bought at any florists' supply shop. This again forms an area into which wet sphagnum moss can be pressed. When the frame of the wreath is thickly lined, set echeverias and big sempervivum rosettes down into the sphagnum. You water this kind of wreath by immersing it in a bowl and allowing it to drain. The circle of rosettes root into the moss and make an attractive feature and a well-rooted succulent wreath can be hung for display. It is wiser to show off a new one flat, and, for the furniture's sake, on something like a circular mirrored tray!

Pumice, or feather rock, which can be bought from building supply companies, can also be used to display sempervivums. They grow excellently on this material, for it approximates their natural home-land. Pumice rock is very sharp to handle, so always use gloves when you are working with it, and you are less likely to cut yourself if you keep the rock wet. Chip and gouge out with a hammer and an old screwdriver small planting holes and drop a little soil into the bottom of them. Try and follow the contours of the rock; this allows for easier hole-making. Plant the sempervivum clusters by gently pressing them

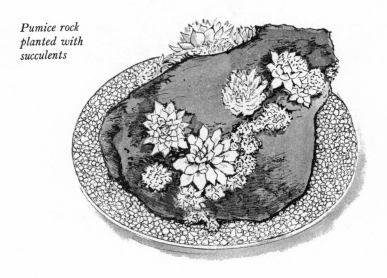

Pumice rock planted with succulents

into the holes; they will take root very quickly and gradually grow into thick rosettes. There is never any danger of overwatering a planting on a pumice rock. You can display it indoors on a pebbled tray or outdoors on your doorstep; either way it will thrive.

With all these specialized and easy ways of growing succulents they make wonderful material for presents. But always plan presents made from growing material well ahead; succulents, like all plants, look much better if they are given time to settle into position and blend their foliage.

In this section it has only been possible to touch upon the numerous possibilities among the succulent plants for an adventurous indoor gardener. Any good specialized catalog will be an eye-opener in the immense diversity of the material available and will undoubtedly lure you to further experiments. This can only be rewarding, and it is a pleasure to be able to recommend easy plants that are lovely, unusual, and can be left to themselves with such ease.

5 ✠ WINTER AND
SPRING BULBS

MOST NEW INDOOR GARDENERS buy their plants either in bloom, or, if they are foliage plants, already fully developed. It seems far beyond their capacity to make any plant grow from a seed or cutting. This is an entirely understandable initial reaction—we all went through that stage—but presently, the desire to be a little more adventurous may hit you. This is particularly likely to happen in the fall when your eye lights upon bushel baskets of bulbs temptingly displayed at every garden center, with enormous, splashy pictures of what they can become. Compared with the price of a potful of flowering bulbs, this basic material seems amazingly cheap; so you buy them, plant them, wait expectantly, and the result is often a great disappointment. Indoor bulbs need rather specialized treatment. Some kinds are quite demanding, and they all have to have their peculiar habits understood.

There exist, however, some easy bulbs that the novice usually can manage without too much difficulty and are well worth trying. These are the paper-white narcissus and a yellow variety called *soleil d'or;* there are also little hyacinths that throw a great many stalks of rather small, sweetly scented blooms and are known, somewhat confusingly, as French Roman hyacinths. There is also the spectacular amaryllis, which make a stupendous show.

These constitute what are known as tender bulbs, those that can't survive outdoors where the winters are cold and long. Even if you live in an area where such bulbs can be acclimatized, they will never be reusable after having been forced indoors. When the bloom is finished you always have to throw them all away. Tender bulbs are imported and have been intensively preconditioned by the grower so that they will flower early, out of their natural season, indoors. The future bloom is already perfectly formed inside. If you cut them exactly in half longitudinally, you can plainly see the embryonic flower stalk and bud. The treatment given these easy bulbs, which includes precooling, is very scientifically controlled and is always effective. But, by being compelled to change its normal growing pattern, the bulb uses up all the vitality within itself not only for the moment but for the future. Thus no easy bulb forced indoors—except the amaryllis, which will be discussed later—can ever recover and bloom again, no matter how good your growing practices may have been or how suitable the climate in which you live.

Paper-white narcissus

Preconditioning makes these bulbs much less complicated for the novice. Because they have been specially treated, they can withstand almost any mishandling, and, as, in most cases, there is no need to consider the future of the bulb itself, they can be grown in the simplest possible manner. You can put them in any kind of container as long as it holds water, and they can be supported with any kind of inert material. Easy bulbs look particularly well in good china bowls; that little-used family soup tureen gives a splendid effect filled with paper-whites—and the fact that there is no drainage problem to spoil the furniture is an extra bonus. But don't think only new growers use these easy bulbs. They may be the simplest and the best for your initial experiment, but sophisticated horticulturists delight, too, in their early bloom, lovely scent, and simple culture.

Tender, early bulbs are usually in rather short supply upon the open market. Ideally they should be ordered ahead from one of the many excellent bulb catalogs available. Failing that, you can probably find them in greenhouses and good garden centers. Try to buy the largest, plumpest bulbs available and always look to see that the tissue is unbruised and without rot. The bulbs should still be covered with the paper-thin outer skins like onions, for, if this has been all rubbed off, they may have suffered very rough handling somewhere along the line and will not grow as well. Always examine the flat part at the bottom of the bulb, known as the basal plate; all roots have to spring from it, and, if it is injured in any way, the bulb will not flourish. Prepackaged sets of paper-whites are also now available, to which, rather like instant coffee, you only have to add water. This might make a good starter present for a child, but one lonely paper-white in a paper pot does not really look or do well. Bulbs, like all plants, do much better grouped.

If you want a succession of bloom from the tender bulbs, buy them as soon as you find a source of supply. They vanish from the market rather quickly, but don't leave those you want for later use lying about. Bulbs, even in their dormant period, survive by drawing upon the moisture they've stored in their tissues. Unplanted bulbs soon deteriorate in dry, hot house air; so keep them stored in a cool, well-ventilated place. If no such location is available, put them in perforated plastic bags, the kind oranges are packaged in, in the vegetable crisper of your refrigerator. But don't put them near the recently washed lettuce. Moisture is a danger; it may set rot going in a bulb. Storage conditions have to be dry. Also do not put them in or near the freezing unit; remember these are tender bulbs that cannot survive hard frost.

Storage should always be in the dark, because light sets the tops growing—the familiar onion can be taken as an example. We have all seen onions sprout and grow without any sign of root action. Bulbs and onions behave alike, and bulbs in which the top growth has begun ahead of root development will blast—that is, the bud will never emerge. During very small experiments, I have found that all these tender bulbs will store extremely well for up to six weeks anywhere low down on the refrigerator shelves as well as in the crisper. Bulbs held in this manner stay dormant, and they undoubtedly leap into action faster once they are planted—more so than those stored in the conventional manner.

Tender winter bulbs are very easy to grow—all you have to do is put them into a container that is deep enough. Many books say 2 to 2½ inches is enough. This shallow depth has always led my bulbs to rise on their own stiltlike roots for lack of space. It seems better to use a container about twice the depth of the bulb and fill it three quarters full of pebbles—the less obtrusive the color of the pebbles the better—and stand as many bulbs as possible on the stones. Don't twist them in, for this injures the basal plate. Top up the stones with water until it reaches the plate but don't let it rise any higher or the bulb will rot. Fill in with more stones so that the bulbs are held upright; they are unlikely to need any more water until heavy root growth has appeared.

Opinions vary about the best treatment once the bulbs are planted. Some experts put their containers, with great success, straight into a cool, sunny window. Others keep them in a cool, dark place until the root growth is well underway. My personal preference is for the cool, dark place, but here you must experiment to find which suits you best. Your aim should always be to get the strongest possible root growth established before the leaves start to elongate. Too warm a location will pull out long leaves, and almost all the failures with tender bulbs come from too much heat at too early a stage. But no matter how good your home conditions may be, you will never produce those fantastic bowls of paper-whites, with huge flower heads carried well above short, strong leaves, that appear in the shops. These have always been raised in a greenhouse and should never be compared with yours!

Even with the most careful attention and regular twisting, paper-whites, which are the most commonly used among the tender bulbs, will grow very tall indoors and invariably will flop over in an untidy, discouraging fashion. To look attractive, the foliage should be controlled by strands of yarn tied to small green stakes. One of the great disadvantages of growing bulbs in pebbles is that they cannot be staked; the little sticks absolutely will not stand upright. There is

WINTER AND SPRING BULBS

nothing more enraging than seeing a well-grown bowl of paper-whites deteriorate into a floppy mess, because the leaves and flowers cannot be supported. For that reason I prefer to grow my tender bulbs in a specially imported bulb fiber, or in a reasonable facsimile of it, which you can make at home. Basically, this consists of damp, not soaking, peat moss, with a considerable quantity of aquarium charcoal added to keep the medium sweet. If you have access to broken-up clam or oyster shells, some of this should also be mixed in to counteract the possible overacidity of the peat moss. Bulbs grow very well in this mixture, which has the enormous advantage of being able to support staking. It's clean and lightweight and holds the moisture much better than the pebbles. The imported material is fortified with extra nutrients for strong root growth and longer-lasting foliage. But if you are using the homemade version for bulbs that are going to be discarded after blooming, the lack of extra food doesn't matter.

Amaryllis

The amaryllis, which is a more expensive tender bulb, needs different treatment. These huge objects are usually not available in the garden centers until November, and, for really spectacular flowers, it is wise to buy the largest you can afford. Amaryllis bulbs, which are usually imported, have also been conditioned so that they will bloom early and successfully indoors, but, unlike the other tender bulbs, they can be carried over for indoor flowers in subsequent years. For good results, amaryllis should always be planted in rich soil with sand mixed in for good drainage; a plant that intends to throw up such a striking flower must have proper nourishment for the roots. Put the bulb in a properly crocked clay pot which is only one size larger than the circumference of the bulb itself; they do not do well in large pots. All the members of this particular plant family flower better when they are pot-bound. Fill the pot three quarters of the way up with the prepared soil and set in the bulb so that the upper half is exposed after the rest of the soil has been firmed in around it.

Opinions differ about the proper procedure to follow next. Many people produce excellent flowering plants by putting the planted pot straight onto a sunny window sill. This method will produce the earliest flowers. I am inclined to stagger the periods when I have these bulbs in bloom, for they are a little overwhelming in mass, by letting some of the newly potted specimens start to root in the cool area of the cellar that holds a temperature of around 60 degrees. The first sign of growth after you have potted your bulb and given it a regular but not torrential amount of daily water is often the bud, pushing up through the side of the bulb. It used to be a very bad omen if leaves appeared first, for that meant there was no flower on the way. Some modern varieties throw leaves first; so don't worry if you get foliage ahead of any show of bud. Keep rotating the pot so that you can thwart its determination to lean to the light, and you will be rewarded with an immense scape of bloom which, for once, you will not have to stake.

After the flowers are over, remove the actual flower head but not the stalk, and grow on the leaves to full and lasting maturity in a sunny window. The pot will need regular watering and an occasional light feed. Again the bulbs show variations in habit. In some the leaves show signs of decay around the end of May. Other plants seem ready to remain lusty and green throughout the summer. Mine do best if they are forced into dormancy by a complete withdrawal of water in June. I put the bulbs in their pots into the cellar where they remain totally dry but in a relatively cool place during the hot weather. This cellar is unheated, so, when the weather outdoors really chills off, I move the pots into a warmer location where the temperature runs in the high sixties. By November there is often a sign of life, or if not, I start them on their way again by rewatering. But I should warn you that this is not the conventional treatment for these bulbs. I came around to the

WINTER AND SPRING BULBS

method after several very irritating experiences of having my held-over pots turn out blind—that is, with no flower. If you read up on this plant, you will find a lot of contradictory advice. In my opinion, the amaryllis is an adaptable plant that will usually respond to any rhythm of growth that is arranged for it. But its good nature has limits. All members of the amaryllis family dislike root disturbance, and the amaryllis bulb resents it the most. For good bloom a second year, you would be well advised only to top dress the pot soil with a very rich mixture containing a dusting of dried cow manure. If you plan to carry over your bulb still longer, repot it during the middle of its resting period when, hopefully, there will be no active roots to get damaged. And never repot all your bulbs the same year or you may have no bloom at all. I do not find that this bulb blends well with other plants; it is too big. But for a splashy, individual show, you can't beat an amaryllis!

Once you have had success with the tender easy bulbs, your new-found self-confidence may lead you to try the Dutch bulbs, the kind that give us such pleasure outdoors in the spring. These are slightly more complicated to bring successfully to bloom indoors, but, to me, there is nothing like the pleasure that comes from the sight and scent of a bowl of hyacinths in the depth of winter—it's almost like having a child; you forget completely the trouble the process has been.

Most of us think of planting these bulbs also only when we see them displayed in bins at the retailers, and then there are so many different kinds that we get confused. It is much better also to order them in advance from a catalog, for then you can discover which varieties force well indoors and save yourself considerable work, and yet get poor results.

Hyacinths are the easiest for the beginner to grow. Huge trumpet daffodils are rather overpowering indoors, in spite of their allur-ing pictures. The bulbs are very big and the foliage grows excep-tionally tall, and these very tall leaves inevitably brown off at the tips with indoor forcing. Small-cup daffodils, which are listed under that general name, will do far better and so will the medium-size trumpet daffodils. Miniature daffodils, though enchanting, are almost impossi-ble to grow well without considerable experience. Keep away from tu-lips, at any rate at first; only the early singles and doubles will bloom without a greenhouse, and even for experienced horticulturists they can prove a menace! Little pots of crocus can give great pleasure; they grow quickly and send out a lot of rather transient bloom. The only difficulty for the novice is to decide which way up to plant them. The indented, slightly bald part is the bottom, and the part with the rather hairy skin covering it is the top. More than one eminent horticulturist have absentmindedly planted their crocus corms wrong side up! Con-

Crocus corm

trary to the usual advice, I don't grow the *Muscari*, or grape hyacinth. This small bulb throws up its foliage in the fall, months before flowering; you will get extremely tired of a very ratty-looking pot long before there is any chance of a bloom.

When you buy bulbs, stay away from those labeled "jumbo" size. These throw up "jumbo" blooms which are often so large that they cannot hold their heavy heads upright and have to be lashed, individually, to the mast. They are usually overpriced and far fewer can be put in a single pot. With hyacinths get the medium-size bulb, and with daffodils try also to get a medium-size bulb but always one with what is called a double nose—that is, two necks—for these will throw several stalks of flowers to each bulb. If you can't plant your bulbs at once, store them, like the paper-white and all the tender bulbs, in a dark, cool place. Again, the refrigerator will do, and don't leave them tightly enclosed in brown paper bags stapled at the top, which is how your retailer may have sold them. When bulbs are sent to you from a good dealer, you will always notice that the bags have had holes punched in them. Bulbs must have air to exist, so you must always tear open a market bag when you get home.

Dutch bulbs don't do particularly well in the makeshift fiber, and they won't flower at all successfully in pebbles and water. Though, once again, the potential flower is already established, they have not been nearly so extensively preconditioned. To produce good leaves and strong flowers, they need a rich compost or a home-improved commercial mix. Unlike the tender bulbs, Dutch bulbs are hardy and can survive very cold winters. If you have a garden and hope to plant your potted bulbs outside later on, add a little steamed bone meal to the bottom layer of the pot soil. This will have no effect on the quality of the flower, but it will provide later food for the leaves that have to

WINTER and SPRING BULBS

continue growing after the flower has faded, in order to plump up the depleted bulb. But don't add any quick-acting fertilizer to the soil as this will only encourage lush leaf growth at the expense of the flower. And don't mix any bone meal in the top of your pot soil, or your planting will grow that unattractive fuzz.

You can use either plastic or clay bulb pans; these are the wide-mouthed, squat pots that have less depth than ordinary flowerpots of the same width. Blossoming bulbs look in better proportion in them.

Growing bulbs calls for a great deal of moving of the pots upstairs and downstairs and into a sunny window. For reasons of weight, and also because they conserve moisture better, plastic bulb pans are proba-bly easier for the novice to handle. Crock the pots in the usual way, fill them three quarters full, and settle the soil with the usual raps. Don't ram it down; if the pot soil is compacted into too hard a mass, the roots will not penetrate but instead will rise up and push the bulbs danger-ously and unattractively out of the pot. Put in as many bulbs as possible for a good show. Books warn against having the bulbs actually touch each other in the pot, but this has never bothered mine. Again, be careful of the basal plate and fill up the pot by dribbling soil in and around the bulbs until only the tops are showing. You should rap the pot up and down as you work and force the soil in with your fingers. Don't use a stick or plant label for fear of piercing a bulb. Remember to look underneath afterwards and clean out any drainage vents that may have got clogged. After planting, there should be an inch between the tips of the bulbs and the rim of the pot to allow for later watering.

If you would like a particularly lavish potful of daffodils, try a planting trick that does not seem to be very well known in the U.S. Use a deep pot, not a bulb pan, and crock this as usual. Then fill in with soil about one third of the way up. At this level, set in three double-nosed bulbs, which you may have to crowd together a bit. Put bamboo stakes into the soil beside each bulb, tall enough to rise above the rim of the pot. Cover the bulbs and put in enough soil to bring the surface up to normal planting level. Then plant more daffodils, using the stakes as guides to prevent you from setting the basal plates of the top layer right over the noses of the lower bulbs. Finish off the opera-tion in the usual way, with a tattoo of thumps and a thorough soaking of the pots; then pull out the stakes. The double layer will root and grow successfully in and around each other, putting out a tremendous show of bloom. The lower bulb shoots will take a little longer to thrust out through the surface layer of the soil; they have, after all, had to grow a greater distance. Once above ground they seem to catch up easily with the upper row and the buds appear at very much the same time. If, as occasionally occurs, the upper row of bulbs comes into bloom a little in advance of the lower threesome, you will still have a

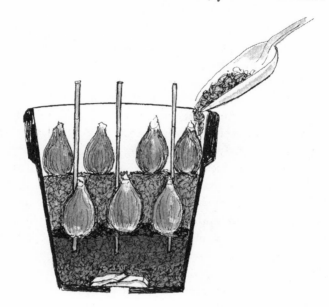

Plant a double layer of bulbs

wonderful show of flowers and a succession of blossom. Double potting is a very common practice among commercial growers who price their pots at so much per bud. But do try it yourself sometime. There is no reason at all why you should have any difficulty, and it may have the desirable side effect of bringing you the slightly unwarranted reputation of being a superlative horticulturist. If you can once get that idea into the heads of your friends, many other shortcomings are often overlooked!

If, in spite of my advice, you buy tulips, pot them up with the flat side toward the edge of the pot. The first large leaf grows from that side, and, always supposing you confound the experts by succeeding, it will fall gracefully out and over the rim. Plant all small bulbs as thickly as possible in a proportionately smaller pot. Nothing looks meaner than a few dreary little bulbs in a large pan!

After planting, you must soak your pans. Set them in a bowl with

WINTER AND SPRING BULBS

water halfway up the sides of the pot and wait until moisture shows on the surface of the soil. Overhead watering doesn't penetrate evenly or sufficiently, and it often merely washes out the newly inserted soil. Failure to soak bulb pans properly is usually the cause of the uneven growth and bloom that plagues many growers. After the whole pan has been moistened, it is equally important to allow a full day for the surplus water to drain out. If you have a garden, leave them standing outside; indoors, put a colander over a bucket and let the pot drain. Skimping the drainage period often leads to permanently saturated soil, and, by now, there is no need for me to go on stressing that this condition sets in rot.

The rooting stage, which all bulbs must undergo, is vitally important with Dutch bulbs. If, like most of us, you have sometime mistakenly dug up a hyacinth in your garden in August, you will have noticed that it has already formed strong roots. Bulbs start growing long before the snow flies, but these same bulbs, which we call Dutch because they were first cultivated intensively in Holland, originated in places with very cold winters—among others, the mountain ranges of Iran, Afghanistan, and Turkey. They still carry within themselves the hereditary necessity of undergoing a period of cold during which, safely insulated underground, they grow yet more roots and without which they will not bloom. If you were to put that bulb you dug up in error into a pot and try to grow it on indoors, no flower would ever appear in spite of the good roots—only leaves, and this would happen no matter how good your treatment. The embryonic bud will never develop until is has been thoroughly chilled. Our great problem, therefore, is how to provide bulbs with this cold, dark period under modern living conditions. In the north, if we stand potted bulbs outside on a window ledge or balcony, the bitter cold will ruin the bulbs, because they are not sufficiently insulated. Elsewhere the temperature may not be cold enough, long enough.

So how best to manage? I often read advice about digging a trench and burying pots in it beneath a load of straw. This is fine for gardeners with gardens, but it involves more space and effort than I am prepared to give—also, it is not easy to buy small quantities of straw. I did do it once, and it worked well—except that the pans could not be got out of the cast-iron ground until late April and then only after lighting a fire on top. For northern gardeners with a garden, the ideal solution is a cold frame where the pans can be buried under a pile of leaves—or even a bottomless box set on the ground and also filled with leaves, with a pane of glass on the top tilted with a brick to allow circulation of air and to shed the snow. If you can contrive conditions of this sort, your bulbs will need no further attention from you. You can also root pans equally well in a cold cellar, unheated attic, or garage. But in that case you must watch that they don't dry out. A good idea is to put the whole set of pots into a plastic garment bag, and then cover with leaves. To make sure of sufficient air circulation, blow the bag up like a balloon before sealing it with an elastic band. This will save worry about the watering.

If you are an apartment dweller with absolutely nowhere cool and dark, try the refrigerator: put the bulb pans on a lower shelf away at the back and wait. Rooting bulbs in the refrigerator is still in an experimental stage. It has worked well for me, though rather messily, and I feel you need a second refrigerator. A pan of bulbs alongside leftover peas and meat has, in some way, a curious psychological impact. Besides, my compost, being very rich, is inclined to harbor earthworms, and earthworms in the icebox I find displeasing. Nevertheless, the process is possible, though rather long and drawn out, and may well be the answer for the lover of spring bulbs with no cool place for rooting. Refrigerator rooting may also prove to be the way in which southern growers are able to enjoy these cool-loving bulbs. Whatever your methods, if you are to have flowers, you must provide this period of cold both for rooting and to trigger off the ancestral drive to bloom.

Bulbs ready for forcing

These considerable efforts should all start in October. Then when we are at our lowest ebb longing for spring, we may be able to produce our own illusion of it with bowls of scented, flowering bulbs. But not, unfortunately, without yet more work. In January the pans should be examined; when some may be found to have roots thrusting through the drainage holes. Bulbs ready for forcing should have a tangle of strong, white roots circling the entire interior of the pot. If you have any doubts, knock out the pots. If the roots are only just showing, put the pot back, cover it up, and be patient a little longer. Bulbs will not force properly until they are heavily rooted. You can find pots with heavy roots and no sign of any top growth. These can be forced by experienced growers, but a novice would do well to put those back. Bulbs are much easier to manage if top growth is a couple of inches along. As the rooting process has taken place in darkness, the shoots will be white. Don't put the pots straight into strong light; this may scorch the tender foliage. Allow them to green up in a cool, sunless position. Pots rooted outdoors are sometimes frozen hard, and the bulbs, in spite of your planting precautions, have been forced up on their roots out of the soil. Don't make any attempt to cram them back. Leave them alone while the soil thaws out and the tops green up; the roots will usually sink back into place unless you set them in too high. Once the shoots are green, move the plants to your brightest, coolest window; keep the topsoil reasonably moist and the pans regularly rotated, so that the shoots don't lean toward the light. The cooler your growing location, the better your chance of getting the flower heads up above the foliage. Complete success in this department is very sophisticated work, and a novice should not be too discouraged if the hyacinths bloom rather low on their stems, in a manner that my mother used to describe as "stuck in the bud." Hyacinth buds can be seen from the start; daffodil buds will be seen after the leaves begin to grow.

At first, the shoots will seem to stand still; then you will notice that the base is lighter in color than the upper part. This means the bulbs are off and running, and the pans should then be given more water and even put in saucers without pebbles so that they can reabsorb surplus runoff—but always beware of permanently sodden soil. Once the buds begin to swell, reduce the watering. If the leaves grow very far ahead of the flower buds, I am assured by my talented friends that the situation can be rectified by putting a brown paper bag, with a hole torn in the top, over the pot and that this will pull the bud up. I have never succeeded with this method, but the fault must lie with me.

Once the leaves have really lengthened, staking is needed. No plant grown in the heat of a house can continue to hold its leaves upright unsupported. Staking is a very neglected art. You need special bamboo stakes, which you can get at any garden or hardware store—not the domestic stake, a broken pencil! You also need green yarn, green to be

Properly staked arrangement

unobtrusive and yarn for the utmost flexibility. Don't put your stakes around the edge of the pot like a picket fence and then lash in the unlucky leaves with a hawser of string. Staking should be unobtrusive; set them inside the pot (being careful not to pierce a bulb) and press them firmly into position as far behind the leaves as possible. Weave and tie in the yarn around the bud stalks and leaves until you have produced a naturalistic, controlled effect. Short leaves can usually be pulled outside or over the yarn so that it is almost hidden.

Staking should be started early; a pot that has already collapsed is hard to rescue attractively. With tall plants like daffodils, it may have

WINTER AND SPRING BULBS

to be done twice; so don't clip off the upper ends of the stakes until the buds begin to open; then cut them so they disappear entirely from sight. A well-grown, well-staked pot of blossoming bulbs, gleaming indoors while the snow is on the ground, stirs a very primitive reaction in me—the scent is spring and the flowers invite a thousand quotations. Bulbs are cheap and the results so rewarding that every novice should try them in spite of the long pull ahead.

If this all seems a little more than you want to undertake, why not start with a simpler experiment by bringing a hyacinth to bloom in water? Growing hyacinths this way was extremely fashionable in the last century when special bulb glasses, in red, blue, and green glass, were manufactured for the purpose. These consisted of a vase with a narrow collar at the neck that expanded into a cup shape in which a bulb could be suspended over water. Original hyacinth glasses can sometimes be found at unbelievable prices in antique shops or even put away on the top shelf in the house of an elderly relative, but modern replicas are also easily obtainable, made of clear glass. Fill the vase with water and add a little aquarium charcoal to keep it fresh. When the bulb is in place, the water should just tickle the bottom of the basal

Bulb glass

plate. Like all Dutch bulbs, a hyacinth in a water glass must have a period in a cool, dark place to make sufficient roots—the back of the lower shelf of the refrigerator does very well. When the roots begin to fill the glass, a slight retopping with water may be needed. And when root growth is really heavy, the vase should be brought into a cool, sunny window and grown on, being regularly rotated so that it doesn't lean to the light—there is absolutely no way in which you can stake a bulb in a glass. If you have managed the cool rooting period properly, you will be rewarded with a good flower head.

This is a good way to get a child interested in growing things, and I can speak from personal experience. I had an elderly cousin who, now I look back on it, possessed a most remarkable piece of furniture. I recall her saying it had belonged to my double great-grandmother: that, alas, takes us back well past the century mark. This was a circular, two-tiered, mahogany revolving plant stand. Around the edge of each shelf were a dozen circular openings with a break in the circumference of each. At some stage in the winter, in a rather stately ceremony, the usual plants were removed from the stand and two dozen white hyacinths, heavily rooted in dark-blue glasses, were produced, presumably from the cellar where they had been rooted—though from what I have been told of the house temperature they could have been rooted equally successfully in any one of the bedrooms! The glasses were slipped into place in their allotted holes and the whole contraption was then moved into the ice-cold bay window of the drawing room. I remember my interest in the development of the roots and buds and the excitement when, on my cousin's monthly "At Home" day, I was allowed to give the shelves the required daily half-turn. This is a very early horticultural memory, for I was still a very little girl. But, formidable old lady as she seemed to me, that same cousin must have recognized my real interest, for it was also at her house that I was called in one day for a special treat—which proved to be something I have not often seen since—an aspidistra plant blooming away at soil level! I wish I knew what had happened to that admirable piece of furniture. I would dearly love to have inherited it. Pleasurable as it may be to grow hyacinths in water this way, the bulbs are completely exhausted by the process and must be thrown away when they have finished blooming.

If you have access to the outdoors, you may want to try to naturalize your forced Dutch bulbs. In that case, cut off only the flower heads, not the stems, when they fade and put the pots in an unobtrusive sunny place where they can still be kept watered. Bulbs will never do well again unless they are allowed to keep their leaves growing until they

WINTER AND SPRING BULBS

wither naturally. When the weather makes it possible, knock out the pots and put the contents into a single deep hole with steamed bone meal in the bottom. The base of the growing stems should be at least an inch below ground level. Don't disturb either the leaves or the roots; this means leaving the crocks and stakes entirely alone. Water the new clumps thoroughly and then forget them. In the fall you can rescue the stakes.

Planted this way, there will probably be some bloom the following year, for the undisturbed root mass will have ripened and established itself in rich soil. If you follow the usual advice and wait to plant until the leaves and roots have entirely withered, the bulbs will have had to ripen in the exhausted soil of the pot and will endure considerably more damage later on by being planted out in ground that has already warmed up. I find bulbs recover far better if they are set out as a compact group and no attempt is ever made to separate them.

There is, furthermore, a particular pleasure in being able to renew acquaintance in later years with a bowl of bulbs you once enjoyed indoors: it produces a very personal involvement. But if you are a gardenless gardener, this particular involvement cannot be for you. Dutch bulbs forced indoors cannot ever be induced to give a repeat performance. If you have no garden, throw them away after they have bloomed and start again next year.

A lot of trouble for a very short period of pleasure? Perhaps. But bulbs bring me a satisfaction that no other plant can equal and, if you will but try, I am sure you will find the same to be true for yourself.

6 ❧ WINTER AND EARLY SPRING

MANY PLANTS that flower indoors during the winter or even in the early summer months have rather special requirements. These are discussed in the chapters that are concerned with their particular culture. In this section, I want to explain how best to handle the more matter-of-fact flowering plants that are usually available at most garden centers during the winter.

For a great many people, a plant collection is incomplete without flowering plants; foliage plants alone seem dull. This problem is often handled by just buying a pot of flowering plants and adding it as a temporary improvement to the plant stand. Chrysanthemums do very well for this purpose and all such purchases will last longer if the amount of water given is reduced as the buds begin to open. But some people want plants that will look well all the time but still give an occasional bonus of bloom. Unfortunately, unless you possess a sunroom or have some special arrangement made for plants, this kind of permanent collection of flowering plants is a bit of a pipe dream.

Plants that will serve as the backbone of a collection, produce bloom, and last from year to year are rare, and those few that do exist are often hard for the novice to handle. Two plant families do fill the bill—African violets and some of the related gesneriads, and some begonias. Many people grow excellent collections of both these families on their window sills. I also grow them, but not on window sills, and I shall discuss my methods in Chapter 10. For novice horticulturists who want to try their hand with these admirable plants, many good specialized books are available.

One tremendous stalwart for any modern plant collection, for permanent use and for occasional bloom, is the spathiphyllum. This is a

WINTER AND EARLY SPRING

relatively new introduction for home growers and can be bought in a large- or a small-leaved variety. Spathiphyllum grows uncomplainingly in poor light in high house heat as long as it is kept very well watered.

Spathiphyllum

The small-leaf variety will throw up so much foliage growth that it soon needs dividing. Fortunately, these plants are also extremely tolerant of experimental work in that area! Flowers appear on the spathiphyllum whenever it is given good light. The blooms, which are white, last an unusually long time and are shaped a little like a small calla lily. When the flowers are over, cut off the entire stalk. This is a shade-loving plant from forest areas, and it resents even the mildest sunlight.

Several spathiphyllums can be potted together to make a spreading accent plant. They enjoy a rich soil well laced with water-absorbent material, and they profit from an occasional feeding. Like all tropical plants, they need as much humidity as possible, and the dry well of stones on which they stand should be kept perpetually moist. Indoors, these plants seem to need no rest or dormant period to do their best: they are always in active growth and apparently always ready to bloom. But for all their tolerance, they are not plants that can be neglected. Deprived of daily watering, spathiphyllums collapse immediately in the most dramatic manner. They usually revive completely as long as rescue comes in time, but, because of their urgent need for steady moisture at the roots, they are best grown in plastic pots. For gardenless gardeners, spathiphyllums will perform best in a sunless window.

Anthurium

Another plant with rather the same shape of bloom is the more leathery-leaved anthurium, which is sometimes called the flamingo flower. This sends up an equally long-lasting spathe of red, white, or pink flowers. Big, well-grown anthuriums are a commonplace in the warmer regions of the United States. In the north they are very expensive plants, and they take time to become important-looking. Well-established anthuriums throw out a steady succession of new leaves, and they are well worth buying in quite small sizes to put together in a single pot with the same rich soil enjoyed by the spathiphyllum. They grow slowly and will take a long time to crowd each other out. These plants also seem to have no well-defined resting period. The small, arrow-shaped leaves change in color as they mature, making the plant interesting in or out of bloom and, unlike the spathiphyllum, they will not stage a Victorian death scene if temporarily forgotten. So, though slightly more expensive, anthuriums may represent a better bargain for someone who is not always entirely reliable about a daily investigation of the needs of each plant!

Clivia

Another excellent foliage and flowering plant is, of course, the clivia, which has already been discussed in other contexts. Clivias bloom in shades of orange and will also set very long-lasting red berries if the blossoms are fertilized. If no berries form, it is probably better to let the blossom stalk wither off of its own accord rather than cut it down. They take up a lot of room even when regularly divided, and, if they are crowded, the fan of leaves gets shabby. But when in bloom they look wonderful massed. One danger is allowing water containing any form of fertilizer to stand at the center of the fan of leaves. This often produces very serious rot in the heart of the plant, and, as this is the area from which all the new growth must come, not only is the plant's future appearance spoiled, but often the growing point is also destroyed. For that reason, do not foliar-feed a clivia and be careful when using a pot-soil feed to keep the material off the leaves. Clivias make marvelous foliage plants and can tolerate poor light or winter sunlight, but if you keep your clivia indoors in the summer protect it from the sun.

When our houses were colder and we all needed much heavier blankets at night, it was occasionally possible to raise camellias for bloom indoors. And they can still be found offered to the unwary as highly expensive houseplants. To buy a well-budded camellia and bring it into the normal house atmosphere is to invite prolonged disappointment. These plants have been raised in a greenhouse and it is impossible for them to adjust. The only way to grow them indoors— and I consider it a time-consuming, boring method of desperation—is to have brought them to bud outdoors yourself and then take them indoors into a very light, cold place for slow acclimatization before the house heat comes on. Even so, to prevent the inevitable plink as the dried-up buds fall off without opening, you must wrap a wisp of cotton batting around the neck of each bud where it joins the stem and mist that wisp daily. Among their many problems, indoor camellias are extremely liable to a pest called mealy bug. These find an ideal rooming area under the cotton, and among your other regular chores with a camellia is an investigation under the cotton for fear mealy bugs may have established themselves. I love camellias and grow a great many of them—but not indoors. If, by all this effort, you do get a few flowers to open, the end result is not worth the struggle. House-grown camellias lose their leaves rapidly and make ungainly plants. Next time you are pressed to buy a camellia, point out firmly that this is not a houseplant and should not be sold as such, for this constitutes a rather expensive, unfair misrepresentation.

If you are adamant enough, you will probably be offered a gardenia as being much more suited to indoor life. Advice about gardenias indoors is very hard to give. They grow well for otherwise inexperienced gardeners in unsuitable places indoors, and faint and fail for experienced horticulturists who seem to be doing all the right things. Gardenias clearly come in easy and difficult varieties, but unluckily there seems to be no way of telling which is which. They all need a great deal of humidity, and the pot soil should never be allowed to dry out. They also need an even temperature and bright light with no sun, but they are such temperamental prima donnas that it is almost impossible to generalize more than that about their care. I don't think a novice should spend money buying such a tricky plant, but, if you are given one and find it does well with you, you've got an excellent houseplant. I am one of those people who can do nothing with gardenias indoors, but the least experienced (horticulturally speaking) of my daughters grows a flourishing gardenia. It is, however, her only plant and I have the feeling that gardenias do best when they can command every ounce of attention and devotion their owners have to bestow. The best indoor gardenias I have seen have almost always been only children! Perhaps this is mere chance, but it does make me feel a little better about my failures. If you are growing good gardenias, go on with your present methods and pay absolutely no attention to anyone else's advice. Gardenias, like camellias, prefer dappled shade if they are taken outdoors in the summer and regular feeding while they are making new growth.

There are now available in the shops various small members of the citrus family with dark-green glossy leaves that do well indoors. With patience, you can even grow your own plants from ripe pips of oranges, lemons, and grapefruit, though it will be a good many years before there will be flowers. Citrus plants need warmth, excellent humidity, and a great deal of air space around them. They don't do well crowded about with other plants, and they must be carefully watched for scale (a pest which, together with mealy bug, will be discussed in Chapter 15). Occasionally an otherwise well-grown citrus plant will turn yellow in the leaves; this also occurs with gardenias. Chlorosis is the name of the trouble, and it means that the plant cannot get at the trace element of iron in the pot soil. The condition can be corrected by several new products now available at garden centers.

Small citrus plants are well worth adding to a plant collection. Their summer care involves more sun than most foliage plants, and they must have a steady supply of water. They can be kept going equally easily indoors. Properly handled, they will reward you with a sweetly scented bloom that occurs throughout most of the winter and small, sour fruit that will ripen and hang simultaneously from the branches.

Citrus plants

There are not many other plants available for the indoor gardener that can be used as a permanent part of the collection and yet be relied upon to bloom. One old-fashioned plant that used to be very popular, the abutilon, or flowering maple, has almost vanished, largely because of an unpleasant habit of leaf drop. A new dwarf variety has much better indoor growing habits, but it is still rather hard to find. Another flowering and foliage plant once very popular that is now making a comeback is the neomarica, or apostle plant. It has a fan of iris-shaped leaves and throws out fragile irislike blossoms on the ends of long

Maranta

leafstalks. Left alone, a small new plant will form where the blossom appeared, which in nature would root when the weight of the plantlet brought it down to the ground. Neomaricas are decorative and long-lived, and they are also very tolerant of poor growing light. So ephemeral is the flower that it is hard to decide whether marantas should be counted as flowering, foliage, or hanging plants. But their style and the grace of the after-flower make them well worth being used for all these purposes.

With a warm atmosphere and humidity provided by a deep dry well, you can grow members of the marantha and calathea families. When happy, these turn into large, spreading plants, some with red veins and others with striped and spotted leaves. They loathe crowding, look better displayed alone, and are tolerant of poor light. Big plants are expensive, and retailers should be pressed harder to provide smaller specimens.

Poinsettias, if you will buy the Mikkelsen variety, now make a very useful, long-lasting houseplant. They used to drop their leaves at the drop of a hat and turn almost at once into ridiculous, bare-legged caricatures, but the new hybrid will last properly clothed for months. To most people, poinsettias mean Christmas, but they can now be classed as very long-lasting houseplants without any seasonal connotation.

Poinsettias can be cut back after they have bloomed and carried on outdoors during the summer. This is another of the short-day plants and to get early color in the bracts, which is the part we usually think of as the flower, poinsettias have to be given that timed control of reduced daylight. It is therefore really impracticable for the novice gardener to try to use the same poinsettia another year. A small word of warning is in order about the leaves of this plant. If you are at the stage of life where you have an infant crawling around putting everything in its mouth, avoid poinsettias until the child has reached a more sensible stage. The leaves are very poisonous, and, if you have mistakenly bought one of the old varieties, there will be far too many dropped leaves on the floor for safety.

Another decorative plant that thrives in warm windows is the aphelandra, which carries a very long-lasting head of yellow blossom. I have not enough experience with it to know whether it will rebloom a second year indoors, but its variegated foliage makes an excellent effect on a plant stand.

All flowering plants need as much winter sunlight as possible, and the cooler the location at night, the longer the flowers will last. In the description of window areas, which is where all the flowering plants do best, the point was made that the more spectacular of the indoor flowering plants need extremely cool growing conditions by day as well as at night. This applies equally strongly to some of the berried plants that we find on sale, such as the Jerusalem cherry and the pepper plant. These will have a very short life in a warm location, for leaf drop will reduce them to hideous skeletons. If you can put them in a cold place they will look well for a surprisingly long time. An extremely cold window also suits the marguerite, or Boston daisy, which can be grown on into quite a large plant with a steady succession of bloom.

The really spectacular parade of winter blossoming plants turns up in the shops in early December, but, even if you see azaleas and cyclamen offered earlier, don't buy them for they will have been too overforced to survive room conditions. This is particularly true of the small pink azaleas that are the first to appear. Brought home, the buds fail to open, and the plant undergoes a catastrophic leaf drop from which it never recovers. Early-bought cyclamen usually have a few miserable flowers and poor buds and are also not worth the price. These failures occasionally come from our mistakes, but far more often they are the aftermath of an attempt by the grower to get the plants earlier to market than their natural growing habits allow. As a result they cannot survive once they have been taken from their special forcing houses. Try and avoid buying any of the deep-winter blossoming plants until January at the earliest; then they will not have been given such intensive forcing and will be much stronger plants.

Azaleas come in two blood lines—the *kurume*, which has a small leaf and little trumpet-like flowers, and the *indica*, which has a larger leaf and bigger, flatter flowers. Both types are sold with flowers in bloom and many unopened buds that are covered with a brown calix. Azaleas need a great deal of water. To get abundant bloom they are grown in a pot-bound state with a tightly packed root mass in the small-

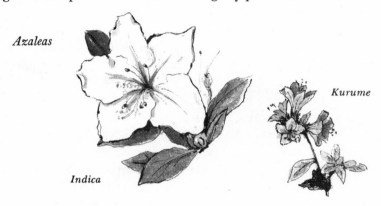

Azaleas

Kurume

Indica

est possible pot. This makes it hard for the roots to get enough water, for there is very little soil left in the pot to absorb any surplus. Azaleas in bloom must be watered thoroughly every day or they will droop dismally. The main danger is dryness at the center of the root ball, and an occasional dunking of the whole pot into a bucket of water, where it should be left until the air bubbles stop rising, will be a great help. Regular misting keeps the bud calix soft and makes it easier for the flowers to come through. Most azaleas drop some leaves when they are first brought into the house, as the direct result of atmospheric change. This usually slows down, and it is not the same as the complete leaf drop that denudes the overforced plants. A well-managed azalea will repay you in a rather irritating way by sending out a lot of green shoots around the base of the still-to-open flower buds, thus spoiling their appearance. This is new growth for the coming year, but it should be nipped out firmly with your finger and thumb; otherwise you won't see the new flowers nearly as well, and while you're at it, pinch off all the faded blossoms.

I used to be afraid to take out these green shoots for fear of ruining the plants for the following year. One day a friend of mine who grows magnificent azaleas came early to take me somewhere and was left alone with my azaleas of which I was rather proud. She couldn't bear

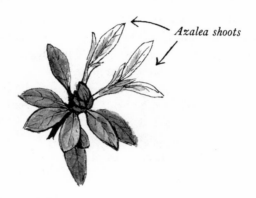

Azalea shoots

them—to her they were a disgrace. First, I gather, she nipped out a few small green shoots where their disappearance would not show, and then, as I learned later, she grew bolder. When at last I rushed in, full of apologies, I found her, glasses on nose, stripping my best azaleas of, what was to me, their future potential. I was simultaneously abashed, horrified, and sufficiently unconvinced to extract a promise that she would give me some of hers if mine died. The promise was unnecessary; my plants were, annoyingly, more shapely and fuller of bloom the next year. Since then I have always cleared off this first new growth; a second crop appears later on. After blooming, azaleas can be allowed to grow on in a cool, sunny place, still with copious water, though for many years I have successfully carried on my azaleas in a cool, but rather poorly lit cellar. In either location they are going to shed a great many more leaves, but new growth breaks as soon as the warmer weather arrives. Azaleas that have been conditioned in a cool place can be stood outside in their pots far sooner than those held in a warm, sunny window. The *kurume* types can be planted in the ground for permanent shrub decoration; they are winter hardy as far north as Boston. During the summer, azaleas, still in their pots, prefer dappled shade and to be watered and fed regularly. By September they need full sun to ripen the wood. It is possible, but not easy, for gardenless gardeners to carry over azaleas, but there will be a very long and rather disenchanting period before there is any return for all the labor. Perhaps it would be better to give them to a friend with a garden.

Cyclamens are the other supreme, long-lasting, winter-flowering plant. These are always extremely expensive and so full of buds that we rationalize their cost by expecting continuous weeks of bloom; their failure to thrive is therefore all the more irritating. Cyclamen cost so much because the growers have had to carry them for so long. Even the smallest size takes eighteen months to come to flower, and the big monsters are at least two years old. This florist, or Persian, cyclamen originated somewhere in the mountainous areas of Iran, where the species and many relatives still exist. In the wild, this particular cyclamen blooms when the nights are still extremely cold and the days bright but chilly. This is why they need such a cool place to do well indoors. Not everyone can produce a really cool growing area, but you will get much more mileage out of cyclamens and azaleas if you will take the trouble to put them into a slightly heated entry way, or an even colder place, by night.

Cyclamens, being very spectacular and having been popular as houseplants for a very long time, have accumulated a good deal of rather contradictory advice about their management. They certainly need a great deal of water, and they will show you at once when their need is urgent by drooping dismally. But the plant does not need to pull up all this water from below, which is so often advised. Unless a pot is partially submerged, it takes forever for moisture to rise to the surface of the soil, and anything as large as a cyclamen needs to have access to a very big supply of water. If you follow the advice and water only from below, you may well for once underwater the plant. The alternative is to leave water perpetually in the saucer, but this does as much harm to a fleshy rooted cyclamen as to any other plant. The official reason for watering from below is the danger of wetting and rotting the corms, the bulbous area from which all leaves and flowers spring. I think this fear dates from the time when houses were very cold and damp, and I suspect it to be advice handed down from English growers. In our hot houses, rot from watering a cyclamen from above seems improbable. This does not mean that water should be poured directly into the heart of the plant; that's bad practice at any time. But I have never watered my cyclamen from below, and I have never had trouble with rot. How to get rid of dead leaves and flowers is another matter on which there is a great deal of cyclamen folklore. There is general agreement that the fleshy stalks should not be left to rot away and that they are best pulled out, not cut off. This is fine, except the instructions usually given will not work. A dead leafstalk cannot just be yanked out; this often brings away part of the skin of the corm with it and that is an invitation to disaster. Instead you have to twist the stem, then pull, and the entire stalk comes free. Big cyclamen get middle-age spread. If your plant is thriving and the buds are continuing to open, staking is needed, because the leafstalks are also lengthening. Use green yarn and small stakes, and the control will hardly be noticeable.

Cyclamens come in such lovely colors that we hate to throw them away if they fade; everyone always wants to try and carry them on. They can be brought through to bloom another year but it takes skill. Once the leaves start to yellow, put the plant in an unobtrusive place and stop all watering. The top growth rapidly becomes a horrible mess, but you have to leave it strictly alone in its misery. As the foliage withers loathsomely away, the pot soil is drying out, and this process of drying is ripening or curing the corm. The whole process is complete when the foliage has withered sufficiently to be rubbed off without injuring the skin of the corm—this usually takes about two months. Throughout the curing process the corm has been dormant, living on moisture stored within itself, and the root system has shriveled along with the foliage. Conventional advice is to leave the pot on its side outside in the shade until August. This, I think, is, again, basically English practice. In the less wet summers and hotter sunshine of this country, the corms often get dried out forever, particularly if they are in clay pots. When I followed this advice and did succeed in reviving the plants in August, I had only very limited top growth when I brought them indoors to avoid frost. This meant months passed before there was a chance of even a single bud. I now start rewatering to renew top growth as soon as the old foliage can be rubbed off, and, at that time, I also top dress the pots. If you want to repot, this is the time to do so. Cyclamens need a rich, well-drained soil, and the corm should be allowed to sit, like a bun, halfway out of the pot. A buried corm enlarges enormously, which is the way the plant expands in the wild, but bloom is not nearly as good. Using this method, my plants are much more advanced when I take them indoors, and I often get bloom by Christmas without any forcing. But each year some corms fail to

WINTER AND EARLY SPRING

revive or do so in such a poor way that they are not worth saving. I do find that I have better luck with plants that have rested in plastic pots, but there is obviously some other basic factor in their survival treatment that I have failed to master. For the indoor gardener carrying over a cyclamen is a gamble, but, for the adventurous, worth trying at least once.

The other plant family that can be coaxed into doing wonderfully well in a cold window are the primulas, or primroses. These appear in the shops in early fall with one miserable head of bloom that eventually fails, leaving a tuft of uninteresting leaves—and we throw it out. This is sad treatment for an outstanding group of houseplants, and it comes about because the plants we buy have once again been forced into totally premature bloom.

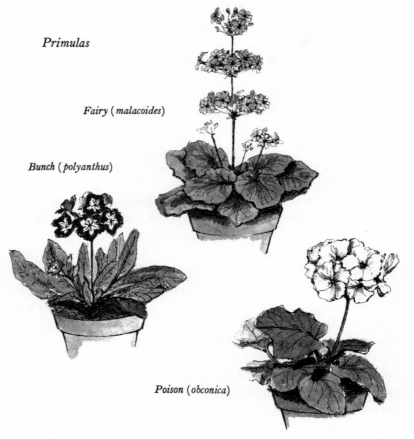

Primulas

Fairy (malacoides)

Bunch (polyanthus)

Poison (obconica)

If you have the facilities, buy primulas when you see them—or even go to a greenhouse and demand immature specimens. Three kinds are usually available: the bunch primrose, the fairy primrose, and the poison primrose. The latter gets its name from the effect it has on some people, as it gives them a rash similar to that from poison ivy. This comes from the oil in the hairs under the leaves of mature plants, and sensitivity usually sets in after handling a great many plants. A casual purchaser is hardly ever affected. Nevertheless, the danger of this particular plant is not enough stressed by the retailers.

Cut off any flower buds from the immature plants and repot in pots twice the size of those they were in. All primroses need a rich, moisture-holding soil, but it must also contain plenty of sand or other drainage material. In nature the plants live in damp places. Not all varieties like the acidity of peat moss, so, for water-holding properties, add wet, chopped sphagnum moss to your mix. Primroses are liable to neck rot if they are planted too deeply, but they also dislike being set so high that the crown rocks. Thus the problem in repotting is to get them settled at the proper level. Primroses should be grown slowly with plenty of water in a bright place without much sun: a cool east window is best. It may take as long as two months, but eventually you will be rewarded with an unending succession of magnificent flowers totally unlike any primrose plant you can buy.

Horticulture of this sort may be much more advanced than you ever expected to attempt, but it is no more complicated than bringing a clivia to bloom and far less difficult than that domineering gardenia. Sometime when you spot an unhappy primrose offered for sale out of season, try the process. Your success will well reward you. Primroses, though they are perennials, cannot be carried over indoors. When the towers of bloom eventually fade, get rid of them.

This section obviously cannot cover all the possibilities of flowering plants that may be available throughout the country. Those I have discussed are the indoor plants I have used over the years that have done best for me indoors and are the simplest for the grower to handle. As you become more experienced, your range will widen—it can go so far as to include certain varieties of orchids that can be flowered in the house. But don't fly too high too soon. Start with fairly simple plants and master their requirements; vaulting ambition comes later.

7 ❧ RAIN-FOREST PLANTS

MOST OF US don't bother much about where our houseplants originated, though we would all improve as horticulturists if we would take that extra trouble. We just assume that plants from every continent and every kind of climate have been so conditioned that they can take the great leap forward and live together under totally unnatural indoor conditions. With most plants this is, in fact, the case. They have been sufficiently worked over by the plant breeders that they will accommodate themselves fairly well to whatever environment we have to offer.

Among the plants whose good nature we take for granted are an immense number from the New World, which has produced many of our best foliage and blossoming plants. The number of invaluable houseplants from this continent is enormous, including as it does all the philodendron family, most of the begonias, the poinsettias, the epiphyllums, and many of the true orchids. And this is only the start of a huge list. A collection of houseplants deprived of anything originating in the New World would be quite sparse, for, with the great variation of climate that exists, the variety of plants is equally spectacular.

One exceedingly important group consists of plants that originated in the tropical rain forests on this side of the world, which are now being offered in increasing numbers by the retailers. But these, unlike many other plants, have not been entirely tamed. It is well, therefore, to be able to recognize them, for although they make excellent houseplants, they will only do so on their own terms.

A plant that originated in a tropical rain forest can be quite properly offered for sale with the recommendation that it will live happily in our even house heat and tolerate rather poor light, for these are two of the growing conditions of its natural environment. To that extent the ancestry of these plants does help them indoors, but there is another side to the coin. Any plant from a tropical environment also possesses a hereditary need for intense humidity, and this is not automatically present in all our houses. Unless you can take care of this problem, rain-forest plants will not do well for you. There are some species that the novice gardener should not even attempt to grow indoors—orchids, for example. These can be managed in a window but not by the unskilled, and most of us would do better to steer clear of them. Rain-forest plants also include many varieties that are freely offered for sale without enough indication of their specific requirements, and, as they usually are quite expensive, it seems important to stress which they are. The particular groups I have in mind include all the bromeliads; the epiphyllum, or orchid cactus, and its close relative, the Christmas cactus; and many varieties of tropical ferns.

In spite of present-day advertising, most of these plants are not novelties—all that is new about them is their easy availability in the shops. Specimens of almost every previously unknown flowering or foliage plant were recorded and sent back by the early explorers very soon after the opening of the New World, and the process continued steadily as the interior was reached. There is, after all, a seventeenth-century picture of Charles II of England being presented with a pineapple, a bromeliad, by his gardener. Occasionally, unfamiliar plants hitchhiked across the ocean in other cargos, and were, in turn, classified. But no matter how they made the immense journey, almost all the so-called new plants have been in cultivation somewhere for over two centuries, sometimes under very special growing conditions. And some of them have previously been through a period of popularity and subsequent decline as houseplants.

There is, for example, a pleasant little bromeliad whose common name, queen's-earrings, or lady's-eardrops, speaks immediately of a more romantic period than our own. This plant was once extremely popular and is a reliable Christmas blossoming plant with a rather unusual combination of red and blue flowers. This, one of the simplest of the bromeliads, was once popular everywhere, but it is now hard to find. Extravagant advertising about new horticultural discoveries should therefore be taken rather calmly. But the inaccuracy of some of the statements does not make these humidity-loving plants any less

RAIN-FOREST PLANTS

attractive indoors; they are well worth their initial cost—if you will meet their cultural needs.

Billbergia nutans

First come the bromeliads that occur in all shapes and sizes throughout the tropical areas everywhere in the New World. Some of them, like the pineapple, grow on the ground, but most of them are epiphytic —their roots attach themselves to the rough bark of the branches or main trunks of trees so that the plants can rise above the savage struggle for light and water that rages continuously on the jungle floor. Bromeliads are spread from bough to bough by birds that eat the fleshy material around the berries and then wipe their beaks to clean them on a nearby branch, implanting the seed in the process. Mistletoe is spread in the same way, but, unlike bromeliads, mistletoe forces its roots into the sap system of a branch and lives mainly off the nourishment being sent up to the tip growth of the host tree. Bromeliads are not parasites; they only use their root system to get a grip. Once firmly established, they accumulate into a rather messy mound, consisting of their own decaying leaves, onto which other extraneous debris from the forest drifts. Bromeliads feed off this rich, self-created decaying vegetable matter that lodges beside the roots. As a family, they come in an

Bromeliads

enormous variety of shapes and sizes and with different flowering habits. The general leaf coloring turns toward the gray-green and the gray-red spectrum. There are huge plants with big sword-shaped leaves and tall spikes of bloom that from a distance look a little like

RAIN-FOREST PLANTS

huge, untidy storks' nests; smaller plants that bloom deep inside their leaves and attract insects for the vital pollination process by putting on a tremendous show of colored leaf markings; and delightful, minute red and gray plants that look like hedgehogs and starfish. If you are lucky enough to see bromeliads in variety in the wild, they present an extraordinary appearance. With their tremendous variation of color, texture, and size, they jostle each other, like roosting chickens searching for a place to perch, on both living and dead branches of trees, weighing their hosts down with the accumulation of debris. In areas where trees are under cultivation, bromeliads are considered a pest, and the horticultural columns in the local newspapers are full of advice about how best to eliminate them.

Bromeliads are extremely tenacious, and they can survive a great deal of abuse either in a pot or on a tree. The roots, which are used both for the viselike grip on the branch and to obtain nourishment from the debris around them, occupy a rather small area in relation to the over-all size of the plant and in cultivation should never be overpotted. One reason why such a small root system can support so much overhead growth is that most of the bromeliads wrap their leaves around each other at the base to form a cup or vase that enables the plant to hold a considerable store of water. In this way they compensate not only for the on-and-off supply of water available to their roots, but also for the fact that, when it does rain, the surplus moisture drains very quickly from the small root system. No matter how torrential the rain, no plant perched upon a tree is ever going to suffer from wet feet! The back-up system of the vases does, however, always get replenished, and the stored water seeps slowly into the heart of the plant. Should there be a drought, this reserve supply also enables the bromeliad to ride out the shortage. These water-filled cups also get full of minute drowned insects, whose bodies dissolve in the water and add nourishment to it, which is in turn absorbed by the plants. If you have ever hung a bromeliad outside during the summer, you may have been surprised, perhaps even slightly revolted, by what goes on inside that cup. Bromeliads are not carnivorous plants in the usual sense: undoubtedly the dissolved insect life helps their growth, but it is not essential for their survival.

The bromeliads that are now appearing in the shops, sometimes in bloom but more often just as foliage plants, are basically unchanged from those still growing wild. Very little hybridization seems yet to have been done, making it important, therefore, to copy their native growing conditions as carefully as possible. The small root system demands that the plants should always be put in small clay pots and never be surrounded by heavy wet soil. If you buy one in a large, plastic pot, knock it out, shake off the soil, and reset the plant, with a great deal of crocking and a soil that is almost entirely made from rough, decaying vegetable matter, heavily mixed with sand. The more roughage the planting mix can contain the better. If you are improving a commercial soil mix, buy a small bag of fir bark, which is used for potting orchids, to add, along with chopped sphagnum moss, to the overfine commercial soil. If your nerves are steady enough, this is one of the planting occasions when it is an excellent idea to increase the area of the drainage hole by chipping away around the edges.

Bromeliads make interesting houseplants. If they are planted properly and their vase or cup is kept topped with water, they will provide not only their own atmospheric moisture but they can also be left unattended for a long time. I would be very cautious about adding fertilizer to the vase water, no matter how diluted, for I have had some disasters after doing this. But I do see the practice advised by good growers. If you live in an area where the water is so heavily chlorinated that you can smell it, fill your watering can at night and let it stand until morning so the chlorine evaporates.

In spite of being unimproved, bromeliads are expensive, particularly if they are in bloom. You can partly amortize the price by the long-lasting qualities of the plant and the flower. They are costly because the grower has had to carry them for a very long time—only mature specimens will bloom. Home horticulturists who buy small bromeliads must therefore resign themselves to using them as foliage plants unless the retailer is sufficiently knowledgeable to be able to tell you whether the particular variety you are buying is naturally dwarf when mature. Unfortunately, bromeliad foliage gets shabby if you try to grow the plant on for a long time to get to flower. It is really better to buy a mature plant. Sometimes it is possible to trick a plant into throwing a bud. Fill up the water vase and put the plant into a plastic garment bag that has no holes in it, keeping the plastic away from the foliage with bamboo stakes. Add a ripe apple and seal the top of the bag with an elastic band. Move the covered plant into a bright, sunless place for a couple of months and, as the apple ages, it gives off a gas that will activate bud formation. There won't be any sign of a flower spike when you do debag your plant, but don't give up hope. As long as the plant was sufficiently mature, a flower bud will eventually form. There also exists a preparation called Omnaflora which is used both by professional growers and amateurs for the same purpose. I am told it works well but I have had no personal experience with it.

After this heady success, unless you have been forewarned, you may suffer a kind of horticultural trauma. Though the flowers remain in bloom for an exceedingly long time, it is nevertheless inevitable that the delighted grower must face the demise of the plant he has cosseted for so long, for it has now completed its allotted cycle. If by chance the flower spike has been pollinated, it will slowly set seed, but always after flowering the leaves begin to die away starting at the outer foliage. The plant remains alive, looking rattier and less attractive every day, until it rises like the pheonix from its own ashes by sending out offsets beside the base. This is how that untidy stork's nest of material collects in the wild. The old plant, though slowly dying, takes an unconscionable time to do so. It stays tenaciously alive and still collects water at the base of its vase. This now takes on an extremely strong smell but does supply moisture to the offsets, for at an early stage infant bromeliads do not form a vase and the necessary moisture has to be supplied by the decaying plant. When the new plantlets can operate alone, the original rosette finally disintegrates. If you can stand the sight and the smell of the decaying plant, you can eventually pot up and grow on the offsets. Personally I think this takes a good deal of forbearance on the part of any indoor horticulturist, but it is not fair to damage the novice's self-esteem by not forewarning him that any spectacular bromeliad must have this messy end.

As a curiosity, bromeliad trees are sometimes constructed from interestingly shaped pieces of wood—driftwood, for example. A small plant is taken out of its pot, the roots wrapped in wet, long-grained sphagnum moss and then tied into position with copper wire. If you want to try a tree, make sure that the planting surface is rough and has a cuplike depression chiseled out. See that the roots of your plant are wired into very close contact with the host wood and keep the sphagnum consistently moist and the plant vases filled; usually the roots will take hold. A tree of mine survived for well over a year, although I had to keep it during the winter months in a totally unsuitable place, a cool, dark cellar and it had also been improperly planted on an iron-hard piece of juniper root on which the plants found it very hard to get a

grip. Bromeliad trees are not really suitable for windows. They take up too much light and space, and the sphagnum is very hard to keep adequately wet. They do, however, look and do very well in a warm sunroom.

One of the plants with which the bromeliad has to compete in the wild is the orchid, or epiphyllum, cactus and its close relative, the night-flowering cereus. These are very spreading, large-size relatives of the Christmas cactus with rather tricky thorns, the difficulty being that the spines are not very obvious until they are deeply embedded in your fingers! This plant bears no resemblance at all to the desert cactus, except that it is succulent and stores water. It likes a rich soil and starts life on the forest floor. As it elongates, it throws its flat, modified leafstalks all over the place with tremendous zest, hanging on tena-

ciously with its spines to whatever mat of decaying vegetation it can
find. In this way it scrambles up toward the light, rooting wherever it
can find nourishment. The epiphyllums make an extravagant display of
enormous flowers that do not last long but that follow each other in a
continuous show. When they are used in the north as a pot plant, the
flowers appear in late spring and, thanks to the work of the hybridiz-
ers, in many lively colors.

The treatment of epiphyllum cacti vary very much according
to the part of the country in which you live. In the north they need sun
in the winter and can be conditioned to quite a cold temperature, so
long as they are kept rather dry. They will, in fact, drop off into a form
of dormancy. Grown in a warm window, the plants should have
regular watering, but being succulent they will fortunately also put up
with a little temporary absentmindedness. In southern areas they need
filtered light in winter as well as in the summer. In the north they can
be summered successfully indoors, but they will do better if they can
be put outside and given at least half a day of full sun, with regular
watering.

The main problem with the orchid cactus is how to handle it in a
pot. Like all the tree perchers, which this plant eventually becomes as
it climbs upward, the root system is small and liable to rot unless there
is a rapid runoff of water. Plants should again be grown in small clay
pots with excellent drainage, and the soil should be rich and full of
decaying vegetable matter—but not as coarse as the mix used for
bromeliads. This is because the orchid cactus root system is not designed to clutch the branches but to root in pads of rich material. Bone
meal should be added for long-term nourishment.

Recently there appeared an account of growing these plants that
called for "soil from a nearby forest" and one part of "well rotted
steer, rabbit, or sheep manure." This is the kind of advice that de-
presses me, because it puts off a gardenless gardener by suggesting
materials impossible for the ordinary grower to find. In my suburban
fastness I have no access to any forest, let alone its soil, nor am I within
easy reach of the droppings of sheep, rabbits, or steers. Yet I have
grown excellent epiphyllums for years without these delicacies, and I
beg you not to be discouraged. Our plants may not be super-scaled but
they can still be quite impressive.

Far more troublesome than finding the correct soil is getting the
plant under physical control. The flat blades (the technical term for

the modified leaves) thresh out in all directions, impaling you with their thorns and taking up angular, uncompromising positions. The length of well-grown blades makes it almost impossible to hold a small pot upright unless rather stringent controls are imposed. Unfortunately, the fleshiness of the blades also makes it impossible to pull them in individually, for even soft wool makes a sharp and permanent cut in the tissue and any damage done to one of the blades can never be hidden. They continue to grow, no matter how bad the injury, but, as their appearance is ruined forever, these plants should be handled with a great deal of care. Recently I have taken to making a bird's cage with bamboo stakes and strands of wool around the outer edge of the pot—exactly the type of picket fence staking I warned you against with bulbs! This holds the long blades inside, though as they elongate you may have to increase the length of the stakes. A controlled pot can turn

Orchid cactus and cage for controlling it

into an unexpectedly good-looking houseplant and this cage method seems the best way to grow an otherwise rather ungainly plant. If the modified leaves become too long, cut them off at a node, which is where the neck narrows. Blades root easily as will be explained in Chapter 11.

RAIN-FOREST PLANTS

The orchid cactus sets bud regularly, but it does like regular misting to simulate the humidity of its homeland. In the unlikely event of no bud set, the next year try an enforced period of dormancy without water or light such as is given to a recalcitrant Christmas cactus; this almost always does the trick. The orchid cactus and the related night-blossoming cereus, which flowers in the summer, will not be forced into bloom out of season, but the show when it appears is always worth the wait.

Another useful group of plants, many of which grow in competition with the bromeliads and orchid cactus, are the tropical ferns. Ferns occupy every continent and are at home in a variety of climates, but very few northern evergreen ferns can be acclimatized to indoor living without being given very special atmospheric conditions, while deciduous ferns, which die back at the approach of cold weather, are no good indoors. The magnificent tree ferns of the Antipodes are expensive and hard to hold to manageable proportions, so the most useful indoor ferns are those that grow in tropical rain forests.

Plants are as much subject to changes in fashion as hemlines; what delights one generation is despised, or even detested, by the next. But fashion almost always turns full cycle, and, while we have no use for the styles of our immediate forebears, we are inclined to admire the taste of our great-grandparents. The present popularity of ferns illustrates this point exactly.

Ferns are now definitely in. They can be bought in variety anywhere, and they are offered to us as excellent houseplants. This, up to a point, is true. Like all plants from the tropical rain forests, ferns find much to like about our style of indoor living; but there's a marked limit to their tolerance where humidity or lack of it is concerned, much more so than the other plants from these regions. This stems partly from the fact that ferns have made no modifications within themselves to enable them to withstand periods without humidity and partly from their method of reproduction. The fern family, which ranges from tree size to minute water ferns, represents an extremely primitive form of plant life. Unlike any other plant making use of photosynthesis, they never bloom and set seed. Ferns, which predate the dinosaur, depend on an older and totally different method of reproduction. Instead of ripening seeds from fertilized flowers, ferns ripen spores inside a covering called a spore case, on the back and along the edges of their leaves or even on separate stalks. When the cases, which always have a brown appear-

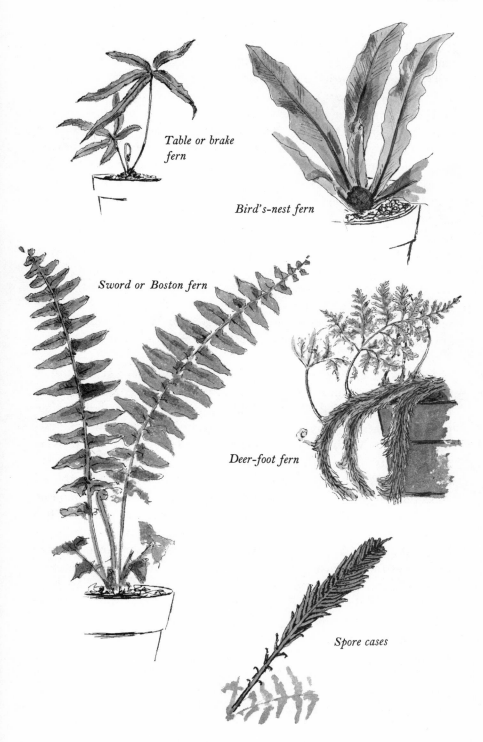

Table or brake fern

Bird's-nest fern

Sword or Boston fern

Deer-foot fern

Spore cases

ance, ripen, they open and the spores themselves float to the ground as minute particles. Under the right circumstances, which involves intense atmospheric humidity, spores grow into curious unfernlike little objects that in turn have to be fertilized; from these tiny objects, an adult fern will grow. In theory this excessively complicated two-part cycle of reproduction can only succeed in a very moist atmosphere, but, remarkably, small self-sown ferns often appear in the pots of nearby houseplants, which must be considered a great tribute to your growing conditions. Incidentally, the ripening spore cases are often mistaken for some horrible form of disease even by quite experienced horticulturists. So, if your fern produces little black dots or ridges that won't scrape off, don't worry; instead, congratulate yourself on having provided them with such good living conditions that they are getting ready to reproduce themselves. Since ferns are particularly liable to a disease known as scale (which will be discussed in Chapter 13) spore cases are frequently mistaken for scale and are attacked with an aerosol bomb. This is the unkindest cut of all, for the fern family as a whole is fearfully sensitive to most of the new spray materials, and, in your anxiety about the possibility of scale, you will almost inevitably kill your once happy plant.

Ferns were at the height of their previous popularity during most of the last century. But even then, though the houses were not dried out by strong central heating, ferns still did poorly because they did not get enough heat by day and they loathed the fluctuations of temperature by night. Many efforts were made to meet their rather persnickety requirements. One ingenious invention, called a "Wardian case," was designed in England in 1824 by a Dr. Nathaniel B. Ward to house his collection of tender ferns. Basically this consisted of a free-standing glass box with a lid, which not only stayed warmer and preserved this warmth better than the open house atmosphere, but also retained more humidity. Furthermore, it protected the ferns from the noxious fumes of that newfangled invention, illuminating gas, which was as poisonous to ferns then as much of the modern spray material is now. There were still fern collections around when I was a child, and I think my rather lukewarm affection for the genus stems from the fact that ferns are always associated in my mind with rather dark, dank conservatories in the houses of elderly relatives, where the ferneries, as they were called, usually lined the house wall. These special display areas were constructed of dark cork over which water trickled rather dismally. Delightful, no doubt, for the ferns but depressing for a child!

Modern hybridists have tried to strengthen the ability of ferns so that they do not have such an intense need for humidity, but this is very hard to breed out of them since it is an essential part of the reproductive system. It is still necessary if you want to grow ferns indoors to provide them with far more atmospheric moisture than is needed by any other plant. Though you may not go so far as to provide a cork-lined waterfall, you will have to make some rather special effort if your ferns are really to thrive. One way is to stand the plants on a deeper tray than usual and surround them with the humid atmosphere provided by moisture evaporating from constantly damp peat moss spread on the stones. But here you run into another problem with ferns (and with all this you may well wonder why they ever became popular in the first place and why on earth anyone is bothering to bring them back): they need daily watering but are very fussy about having wet feet. Their roots rot very quickly if the pot soil becomes stagnant. Ferns grow naturally in damp areas, but they always stand on mounds above water; they will not grow in wet ground—hence the elevated cork-planting areas of my youth. If you are using a pad of wet peat moss, don't stand the plants actually upon it; instead, put them on inverted saucers that in turn lie on the peat moss. This means that the surplus from your daily watering chore will never accumulate around the base of the pot.

To look their best ferns cannot be crowded; they should not be crammed into the front of a plant stand. One highly desirable antique that occasionally can be found still unappreciated by the dealers is the elegant wire fern stand. Fern connoisseurs of the past who did not go in for cork waterfalls displayed their plants in these so as to give the fullest effect to the airy foliage without crowding. I have looked everywhere for a fern stand without success. My friends seem to pick them up at will, but the prize continues to elude me.

The modern hybrid of the Boston or sword fern is far too often sold as a filler and this is a most unfortunate way of using a good plant: the tremendous Boston fern of memory did so well just because it was standing alone on its bamboo plant stand! Crowding ferns does damage to the fronds or leaves, which are extremely delicate. Being brittle they get broken and brown and the over-all appearance of the plant is ruined unless they are cut out. Cutting out fern fronds usually means damaging yet more—it becomes a vicious circle.

Even when you've taken care of all these problems—sufficient moisture, enough elbow room, no wet feet, and even warmth—ferns make

RAIN-FOREST PLANTS

yet another demand upon you: they need good indoor light but not sunlight. Strong sunlight yellows the fronds, but don't imagine that ferns can be relegated to a dark corner; if you do that, they will also die! Fortunately, they are kind enough to grow extremely well under artificial light, but this is absolutely the only concession they have made to modern conditions; otherwise they hold sternly to the way it was done in prehistoric times.

Ferns need a rich soil full of humus. Compost containing a great many odds and ends suits them very well. For a home-improved mix, add plenty of chopped sphagnum moss. Since they dislike stagnant soil, give them very good crocking as well as additional sand in the potting soil. Small ferns are now very much in evidence at most retailers and should be carefully examined before they are bought. These plants suffer severe damage if they are offered for sale with the modern labor-saving device of little or no crocking.

You can choose from four main groups. The easiest are some of the many hybrids of the sword or Boston fern, which made its first appearance as a stowaway on a cargo ship coming to Boston from the West Indies; hence the common name. If you do all the right things, you may find you have on your hands a quite unexpectedly large plant. Sword ferns increase by spreading sideways with the fronds pushing up through the outer edges of the root ball. Any of this group can be easily divided; otherwise you will have to be constantly increasing the pot size. As this type of fern expands, the central fronds die out and the plant looks shabby; you must therefore expect to give it rather finicky attention. In spite of their ancient method of reproduction, ferns also come with back-up systems to ensure survival of the species. Sword ferns, when mature, send out long, skinny runners that root when they touch ground and grow into adult forms that can be cut off and grown separately.

Another family of ferns, called the davallias, spread by means of rootstocks known as rhizomes. These have something of the appearance of fur-covered claws, and they too expand slowly outward, rooting, and throwing up new top growth as they spread. Indoors, these silken fingers creep down the sides of the pot, giving rise to the common name of deer-, rabbit-, hare-, or squirrel-foot ferns. They make interesting, if slightly sinister-looking, plants and are best displayed high, where the rather menacing rhizomatous growth can be featured.

Yet another family of pot fern now available everywhere is the bird's-nest fern. This spreads from a black fibrous center with large, single, upright leaves and, as the plant thrives, the leaves grow larger

Staghorn fern

and taller. This species cannot be divided without mutilation; if you are doing well with one, you will either have to find it a happy home or pot it up. The final, relatively easy group is the small brake, or table, or pteris fern. These are the little ferns that used to be planted at the base of the old-style poinsettia to hide the inevitable bare legs. Brake ferns never grow large, and they have been rehybridized into a great many very subtle colors in the gray-greens. They used to be grown by the thousands for table decorations for banquets, but they have only recently reappeared in general use. They are unusually tenacious for such a specialized family, and, despite their complicated reproductive cycle, it is they that appear unasked in the pots of neighboring plants. If you are new to ferns, don't be persuaded to buy either the fragile maidenhair fern or a staghorn fern attached to a slab of wood. Neither is going to do well in your window. Maidenhair ferns are very delicate.

RAIN-FOREST PLANTS

Like allergic children, they suffer from everything and catch everything; they take a lot of understanding, and you must graduate to them when you have mastered the culture of the others. The staghorn is a fern that has modified itself to cling to trees. A lower leaf forms a sort of membrane-like suction cup that holds it to the host bark. This leaf clings tightly except at the top where an opening is left, into which natural debris will drift and on which the plant roots will feed. The unmodified leaves form the fronds from which the plant gets its name. Staghorns cannot survive on a slab indoors; bought this way they are nothing but a waste of money and something of a fraud. But they will do well and look extremely dramatic if they are planted in rich soil in one of the new types of hanging pots that has a saucer attached. This provides them with the needed humidity and the modified leaves will soon creep over the edge of the pot presenting a very unusual appearance. Staghorn ferns need plenty of water and considerable misting in a warm window; but don't let it be a sunny window. There also exist other small wood ferns that cannot survive long in our indoor atmosphere no matter how hard we try to please them. To grow them, and give yourself the minimum of trouble, try a terrarium, which is nothing but a small modern adaptation of Dr. Ward's big glass box.

A terrarium can be any size ranging from a brandy snifter to a fish aquarium, but it must have a tightly fitting lid. Inside, you make a miniature landscape, usually trying to reproduce a woodland scene, and, though terrariums are occasionally used for some of the gesneriad family, they do best and look the most effective when planted to little wood ferns, mosses, and lichen. To make a terrarium, put a two-inch layer of gravel on the bottom to form a dry well for drainage, and incorporate a considerable quantity of charcoal into this gravel to keep any surplus water sweet. Over this spread another two inches of sand and then design your naturalistic scene with hills and ravines, building them up with layers of rich, textured soil. Fond as I am of compost, this is not the best material for a terrarium. The natural weed growth in it would flourish too rampantly. A special terrarium kit complete with soil and plant material can be bought, or, if you are making your own soil mix, add peat moss and chopped sphagnum moss to a commercially sterilized soil. A few moss-covered stones and sticks make effective little accents. But do please steer clear of gnomes or any artificial additions. Try to keep the glass inside clean, because it is not going to be able to be polished later on. Once the soil layer is in place, plant the tiny wood ferns or fragile tropical ferns extremely neatly and tidily making a small hole in your stratified soil and lowering the plantlet gently into place. After planting, spread sheet moss, which can be bought from a florist, gently over the soil layer so that it comes into growing contact with the soil and completes the effect.

If you dig plants from the wild, be very careful that you don't take those that are on the conservation list. Our land has been badly enough ravaged by roads, shopping centers, and housing developments without having horticulturists add to the destruction. You can always find out which plants are protected by consulting with your local horticultural society. If you are able to dig small wild plants, try to keep as much soil attached to the roots as possible; there is a close interrelationship between the bacteria that are in woodland soil and the health of the roots of plants that live in it. Once everything is in place, spray the interior lightly with a fine mister and put on the lid, leaving from half to a quarter of an inch open for air space.

The box will need very little further attention if it is put in a north or east window. Properly planted it will hold a good moisture balance for about three weeks. If the interior mists up, the planting is too wet—when that happens, remove the lid all day. If the moss appears too dry, a very light misting will suffice. Well-planted terrariums have a long life; they create their own humid atmosphere, and the small,

RAIN-FOREST PLANTS

delicate ferns will amaze you with their vigor. Dr. Ward stumbled on something extremely effective, and we can still profit by his skill today. Don't overlook the pleasure and the lack of trouble you can get from a terrarium, and don't rule out ferns because they are so fussy. Once you master their needs, you will never want to be without them, and there is no need for you to fail.

8 ❧ LATE SPRING AND EARLY SUMMER

EVERYDAY LIFE provides lavishly for two of our five senses; we have sights and sounds in abundance. By comparison, the other three—taste, touch, and smell—are rather short-changed. Yet nothing can equal a scent or a seasoning for inducing a stir of memory that otherwise may have been entirely forgotten. In my own case, the rather unusual, heavy smell of ivy in bloom vividly recalls a peat shed near a house my family rented one summer, and I can visualize rooms and furniture I knew for only a brief two months. This photographic image reappears only when memory is reactivated by that particular hot, drowsy scent. At any other time my recollections of that house are rather vague. A touch of sage in a seasoning brings back a sense of impatience and the feel of chairs covered with slippery horsehair in my grandfather's dining room. He still held to the old custom of roast goose at Christmas and also to the old-fashioned view that children were served last!

Most of us have memories that are triggered off in this way, and I think it important for our inner well-being that we use the pungent variations of taste, the sensuous pleasures of touch, and the heightened perception induced by scents for this very purpose. Serenity is something we all need and search for, and one way to achieve it in a small way is to use all our senses not only for immediate pleasure but also to store up an accumulation of experiences and memories on which we can draw from time to time.

People who grow things are fortunate in this respect, for plants exist that can serve all these needs and produce a lasting impression, perhaps even on our own descendants. Memory-inducing plants need not be only those that are grown outdoors. There are aromatic potted plants that are a delight to touch, and of course there are the culinary herbs.

To consider the last first, what about herbs indoors? How well can they be grown? Fundamentally, herbs belong outdoors. The use of these plants for medicinal purposes or for seasoning is rooted in antiquity and is one of the few surviving links, kept alive in the Middle Ages by the monastic orders, between the gardens of the ancient world and those of today. Wherever groups of people have collected, whether in the ancient civilizations such as the great urban centers of Mesopotamia, in the later classical world, or in pioneer societies of the kind that colonized the United States, herbs have always been considered essential both for health and as an addition to the diet, and their cultivation has been continuous. Growing them indoors, however, is another matter. It is difficult and often something of a disappointment, for, much as we wish they would acclimatize themselves, herbs are not really indoor plants.

We are all familiar with the dream kitchens paraded before our envious eyes in the glossy magazines. In them the over-all effect is often pointed up with little groups of potted herbs clustered together in the most inappropriate place, sometimes on a counter or decorating a dinette table set back inside the room. These locations are staged entirely for the delight of the photographer; the plants wouldn't survive there an instant. The only way you can grow herbs indoors is to put them in the coolest, sunniest place you possess, and, if you must have them in the kitchen, try the window sill over the sink where they will get the maximum benefit from the surrounding humidity. The only herbs that can be used decoratively around a kitchen are strings of dried herbs—anything growing in a pot needs light.

Herbs already potted up can be bought in variety from any good greenhouse in the spring—even the most languid horticulturist is made aware of this when those unhappy, overforced chives, miserably stuffed into small pots, appear in the food markets. Unfortunately, herbs are not so readily available in the fall when most of us are getting ready to refurbish our plant collection. This is because many herbs are either annuals, which of course die in the autumn, or deciduous perennials, which also will not grow during the waning months of the year. Others that we use originated in the Mediterranean and during the winter require a cold location so that they can go through their natural period of dormancy. Most herbs, like bulbs, will not revive and grow well unless they have had their statutory period of cold. The only herbs that can be considered as houseplants are the bay and the rosemary, both of which are evergreens and prefer cool treatment but which will survive as a permanent part of a collection. If you are thinking of using these

Chives

Mint

Savory

Thyme

Sweet marjoram

Rosemary

for actual cooking purposes, look them over rather carefully before you incorporate portions of them into your dinner. Bay is extremely liable to scale, and rosemary often harbors the mealy bug, particularly at the end of a long winter indoors. This is a form of wildlife seasoning that I do not feel adds appreciably to the food.

If you cannot find pots of herbs in the fall but you have access to someone's outdoor herb plot, it is possible to dig small clumps of some of the perennial varieties and put them in pots with a light, sandy soil. You must then set them in an unheated, or at least extremely cold, place, such as an entry way, and slowly reduce the water you give them. The plants will look miserable, as they lose most of their leaves and drop into dormancy. But after a period of rest in this really cold place, during which time they must of course be given only the minimum of water, the clumps can be revived into fresh growth on a very sunny window sill. The list of herbs amenable to this treatment is not very long. It includes mints, thymes, chives, winter savory, and, for a very short indoor life, sweet marjoram. There exists, by the way, a much larger and more interesting garlic chive that you can also grow in this fashion. If you are going to use snippets of this, do make sure all the family eats it, not only you. Sage, which is a close cousin both of the lantana and the red salvia of the garden, grows untidily and often loses its leaves indoors. Nasturtiums, one of the many plants that are both decorative and edible, are sometimes counted as herbs. I find these very hard to grow in pots at all, even in a greenhouse, and I have had absolutely no success with them in a window.

This, I agree, is not very encouraging advice, but, if you will reconcile yourself to their short life, you can get considerable pleasure out of growing herbs indoors, particularly if you grow them under an artificial light unit. The way to use these for intensive growing is discussed in Chapter 10; but it is worth stressing here that perennial herbs are one of the groups of plants that do better grown under lights than in a window. A special lighting unit is also the place to sow seeds of annual herbs, some of which will do reasonably well if they are started during the early spring months. There are now available commercially a good many herb packages specially designed for easy indoor growing. Experimenting with some of these kits, I was distressed to see how difficult it would be for the complete novice to use them. Many of the misguidedly combined packages of seeds would indeed germinate very easily and grow away quickly, such as mustard and cress—the makings of the authentic Edwardian sandwich—and chervil, basil, and fennel. But with these fairly simple seeds, there were also included packages of parsley and dill, both of which take an extremely long time to germinate and should never be combined in a single unit with the others. Parsley seed, in fact, can often be coaxed into action only by pouring boiling water over the seeds to crack the hard outer casing. To be able to use either of these herbs indoors, an extraordinary amount of patience would be needed. So I can't feel that these mixed combinations of herbs are really useful for the novice grower, and the way in which some of them are advertised might even be described as misleading.

But these possible complications should not deter you from trying to grow herbs indoors. You may well succeed where others have failed. If you love to cook, or have children who may learn to love the smell and taste of the plants that have been in use throughout the world for so long, even a very short stay of a few herbs in your window garden is well worth while.

Herbs have the two-part advantage of tasting and smelling delightful; the only thing they lack is feeling equally pleasant to the touch. The blind get great pleasure from both scented and touchable plants and we, who are fortunate enough also to be able to see, should cultivate the habit of enjoying the feel of the leaves of some plants. There are, for example, woolly leaved kalanchoes, which have all the advantages of being succulent and make delightful indoor foliage plants. These come in several sizes with gray-brown foliage and are an excellent addition to a plant collection as well as giving a delightful sensation when the leaves are stroked. Some begonias have velvety leaves.

Aromatic plants are a delight, although there is not a substantial list of candidates for long indoor life. If you have a really cool place, such as an unheated sun porch or sunroom, the box and lemon verbena both make delightful plants. The cool location is essential in order that these plants, which are not really houseplants, can have a period of dormancy in the fall. During this time the box will stand still and need almost no water, and the lemon verbena will drop all its leaves which even in decay smell delightful. At the turn of the year both can be brought indoors onto a sunny window sill, where they will start again into active growth and perfume the room.

From the time of my great-grandfather it has been a family custom to take cuttings from whatever plant of lemon verbena then existed to anyone who was setting up a new household. Four generations, two world wars, and ten household moves later, my brother still owns a thriving descendant from that walled Canterbury garden. The smell of my plant automatically brings back a time when the sun always seemed to shine and the garden be ablaze with flowers. I have made cuttings from my own plant for my own children, and I hope they will for theirs. It is this kind of continuity I cherish. Fragrant plants call for a tradition of this sort and you can so easily start one for yourself.

LATE SPRING AND EARLY SUMMER

One plant family that manages to combine both the pleasures of touch and the delights of smell is the variety of geranium with scented leaves. These look nice, grow well, feel soft to the touch, and have a haunting fragrance. Geraniums with scented leaves are members of a large family that exists in many parts of the world, although most of

Scented geraniums

Peppermint

Lemon

Rose

those we grow indoors originated in Europe. They need a light, sandy soil without too much water-retaining material added to it, a cool location with bright light, and plenty of water. Whereupon, if you are not alert, they will proceed to take over the house, for they are rampant spreaders. Scented geraniums, as they are a little inaccurately called, need constant cutting back. You can put little pieces among your clothes, in your linen closet, and on state occasions in finger bowls. The small pieces also root exceedingly easily, and they can be turned into extra little plants by the process discussed in Chapter 11. A small pot of any of the scented geraniums is one of the nicest presents you can send a sick friend. One was sent to me years ago and I still have many of its descendants. Even withered and dry, the leaves continue to smell sweetly when crumbled. So never toss out the extra odds and ends; if you don't want them, give them away. You will be surprised at the pleasure such a simple present produces.

In a plant collection, the pots should be set where you can brush against them or finger them very easily and get a waft of peppermint, lemon, nutmeg, or rose, combined with that distinctive bittersweet smell of geranium oil. These plants are carried by most greenhouses and will give you almost no trouble. You will not gain anything from the flowers, which are small and undistinguished, but, except for their capacity to bully you—and all the other plants around them—they are very good indoors.

For most people, however, the word geranium means those flowering plants that are grown by everybody everywhere. If all the geraniums bought each year were laid end to end, they might well span the continent. But unfortunately most of them would not be grown particularly well, for this is a much misused plant, and I think our treatment of it needs some new thinking.

Geraniums, as we know, constitute a large plant family. Apart from the scented plants we have just discussed, there are many wild varieties with some of the same characteristics here and in Europe. The kind most commonly grown in pots for their bloom, however, originated in South Africa and is called a zonal or horseshoe geranium because of the markings on the leaves. As houseplants they are great favorites and thousands of potted plants are bought each year. Unfortunately, most of us just pick up what might be called the old red and pink cemetery variety, ignoring the fact that the plants now come in much better colors with more weatherproof flowers and in types which give us better bloom. The slow use of improved geraniums is partly due to our own inertia, but the newer plants are hard to find and more expensive if you do discover a good source of supply. This is because the stock can only be built up by vegetative reproduction—that is, through cuttings —which is a long and time-consuming process when you are attempting nation-wide distribution. The higher price is also the result of many of the new types having been patented so that the local propagator has to pay more for the basic stock. The reason behind this slow method of increase is that geraniums in the past have not come true to color or type from seed. Very expensive, hand-pollinated seed has long been available. This produces interesting varieties and clear colors, but, as it is impossible to tell what the colors or shapes will be, geraniums from seed have not been commercially possbile. One excep-

LATE SPRING AND EARLY SUMMER

tion to this rule is a geranium developed by Pennsylvania State University, but this comes in a bright red color that is not universally admired. The explanation for the difficulty lies in the cultural history of the zonal geranium we use today. The first wild species, or unimproved plant, was sent to England in 1704 and a second, slightly different, wild plant, also from South Africa, followed in 1710. By 1730 the plant breeders had succeeded in cross-pollinating the two wild plants and thereby produced the forebears from which all our modern-day geraniums have been developed. But any plant that has

Geraniums

Zonal

Variegated

Miniature

originated through the combination of two blood lines and then has been crossed and recrossed by still further interbreeding cannot be trusted to produce offspring that look like its parents. With Mendelian perversity, the seedlings almost always revert to all that is the worst in the characteristics of their forebears. They also suffer from another quite usual failure among hybrid plants: the seed tends to be infertile.

Recently there seems to have been a breakthrough; a new outdoor bedding geranium has been developed that does come true to seed and also germinates freely. The new plant also has another good characteristic of not needing to be pinched back in order to make it bush. But it grows to flowering size here in the north much more slowly than the conventional geraniums, and the colors are not as yet very exciting. If, however, true color can be bred into fertile seed for bedding geraniums, then we must obviously be on the threshold of a similar advance for the pot varieties.

The usual horticultural advice about geraniums is to grow them in full sun in rather poor pot soil and to go easy on the watering. Zonal geraniums are strongly succulent, as you can see from their swollen stems, so the conventional advice seems to make good sense. For many years I followed it and grew good plants, but after I came to this country I lost my touch. My geraniums were a disgrace, with yellowed leaves, poor flowers, and a general look of starvation. I found this very disheartening. The treatment I was giving them was suiting my other succulent plants and had always previously produced good geraniums —but I was now in America, not England, and the clue obviously lay in the difference in the climate. A little more investigation, once I had reasoned the matter out that far, showed that the original species of plants set flower in their native South Africa after abundant rain, when the days were bright and the nights still quite cool. I decided that my failures came from the fact that the advice I read here and the method I was following were based upon English horticultural practices. These had been worked out under conditions that were much more akin to the climate at the time of year in South Africa when the ancestors of our plants were in bloom. Full English sun, for example, bears very little resemblance to full American sun in most parts of the United States, and hot weather in England is almost always followed by cool dew at night. Also, in England there is usually enough summer rain to make heavy watering of potted geraniums unnecessary. In America the summer conditions are not at all the same, except on the West Coast where magnificent geraniums are grown. We have hot days with blistering sun and equally hot nights. Geraniums in full sun obviously lose a great deal of water through transpiration from the big leaves, and there is no dew here until late in the year to replace this loss automatically. It therefore falls to the lot of the root system to replace this water loss daily, and to achieve this they obviously have to be kept adequately supplied with extra water as well as additional nourishment. With any heavy water loss through transpiration there also occurs a loss of the soil trace elements essential to good growth. I began to see where my mistakes lay, and I changed my methods. I now pot my plants in rich soil so that the roots have a good supply of food available in spite of having to have daily watering. I also set the pots where there is full morning sun but none in the afternoon. This gives the leaves a chance to cool off a little before dark. My geraniums are still not as good as those I used to grow, but at least they no longer shame me.

All this should have been obvious to me from the start, because I was well aware that geraniums grew magnificently on the West Coast. I ought to have equated this fact with the humidifying presence of the coastal fogs and the less intense sunlight. One other thing that I learned from my problems with this plant was that succulence in geraniums is not provided in order to enable them to adapt to hot, dry periods when they are in bloom; rather, it exists in order to enable them to survive during the dry months when they are at rest. Old-fashioned growers took advantage of this built-in heritage when they wintered their plants in bundles hanging upside down in an earth cellar. The cool conditions and humid atmosphere, rising from the earth floor, kept the geraniums dormant and the succulence kept them alive. In our modern, finished cellars, this method does not work. But it is still perfectly possible, if you have a really cool place, to carry over old plants still in their pots with hardly any water all winter. Geraniums treated this way are revived in the spring by bringing them into the warmth and giving them heavy watering. When the stems start to plump up, small shoots will break. This is the time to repot the plants, cutting them back fiercely to an outward-facing break so that the new shoots will not grow inward toward the center and crisscross each other. Like all succulents, geraniums require good drainage, and, for me, they do best in well-crocked plastic pots in which the earth cannot heat up and dry right out. A home-improved mix should include an all-purpose commercial soil with an equal amount of water-absorbent material added, and a healthy handful of sharp sand or perlite for drainage. After repotting, the plant can be grown on in a sunny place for summer bloom. You cannot, however, take pots of geraniums that have blossomed well for you outdoors all summer and expect them to continue flowering indoors. This is too much. Even in the sunniest window, the leaves will yellow and fall off, for the plant has done its share for the year.

If you have a cool, sunny winter window you can perfectly well have winter-flowering geraniums if you will prepare plants particularly for their role. Over the years I have noticed that a great deal of horticultural advice is faithfully repeated year after year even though it is not particularly good. Winter geraniums illustrate this point exactly. I frequently read that cuttings should be made in August from summer geraniums for winter-flowering plants. This is fine if you want a small, skinny little plant, but a cutting taken so late is not going to be a really satisfactory flowering plant. It is much better to set some plants aside for winter bloom when you buy your annual supply in early summer. Treat them exactly like the others, except they should be strongly pinched back to make the plants extremely bushy. Remove every flower bud the moment it forms; don't let these plants bloom. This is a process that can be carried on indoors in a sunny window or outside. The plant will respond to this highly frustrating treatment by growing very sturdy stems and a strong root system. If it becomes intolerably pot-bound, some of the lower leaves will turn yellow. In that case move the plant up one pot size, but try always to keep geraniums in tight boots; they flower much better that way. If you repot, ram the new soil down very firmly; geraniums benefit from hard potting. By late August let the flower buds develop and, as usual, bring the plants indoors ahead of turning on the house heat. Once allowed to go ahead and bloom, these specially treated geraniums make up for their long period of frustration by an immense torrent of bloom that will last for many months and will be much better than any cutting.

All zonal geraniums need regular tip pinching while they are in their growing-on stage. This keeps the plants stocky; a geranium left unpinched will elongate into a rather unattractive climbing plant—this, incidentally, is the reason why geraniums can be easily trained into standard forms. When buds form, a soft pinch of the growing point just above the developing bud keeps the lower stems sending out new growth, while it holds the top of the plant in check. A soft pinch also has the advantage of sending all the nourishment into the bud and turning that into a much larger, longer-lasting flower than appears on an unpinched bud. Zonal geraniums need good air circulation or the leaves will become moldy, and they always need careful grooming. Don't splash around when watering. This not only makes brown spots on the leaves but it also ruins the flowers, if water rests on them. So, though this is a very common plant that everyone thinks he can manage, you now perhaps appreciate why geraniums usually never quite come up to expectation. They do, in point of fact, need a considerable amount of attention.

Most zonal geraniums are grown in pots, in beds, or in window boxes, but there are a few colored-leaf varieties that are grown as hanging plants—these will be discussed in the next chapter. There are also a great many geraniums with variegated leaves that can be used either as foliage plants or in combination with zonals for a more decorative effect. Almost all the plants with variegated leaves have less important flowers.

Excellent geraniums for bright winter windows are the miniature varieties. To buy these, it is usually necessary to get a catalog from a geranium specialist, but a search among the neighborhood retailers sometimes turns them up. Miniature geraniums come in a great variety of colors and, oddly enough, with a great variation in size also—they range from the small and dainty to a thimble size and they all do better indoors than their larger relatives. Miniature geraniums are also much more tolerant about being expected to bloom throughout the year. After a long summer of flowering, you should trim the plant back lightly, cut off all the oncoming buds, and repot the plant in fresh soil —but probably in the same pot size. These little plants will not then demand a long, leafless period of dormancy. Instead they will stand still, holding onto a few leaves for some weeks; at this time you must, of course, reduce the watering. The moment new growth starts, which won't take long in a warm, sunny location, step up the water and fresh buds will appear. Heavy bloom follows when the days begin to lengthen. Keep rotating your pots for even growth, and like all geraniums keep them well groomed. Miniatures, incidentally, flower extremely well under an artificial light unit.

Another variety of geraniums, or pelargoniums, as these are more correctly called, are the regal, *domesticum*, or Martha Washington geraniums. In spite of the variety of names, these are all the same plant. Regals are now making a comeback after having had a previous period of great popularity. Old gardening books are full of mouthwatering descriptions of the colors once available, but only recently have the plant breeders on the West Coast, and also in Europe, begun to reintroduce these fine old forms, some of which, unfortunately, are gone forever. Regals are not nearly as succulent as the zonal variety, and the leaves are thinner and lighter in color. Occasionally a plant can

Regal geranium

be found in which the leaf bears a horseshoe marking, and the flowers, in which each individual floret is much larger, usually carry a dark blotch. In the best of the new introductions the blotch has been feathered. A rather small, uninteresting variety of this plant, which oddly enough is quite easily available in comparison with the difficulty of finding the others, is called a pansy-faced geranium, which gives an indication of the appearance of the flowers. Regals need slightly different culture from other geraniums, and this may be one of the reasons why they fell out of favor. Their best use is either in a bright window or on a sun porch; previously they were used as splendid conservatory plants. They are too fragile for outdoor growing for the flowers are ruined by wind and rain.

Regals have a tremendous flush of spring bloom; the plants can hardly be seen for the mass of color. That used to be the end; after this one show no more flowers appeared. Nowadays the story is a little different. If a plant is cleaned up and fed after the first burst of flowering is over, there will be sporadic blooms all summer. These are excellent plants for a bright window; they do not like full summer sun at all, and gardenless gardeners would do well to seek them out. At all stages they need different treatment from all other geraniums. As they are only mildly succulent, they cannot be carried on in a cold cellar with very little water through the winter, but, if you keep them in active growth in a warm window, they are apt to turn into very large plants and be rather liable to a pest called white fly, which will be discussed in Chapter 13. If you have a plant you want to save, you had better perform an activity known as potting back. This is done in the fall and involves knocking out the plant, shaking off all the old soil, and root pruning it quite strongly, cutting back a similar amount of top growth at the same time. The plant is then reset, with the usual geranium soil, but in a pot at least one size smaller than it was in before. The shocked plant should then be stood where it gets good but cool light and be given very little water. By the turn of the year, strong new growth will be underway, and the plant can then be potted back up, if you want to have a large plant. It isn't necessary to clutter your window sill with enormous pots to get very lavish bloom, for the regals, like all geraniums, do not mind being pot-bound. The first new growth can be pinched out in the usual way to promote bushiness, if you are dealing with a small cutting. But if the plant is growing well, it will bush out without your help. Too much pinching out is fatal to regal pelargoniums, and this I am sure is the reason why many people fail with them. It is not nearly enough stressed by those who sell them to us that this plant does not throw a bud below the growing point but that the growing point itself develops into a flower. If you mistakenly treat a regal like an ordinary geranium and go on pinching it back several times, you will take out all the flowering points and get absolutely no bloom. I found this out the hard way when I was trying to make a particularly symmetrical plant, and I have seen plants in very good greenhouses with which the same mistake had been made. When you buy regal geraniums, always look extremely carefully at the very ends of all the stems. If the plant is at all mature, the tiny buds are always visible. I suggest you do not buy one in which you can see no bud—it may have been wrongly handled. The height of the plant, if it is an old one, will depend on the extent it was cut back in the fall, and, in the case of a cutting, on the amount of additional food that is supplied. Enormous young plants can be produced from a single cutting by a kind of forced feeding, but the natural rounded shape of a plant left alone always looks better to me.

The other houseplant that brings a great show of bloom in the shops in early summer is the hydrangea. The flowers are very long-lasting indoors and are quite elegant even after they begin to fade. The round mopheads of bloom are not admired by everyone, so you should remember that there also exist flat-blossoming types which are worth searching out.

Hydrangeas

Flat

Mophead

Hydrangeas demand a great deal of water, and they dislike the hot sun. They are at their best outdoors in huge tubs in climates where the evenings are cool, but they do fill a rather vacant period in the sequence of blossoming plants available for indoor use and are certainly worth buying. I am not, however, sure that they are worth trying to carry on. Even with a greenhouse and a cool cellar I have found them very tiresome. After they have finished blooming, hydrangeas need repotting in a rich soil with good water retention, and the canes should then be cut back hard. New growth will come at once and should be allowed to grow and ripen in the full sun; this will mean daily gallons of water for the plant, for this is one that is anything but neglectable! The plants must remain outdoors until the first frost strips the leaves. They must then be wintered over in a really cool place where they can be kept sufficiently watered to keep the canes alive but not in active growth—this is quite a trick, particularly if you ever want to take a winter holiday! But if you want flowers the next year these canes must not die; flowering shoots will only grow from the ripened wood of the previous year. Hydrangeas are very tenacious of life; if you muddle it and the canes do die, the root system will probably survive and send up

LATE SPRING and EARLY SUMMER

nice, strong-looking growth in the spring, but this new wood is not blossoming wood and never a bud will set!

In fact, to carry over a hydrangea is often a bore even for the experienced grower and the novice gardener really had better leave it to the professionals.

9 ❧ HANGING PLANTS

THE APPEARANCE of any plant window is always improved by the softening effect of hanging or trailing plants, either suspended by hooks or grouped around the framework. In previous chapters various possible candidates for these locations have been mentioned. It is important to be careful when choosing plants that you want to hang; not only are many house plants quite unsuitable for the purpose; others, even though they trail by nature, cannot survive the rigors of being used indoors in this way.

Hanging plants can range from the very simple, like the trailing pothos, to the highly dramatic staghorn fern or donkey-tail sedum, but they all have to contend with greater growing problems than any other indoor plant. By the very fact that they are hung, these plants are continuously enveloped in the rising hot, dry air of the room, and they cannot be given any of the additional atmospheric moisture we produce for our ground-level plants by standing them on deep dry wells. Also, we usually don't have enough space to group several hanging plants together, so they cannot even help each other through the process of transpiration. Hanging plants are also a great nuisance to water properly and are some of the very few indoor plants that are hardly ever in danger of death by drowning. In point of fact, they often slowly die because of lack of sufficient moisture at the heart of the root ball. Hanging plants dry out quickly, long before the novice gardener watching the soil surface of his plants at ground level expects. For that reason, it is almost essential to use plastic pots that hold moisure much longer and convert them into hanging pots by means of special clamps that can be bought at any garden center. The alternative is to use a pot specially designed for hanging and there are all kinds now available for

HANGING PLANTS

this particular purpose, and new ones are appearing daily. Indoors you obviously cannot use the hanging basket made either of galvanized iron or sometimes of plastic mesh. These have to be lined with sphagnum or sheet moss to hold in the planting medium, and they drip freely, without any means of controlling the water, as well as shed sphagnum.

They are thus totally unsuited for indoor work. Lined baskets of this sort can be used only in a greenhouse or out-of-doors and even here their culture is more difficult than a hanging pot and not easy for the novice grower to manage.

The word basket, which is always used for hanging plants, does not connote anything woven or of wicker. It is the generic term applied to any container that holds hanging plants. The open-work type just discussed may have given rise to the origin of the term, but even these have never, to my knowledge, been made of a material that would rot away as quickly as baskets, in the sense that we mean the word.

A new, useful hanging pot comes with a saucer permanently attached to the base of the pot, with enough open space around the outer rim to allow for any overaccumulation of surplus water to spill out. Unless you are far too lavish with your overhead watering—a fault that very rarely occurs—this pot will catch all those drips that are otherwise such a problem, and the attached saucer also provides a reservoir for surplus water that can evaporate around the plant. In theory, this saucer constantly full of water should do damage to the soil structure inside the pot; in fact this does not seem to happen, probably because hanging plants use up the extra water extremely fast and the soil does not get sodden. I have one small objection to this type of pot—there is so much of it. Unless the plant inside is extremely large and full, this new type hanging in the window usually looks more pot than plant. Small pots are better proportioned for indoor hanging plants.

If you have to repot a hanging plant, and unluckily they are incredibly prone to noisy, messy disasters, take off all the apparatus by which it is suspended before you set to work. This apparently is not as obvious as it should be. And because novice growers often find it very hard to get clamps or wires back into position afterward, they try to work with them still in place. You will probably do more damage to the plant potting it up with wires getting in your way than you will struggling to get those same wires back into position afterward. The business of planting a pot with the wires already in place also does irreparable damage to my temper.

The only problem with the hanging clamps is getting the inner prong over the molded inside rim of a plastic pot. This does have to be done with care, for I have broken many plastic pots trying to force them the wrong way. The trick is not to try to put them on straight, but to insert them at a sloping angle, for then the rim of the pot will slide safely between the straight prong and the curved outside hook that holds the clamp in place over the outer molding.

Getting the wires off the new hanging pots which have those attached saucers is also an annoying procedure. The holes through which the wires pass are very small and are set on the outer rim of the pot where they can get broken extremely easily. If this happens, the pot cannot again be used to hang plants, for there is no other way to attach the wires and no molding to hold a clamp. So be careful as you untwist the wires and even more cautious as you pull them out. When you have finished planting, the wires have to be threaded in again and twisted at exactly the same place as before so that all three are the same length. If one wire is shorter than the others, the pot will forever list unevenly and look unattractive. What's more, all the water will spill away as you try to keep the soil moist. This wire business is a nuisance and I am sure I am not the only person to be irritated by it!

Another approach to solving the problem of giving a hanging plant enough water and extra humidity is to attach three brass chains to a clay saucer. Then an ordinary clay pot can be stood on the saucer and the foliage carefully worked through the chains. This combination also looks a little overwhelming in an ordinary window, but for people who loathe anything except clay pots—and there are plenty who feel that way—it is a possible solution. This kind of pot is no harder to plant than any normal ground-level pot.

You can also hang your plants in the kind of muzzle made for a biting horse or donkey. Nets of this sort are usually the work of local craftsmen. They can be used to hold a solid container into which the pot with the hanging plant is slipped, or they can take the hanging pot itself. If you use a net with the pot alone, it will not last too long, but, even with a solid container, the useful life does not normally extend much over two years. With the solid container, make certain that the water level inside is not rising and drowning the plant. Between that danger, and the sinister crash in the night as the net gives way, I am inclined to suggest that you use this particular method of suspending plants with some caution.

Getting sufficient water and humidity are the worst problems that confront any hanging plant; another is continuing to have sufficient nourishment within the pot to grow well. Hanging plants lose the nutrients in the soil much faster than ground plants; the rapid runoff of surplus water leaches out essential food elements. When a pot stands on a pebbled tray, some of these nutrients are reabsorbed by the plant from the moisture that evaporates around it. Since this cannot happen with hanging plants, they need to be fed more often than other house-plants, particularly when they are in active growth. Because of the drip problem, it is really more sensible to use a nonorganic, water-soluble food that has no smell and will not ruin the floor!

Ideally, a hanging plant needs to be thoroughly watered every day. To do this properly, you have either got to take the plant down each time or stand on a ladder—if it is suspended at any height. It's only the fantastically dedicated horticulturist who will tie himself to such a program. Holding a watering can overhead with enough water in it to satisfy the plant almost always ends with a torrential cascade down the sleeve and this, in a nutshell, is why overhead plants are usually underwatered! I compromise. I use the limited overhead method and give each plant a dribble of water daily, but I also mist them each time; this keeps them in much better shape. I also try to touch the soil in the pots very regularly, and, as I suggested earlier, if a plant feels unusually dry, I put in some ice cubes, which slowly seep into the soil. Every now and then I take the time and, let me at once add, the fearful trouble to take down all my hanging plants and dunk them in a bucket of water until the air bubbles stop rising. This washes off the accumulation of house dust, which is far worse with hanging plants as it is carried upwards with the rising air. It also gets rid of red spider and other mite diseases that are very apt to attack hanging plants and refreshes the plant enormously by cleaning the foliage and getting the entire heart of the root ball wet. This is a very messy proceeding and you must make provision for the surplus water to drain away before you hang them up again. As with bulbs, an old colander on a bucket serves the purpose.

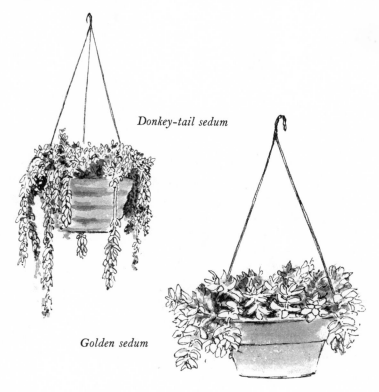

Donkey-tail sedum

Golden sedum

HANGING PLANTS

All this advice can be quite correctly interpreted as suggesting that the novice indoor gardener will have trouble with most hanging plants. For that reason I recommend that, for a first attempt, you use some of the succulent plants that we have already discussed. Most books don't suggest succulents as hanging plants, but for me certain varieties have

Stapelia

done extremely well in windows—particularly the sedums and the interestingly angular stapelias. Both can survive abuse, neglect, and inadequate water and still grow into very good-looking plants. I think nothing looks more ridiculous than a small hanging plant in a large pot —unless it is a minute hanging plant in a small pot swinging from an enormous clamp. So the fact that these succulents increase in size quite rapidly makes them even more desirable.

Hanging plants that flower well indoors are rare, but here again one of the big families of succulent plants can come to the rescue. There is an ever-increasing list of new varieties of the now totally misnamed Christmas cactus. The so-called Thanksgiving variety starts to flower in November and, by careful selection of the different species, bloom can be maintained until late spring. Most of these new kinds are still rather small plants, and for a more interesting effect, it is worth buying several of the same variety and potting them together. Remember, the basic rules for potting succulents are not quite the same as for other plants and that a great deal of extra crocking is needed in the pots.

Christmas cactus

There are also magnificent hanging gesneraids, such as the columneas and other related species, which I am told will bloom indoors in a warm, sunny window. But as I have not grown them myself, I can only report that they do exist. Anyone who grows good African violets would do well to look into the possibilities of these plants, for they are most spectacular.

There are very few bulbous plants that serve as good hanging plants indoors. If you have a cold, sunny window, some members of the oxalis family may flower for you, but since these plants close their blossoms by night, I really cannot entirely recommend them for an interesting display. In the fall, the *Campanula isophylla*, or star-of-Bethlehem, often appears in the shops. This is an attractive plant, but it usually comes in a very small pot and does not look well swinging a little dismally in a large window. It also gets untidy very quickly, because it needs daily grooming. The flowers last an extremely short time though there is a long succession of buds which will open indoors. I have seen enormous specimens of this plant, but they usually come from private greenhouses.

The sparseness of the possible flowering plants makes hanging foliage plants important in a window, and here there is much more choice. In a warm, sunless location you can use many of the trailing pothos and philodendrons. These are by nature climbers, but they will

Spider plant

also trail. They look best on a bracket beside the window frame, and for good effect they must be kept strongly pinched back so that the plants are full of bushy, young growth and do not degenerate into two or three stringlike stems. The spider plant with green and white foliage also makes an excellent hanging plant. As it grows, long runners appear with small plantlets at their ends. These in nature take root wherever they touch the ground. You can increase your collection by severing one of the runners leaving a great deal of it still attached to the infant plant, and then potting the baby in a small thumb pot.

The cissus, or grape ivies, make big hanging plants providing you get the proper variety. These become ungainly if they are happy, they reach out in all directions, catching in your hair as you try to water the window plants and vanishing into the curtains if they are placed anywhere near the frame of the window. For a good appearance, you must keep a prospering grape ivy under firm control. All hanging plants invariably turn toward the light, and the more rampant growers

Wandering Jew

will turn their backs to you very quickly. Try to reverse the way they face each time you take them down.

For a touch of color with winter hanging-foliage plants, use some of the wandering Jews that now appear both as tradescantias and as zebrinas. These produce strong trailing foliage in assorted shades of green and purple. They are extremely accommodating plants that can be used summer or winter alike and grow to very large sizes. I don't think they have been sufficiently appreciated in their many new forms. The misnamed Swedish ivy can also be grown into quite a spectacular hanging plant, with a bonus of small white flowers in the fall. This I have found to be a very slow grower and, unlike most succulents, it needs plenty of water to stay fresh and green. There is a variegated variety but this does not spread so well.

Several of the fern family can be grown as hanging plants and with sufficient humidity will look very effective. All the davallias, the kind that have the woolly, creeping claws, look well suspended, and so does a properly planted staghorn fern—by properly planted I mean not on a board. With ferns you will have to have your mister always at the ready.

The plant most often used as a trailer, the common ivy, is the one that dislikes the house the most. Ivy has now many new hybrids, some of which are multibranching. These varieties throw out lots of little bushy stems without constant pinching and are better for indoor use then the older types. But none of them do well for me as hanging plants. All ivies are prone to attacks of red spider and the spider mite. The most vulnerable is the unimproved English ivy, which unfortunately is by far the most commonly offered for sale. If you buy one of these, nothing will look worse in a shorter time if you try to make it hang high in the window. If you grow ivy at ground level in a cool window and train the shoots upward, then you may get a delightful plant that will eventually frame the area and send out waving side shoots. You can also grow a philodendron much better this way than by letting it drip in the usual dismal manner.

For the indoor winter window, foliage hanging plants are best, but this is not the case in the summer if you have a balcony or any outdoor area where plants can be hung. Here flowering hanging plants come into their own with many profuse bloomers to suit whatever exposure you may have. These plants have the additional advantage of not taking up much-needed space for chairs if your outdoor area is small. Like their winter counterparts, summer hanging plants call for a great deal of attention, and, if you want carefree porch or balcony gardening, don't try them. They demand a fussy schedule that has to include daily watering, a certain amount of careful feeding, and regular cleaning up underneath them. Normally I resent plants that demand so much from me, but I find summer hanging plants so rewarding that I grow them in quantity.

Most of us have neither the time nor the facilities to grow good baskets of summer-flowering plants ready for the first warm days when they can go outside. It is better to spend a little money on a few judicious purchases. Enormous plants are usually available even in the north by mid-May. These have been forced into premature bloom in a greenhouse and are lush and full of bud and almost too heavy to lift. If you do weaken and buy one of the elephantine baskets, make sure that you have a really strong hook on which to put it. These forced baskets, having been grown under perfect conditions, usually have a huge spread all around the pot. This makes it almost impossible to hang them up against a wall without breaking part of the foliage; yet if we hang them free-swinging, their proportions are so gigantic that they overwhelm everything else. I trim these early baskets back. For one thing, having come from a greenhouse, they find life outdoors so early in the season very hard. The young tip growth is very susceptible to injury from sudden changes in temperature and the burning effect of wind. If you will cut your dinosaur back, not only will it fit your space better but also you will be removing the part most vulnerable to the weather. New growth will soon appear, and you'll never know that you ever laid clipper to the plant! Nevertheless, you would be wiser to resist the temptation these plants offer and get much smaller, budded plants from a greenhouse nearer the time for evening outdoor living, if you want your plants to grow without a check.

If you decide to buy small plants and make your own hanging basket, be very sure that you are buying trailing varieties of the plants you choose. Both the fuchsia and the lantana, for instance, exist in upright as well as weeping forms. It is possible to train an upright plant so that it will droop by allowing the stems to wilt and then hanging weights upon them before you rewater. This is far too complicated and time-consuming for any amateur; concentrate instead on buying the proper type of plant!

The soil for an outdoor hanging basket must be very rich, for the nutrients leach out even more rapidly in summer heat. To any commercial soil mix, you should add an equal amount of water-retaining material, such as wet peat moss or wet sphagnum moss, and take care to provide good aeration with plenty of sharp sand or perlite. For heavy feeders, like the fuschia, add a dusting of dried cow manure. A homemade summer hanging basket can be made of more interesting plant material than those already grown on for sale, but homemade baskets need a long growing period before they look their best. To do well there has to be heavy root growth, and until that exists the foliage will look poor and the flowers be almost nonexistent. Commercial growers are able to get this heavy root growth by starting their plants early, but this is impossible for the indoor gardener. That is why almost all of us buy our flowering baskets already well advanced and put up with the rather uninteresting varieties that are the most readily available.

A little care needs to be taken about the exposure in which the plants hang. Full summer sun all day long is very hard on a hanging plant. Among the few that can take it are the rather hard-to-find plumbagos, which bloom in blue and white tubular flowers shaped like a phlox, and a dull yellow-orange plant called a thunbergia, which looks a little like flowering string and demands gallons of daily water. If it doesn't get it, this plant takes on the most devastatingly miserable appearance. Trailing nasturtiums love full sun, if you are numbered among those who can grow them in pots. Potted nasturtiums give me great trouble; I have tried many methods but I always end up with a plant that has a lot of dead leaves and poor flowers but a fine show of plant lice! I have no trouble with nasturtiums in the ground. They self-sow aggressively and have to be pulled out, but I cannot discover the secret of growing them well in pots. Happy nasturtiums are a delight, trailing and tumbling over the pot rims, but few people manage them well.

Another trailing plant that thrives in full sun is the purple, or rather the magenta, lantana. Lantana is a weed in some parts of the country, so those of us who use it as a potted plant can only ask you to excuse us. The mauve-red color is regarded with distaste by a lot of people. Purple seems to be the basic color of many wild plants; only as they are "improved" do "better" colors emerge. The magenta seedlings that plague growers of phlox are an example of the way in which hybrid seed reverts to this primitive color. If you have an azalea that has been grafted and if the rootstock is allowed to grow and blossom, the chances are that the color will again turn out to be magenta. My mother used to say that she had no difficulty at all in visualizing the Garden of Eden—all the flowers in it were obviously magenta. For that

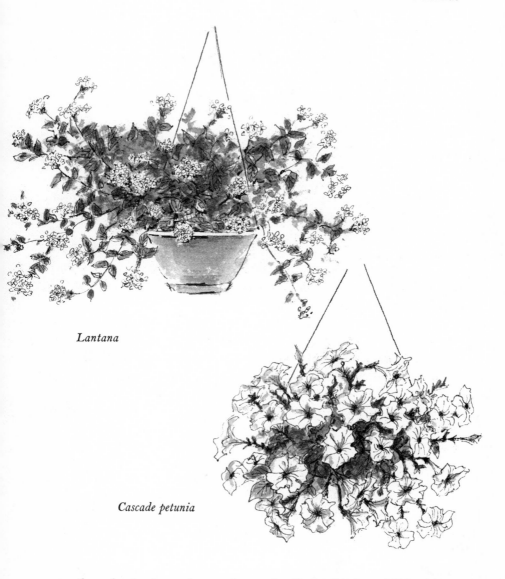

Lantana

Cascade petunia

reason the color is always known in our family as Garden of Eden! But if this rosy purple is set close to white, the combination of the two can be extremely pleasing. With the purple trailing lantana, the hanging plant to have nearby is the white cascade petunia. Both plants do very well in full sun in hanging baskets but both need plenty of water.

Basket petunias are now available in many colors. Try to buy the "F1," or first filial, hybrids. These are slightly more expensive plants,

HANGING PLANTS

but they have been extremely carefully bred for good growing qualities. You have to take just as much trouble with inferior plants as with good ones, so why not be rewarded by having the best possible varieties? Here again we must produce a little customer resistance to get our retailers to understand that we really expect to be able to buy the best plants available by refusing alternatives. After all, if you are willing to pay the small additional cost, surely the shops and greenhouses can take the trouble to grow the proper stock. It is surprising that people who wouldn't dream of being talked into buying inferior material in food or furnishings will meekly accept very poor plants.

Plant growing is a business like any other; it must make a profit. I am full of admiration for the effort and skill that goes into producing the plants, but I resent not being allowed to buy the best if I want to do so. The solution to this problem is up to us. We should read the accounts of the innovations and ask for them by name regularly, like a dripping tap. If your dealer can't or won't get them for you—go elsewhere and tell him why you are leaving.

The F1 petunias make much more even growth than the older varieties, but even they eventually get leggy. In midsummer you should cut the pot back quite drastically and feed it thoroughly. It will soon send out a burst of new growth and revert to a well-rounded shape. But let me again emphasize that these plants will not look presentable unless they are sheltered not only from driving rain but also from strong winds.

The list of hanging plants that thrive in half a day of sun or very bright shade is much longer. An excellent one is the browallia, which can be had in white and gentian blue; another is the trailing blue lobelia. A hanging lobelia will not stay with you all summer, for it dislikes the heat of the dog days. Browallia lengthens out and gets a little stalky but will give a good account of itself all summer long, unless there is a very prolonged heat wave, in which case it too may go over.

The most rewarding plant for half a day of sun is the ivy-leaved geranium. There are several types of these vining or trailing geraniums, some of which are grown mainly for their colored leaves. With them, the less water—though not, of course, to the point of no return— the stronger the color of the leaves. These trailing, fancy-leaved geraniums make rather small hanging plants; the foliage spread is not really thick enough. Most of them are better used outside in window

boxes where they combine well with their larger, zonal brethren. A few
colored-leaf zonals with small flowers spread so widely in their pots
that they, too, are often offered as hanging plants. If you can set these
so that they are suspended at eye level or even a little lower, they are
admirable plants, for they are covered with flowers the whole of the

Ivy-leaved geraniums

summer. They do not look nearly so well hung up high; the stems
never trail and the flowers can hardly be seen. These excellent plants,
which now include some new dwarf forms, are really better used in
planters and window boxes where their spreading habit makes them
particularly acceptable.

Far better for a hanging basket is the plain green-leaved ivy geranium. These range in color from white through mauve to the various
shades of red and pink and they come with double or single flowers.
Those in the red and pink shades are the stronger growers and, as with
all plants, the doubles hold their flowers better. Ivy geraniums respond
extremely well to soft pinching and can usually be bought full of bud
and raring to go. Our job is to keep the growth thrifty by continuing
the pinching-out as we see buds forming on the ends of the shoots.
This will force a continuous series of new flowering breaks along the
stems. Any ivy geranium allowed to elongate without pinching soon
turns into a ludicrous sight.

Ivy geraniums grow into complete blankets of flowers where the
climatic conditions suit them; they do particularly well along the West
Coast, for they do not like searing heat day and night. In the East the
show is less dramatic but can still be extremely good. I usually hook
several pots into each other so as to produce a very full effect. The
difference between one well-grown ivy geranium in full bloom hanging
alone and two others hung at different levels beside it is astonishing.
This can be easily managed by putting three hooks side by side and
then cutting suspension links out of wire coat hangers so that the
plants hang at slightly different levels. Try the effect. You'll never
hang an ivy geranium alone again!

One problem with these plants is a continuous series of yellowed
leaves that appear at the base of the stems. This is not a sign of poor
culture on your part; it is basic to the growth cycle. Cut them out as
you clean up the plant. Ivy geraniums need continuous dead-heading to
keep the flowers coming. This is true of all plants, but where heavy
summer bloom is required it is essential. Dead-heading a plant means
preventing it from setting seed, which it is much more likely to do
outside than indoors. Once a plant has set seed, it has achieved its
mission in life and ceases to flower; it then turns all its energies toward
ripening the seed pods. Your wishes and its interests cease to coincide.
If you cut off the dead flowers before the seed can form, the plant,
incurably optimistic, will throw yet more bud and try again. And you
and it can repeat the process all summer long.

In poor growing seasons, particularly if there has been a great deal of rain and very little sun, ivy geraniums are inclined to flower in spurts and then take a rest before they try again. If you are growing several grouped together and it seems to be one of those years, you can keep a continuous show going by cutting all the buds off some of your plants as they form and making them throw a fresh set. This will stagger the periods in which your plants are in flower and give the display a better appearance. Ivy geraniums are not succulent enough to be carried through the winter in a cold place with very little water, and since they loathe indoor life—all the leaves turn bright yellow in a few days—they cannot be held in a window. Unless you have a cold, bright window where you can attend to their daily needs, it is better to buy fresh plants each year, particularly as those plants take time to reach really good proportions.

The other familiar plant for bright shade is the hanging fuchsia. These are also plants that flower on new wood with a tremendous

Fuchsia

succession of bloom. But unless the terminal points are carefully pinched several times during the very early stages of growth, the plant will just have a few long, thin stems. The plants we buy have been brought to their floriferous best both through careful pinching and also

HANGING PLANTS

by very heavy feeding. If they are to continue to give a massive show, fuchsias need a regular supply of plant food in their pots. They also need a great deal of water and can be depended upon to show instantly when you are giving too little. A fuchsia wilts as dramatically—and as quickly—as a spathiphyllum, and, if this is allowed to happen too often, flower production will fall off. Fuchsias come in a beautiful variety of shapes and colors, but are extremely messy plants. The withered flowers litter the ground below them all the time, and you must also keep seed pods constantly clipped off or black fruit, like a small cherry, will form and the flowers will cease. If you are house proud, this may not be the plant for you. Fuchsias also cannot be carried on in bloom indoors. They are extremely determined about their period of dormancy and they have not yet been recycled so that they will flower during the winter. When the weather cools off, fuchsias drop their leaves and look horrible: at this stage they need rest in a cool place. The dormancy, though fierce, is often quite short-lived and new growth sometimes appears as early as January. The old plant must then be cut back to a new break and grown on for months in a cool place with no chance of bloom but an ever-open invitation to innumerable bugs! This is no job for the gardenless gardener; if you have found a variety you particularly like, it is better to give it to a friend with a greenhouse and ask for some softwood cuttings to be made for you the following year.

For a northern exposure or a location that gets really very little sun, hanging tuberous begonias cannot be beaten. This is not quite the

Hanging tuberous begonia

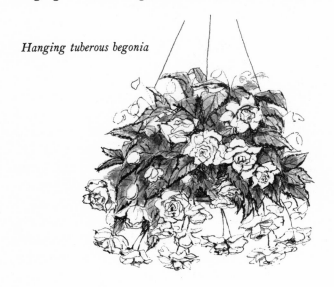

same plant as the tuberous begonia that is used as a bedding or pot plant. The tubers of the hanging varieties are harder to get and much more expensive. The method of growth is exactly the same as the upright varieties which are discussed in Chapter 10, but more stems will develop and these will eventually fall gracefully over the sides of the pots instead of having to be staked upright. The hanging tuberous begonia needs a very rich planting soil; I read that fish meal should be incorporated in it, and I know the plant relishes regular feeding with a fish emulsion. When cooler weather drives us all indoors, put your plant into a dark place and withhold water. When the stems have withered sufficiently to be rubbed off without difficulty, the tuber is cured. Store it in its pot in a cool, dark place and take an occasional look at it. If the tuber shows signs of shrinkage, that is if it begins to wrinkle and get flabby, spray a little water on the tuber but be very careful not to wet the pot soil. This usually plumps up the tuber.

Achimenes make excellent flowering baskets for bright shade. The method of starting the tubercles under lights is discussed in the next chapter, but I have grown an ever-increasing hoard of untouched achimenes in the exact duplicate of the sphagnum-covered planks on which I grow succulents. They have done extremely well growing in this sterile medium for several years, but the plants do need very considerable feeling and they must be pinched back when young or they will get straggly. It is particularly important to take the planks down and lay them flat when feeding. Planks with achimenes react very unpleasantly to a build-up of fertilizer salts at the base in the sphagnum. White fly, discussed in Chapter 13, can be a nuisance with achimenes. I start my planks in late May, the first buds show in late August, flowers continue for at least two months and, in a frost-free area, the display would be much longer. When the flowering ends, the planks are left on their back on a shelf and entirely neglected all winter long. Nothing has ever given me so much pleasure in so small an area, and the fact that these plants must have a sunless location makes them extremely suitable for porches or balconies that are not very bright. Small individual pots will flower for months indoors under the lights and this is a good way to build up a stock of the newer and more expensive varieties for future hanging plants.

Achimenes also make an extremely floriferous hanging basket for late in the season. These plants should not be started into regrowth until the hot weather has arrived and your other plants are already outdoors. This makes achimenes an easier plant for the gardenless gardener to grow than some of the others, and, as they can hardly ever be bought already planted in the commercial greenhouses, the late-starting habit is a great advantage. You must search the catalogs to

Achimenes on a plank

find them, and most of the trailing varieties—for they too come in both weeping and upright forms—are usually rather Garden of Edenish in color. They give such a breath-taking display, thickly planted, that this is no disadvantage.

But do let me re-emphasize that none of the plants you use to flower outside during the summer will continue the process after you have to take them indoors. They are exhausted, shabby, and ready to collapse. Those that grew from tubers should be dried off. As for the others, take a hint from their appearance, don't demand anything more from them. Throw them out. Next year you will be able to be more selective in what you buy as a result of your initial experiments.

10 ❧ USING A
LIGHT UNIT

RESEARCH, which has shown that a properly balanced artificial light can be used as a substitute for sunlight, has opened a new dimension for all horticulturists. We now know that even the simplest arrangement of extra light not only dramatizes the appearance of any group but also helps the plants to grow better. This has freed us all, experienced growers and novices alike, from the necessity of having suitable window space.

Horticulturists are not unlike the plants they grow, basically a little conservative and disinclined to be recycled. But even the most unreconstructed indoor gardener has come to realize that plants given artificial light will grow well in otherwise dimly lit locations and that lights can be installed in plant windows so as to prevent the flowers from turning their backs upon the room. This supplementary use of light is now accepted everywhere, and the various ways it can be applied to indoor horticulture have already been suggested. Artificial light can also be used, entirely upon its own, to grow excellent plants and to enable us to indulge in a variety of horticultural skills in such improbable places as warm or ice-cold cellars or windowless passages. The excuse of having no light will no longer get you out of trying to grow plants!

Light units for indoor horticulturists are easily available in very simple forms, and shelved and lighted carts also exist for people who want to try this kind of growing on an intensive scale. If you can once induce yourself to try a simple unit, you will find you can grow excellent foliage plants. It is a little more difficult, however, to grow plants to full cycle so that they will set bud and bloom. If we turn to the experts for guidance in this problem, we are inclined to run into a contradictory blitz of advice about candle-footage and light rays, which fails to give the new grower any sense of security! Don't let all this scientific jargon put you off. I don't understand any of it myself, but I have used lighting units for years with the greatest success. I am sure you can do the same. The technicalities are very important to the plant breeders, and all the knowledge they are acquiring will eventually be greatly to our advantage. But at present all we need to know is what works. Fortunately enough experience has now been accumulated to make this fundamental aspect of the problem clear. It is an oversimplification of a complicated subject, but it will suffice to say that plants grown under special fluorescent tubes, prepared particularly for horticultural purposes, will set bud and bloom. Plants will also complete the entire growth cycle with a lighting combination that contains "daylight" and "cool" fluorescent tubes. Light units with only cool, white fluorescent tubes will bring on strong, healthy plants, but there will be no bud set unless some incandescent lights are added.

The special horticultural tubes give off a curious purple glow that not everyone finds attractive. Thus it is important to realize that there is another combination that can be equally effective indoors. The special horticultural tubes and the daylight and cool tubes are available everywhere: the combined fluorescent and incandescent units can be bought from many dealers or even constructed at home. If you are a little skeptical about the whole business of artificial light, try a very simple experiment for yourself. Put an ordinary dime-store philodendron in a pebbled saucer on a table where there is not enough daylight for good growth but where a lamp will shine on it every evening for a good many hours. The one by which you read would be the best because presumably you turn that on without fail—maybe in these times it might be more realistic to suggest the lamp that is always turned on when you watch TV! Take care not to put the plant so near that it will be burned by the heat. Put another philodendron at the same stage of growth somewhere else in the room where it gets whatever daylight is available but no lamplight, and treat both plants identically as far as the culture is concerned. In a remarkably short time you will find that the plant that is getting the lamplight looks much sturdier, with strong new shoots and better-colored leaves than its twin. African violets treated in the same way will also show a marked difference in their growth.

If this experiment convinces you, then you can give yourself even

USING A LIGHT UNIT

greater pleasure by buying a simple horticultural lighting unit. They are available at all good garden centers and come equipped with a reflector to cut the glare; they are adjustable in height. They need to be used with a tray underneath them, and this is usually part of the complete package.

Light unit

Plants under any form of light transpire very strongly and need more water than usual. It is therefore a good idea to make a deep dry well with at least two inches of sand or aggregate in the tray. Some trays come with built-in plastic wicks that lead into a small water well, and these certainly help in keeping the dry well moist. But plants under lights are not for the absentminded or casual gardener; they need dedication.

Fluorescent light tubes can also be arranged to make growing areas underneath cabinets or can be built into pieces of furniture. These arrangements look extremely effective in all the pictures I have seen of them, but fixed units of this kind are harder to handle partly because of the lack of free air circulation and also because they are not flexible in relation to the height of growing plants. A novice gardener would do better first to master the technique of growing under lights with one of the commercial appliances before graduating to any custom-built affair.

What are these techniques? What's so different about them? First is the realization that, to be effective, lights must be close to the plants. Unless you have enormous facilities, this rules out growing tall or billowing plants; you will have to decide upon rather small ones. Next comes the question of light hours; how long must the plants be lit for their best advantage. Here again expert advice is hard to pin down. With my own flowering plants, twelve to fourteen hours of light in every twenty-four hours seems to suit them best, but a period of darkness is an absolute necessity. The distance the tip of the plants should stand from the source of light also produces different opinions. My lights are suspended about 7 inches from the plants; otherwise, all I see is the reflector. If plant leaves begin to curl they are getting too strong a light, and the unit should be raised higher. If the stems elongate, the lights are too far off.

You must also bear in mind that these lights are the equivalent of strong sunlight, and a unit arranged for display cannot be mismatched with sun-loving and shade-requiring plants. The only way in which you can combine plants that enjoy bright light with those preferring filtered light is to group the shade-lovers at each end of the lighting tubes. The intensity of the light diminishes outward from the center.

In a warm place, two excellent plant families do well under lights: African violets and begonias. I grow these particular plants in this way for I have no other suitable location that is warm enough for them.

African violets are a cult; they are grown by the thousands everywhere by amateurs who often otherwise are not interested in plants. And like most cults, they produce very strong reactions both for and against. Badly grown African violets are very dreary little plants, but a few sturdy, flourishing pots full of bloom are wonderfully useful as temporary decorations for the table. I refuse to feel that I am betraying my fellow horticulturists because I enjoy raising some good specimens! The family of gesneriads, to which they belong, contain many other very floriferous houseplants that do well under light, some of which I have also grown but not long enough or well enough to be able to give any good advice about them. Many of them have rather different growing requirements from the African violet, and, if you are interested, you would do well to read some of the books dealing entirely with the culture of the gesneriad group.

USING A LIGHT UNIT

African violet

African violets need good light and warmth to flourish. Inadequate window-sill daylight during the short hours of the winter is almost always the cause for lack of bloom and long, thin, stalky leaves. These plants can stand a room temperature between 65 and 75 degrees, but, like all houseplants, they will be sturdier if there is a drop at night. Any temperature below 65 degrees will inhibit bloom unless the plant has had long, slow conditioning. Practices that suit other plants cause distress to African violets, which is, I imagine, why they are not favorites among many horticulturists. African violets, for instance, dislike cold water, and in the coldest months they should be watered with tepid tap water; otherwise the leaves will be spotted. It is not, however, necessary or desirable to water them from below. Novice growers should start with plants that have plain leaves; they are easier to manage than the varieties with frilly or curly leaves. For longer-lasting flowers it is always better to choose plants with double blossoms, for these hold on longer than the single flowers. I have always used plastic pots for any plant grown under lights in order to conserve moisture. I was interested to learn that one of the main professional growers of African violets in this area also advocates plastic pots, though for a different reason. He grows his plants in a sterile medium that has to be fed regularly and he finds that clay pots often absorb fertilizer salts in sufficient quantity to damage the leafstalks resting on the rims.

African violets are mildly succulent. If you look carefully at the leaves and stems, this becomes obvious. In consequence, they must have soil with excellent drainage so that the surplus moisture rushes through. Rich compost very heavily laced with sand works well for me.

The commercial mix sold specially for African violets needs the addition of both sand and moistened, milled sphagnum moss. I would not add peat moss, as the mix itself is basically peat. A recommended soil-less mix consists of equal parts of peat moss, perlite, and vermiculite with a dusting of ground limestone, and I am told that plants in this mix need no crocking—a piece of information I can only pass on without comment! It is important to point out that any soil-less mix means more work for you, because, having no nutritional value, plants growing in it have to be fed regularly. This is why I prefer compost or an improved commercial soil, but it is unfortunately also true that my plants bear no resemblance whatsoever to those grown by any local expert! Since the plants are succulent, they need water only twice a week even under lights. Good plants are grown to a single crown; the additional side growth can be cut or pulled out and rerooted in a manner that we will deal with later. Those flat show plants that look like Victorian bouquets are produced not only by keeping the plants to a single crown but also by pulling out individual leaves from the outer ring in order to keep the whole shape symmetrical. As the succulence of the African violet is largely concentrated in the leafstalk, it is important not to cut off any leaves. Like a cyclamen stalk, the fleshy part left attached to the plant may rot back.

If your plant grows well, it will eventually refuse to lie flat no matter how much you may have plucked and pulled. As it gets older it will rise on a stalky neck. At this point I throw mine out, and start again, but if you are very much attached to some stalky variety, repot it more deeply than it was before and get the neck down below the soil. Unlike almost every other plant, African violets do not resent this change of growing level. As with all succulents, do not water it after repotting for at least a week.

I have also found that African violets grow unexpectedly well on pumice rock, inserted in exactly the same way as the sempervivums. Planted this way the leaves almost always stay flat, hug the rock, and spread out into very large plants, as long as they get sufficient warmth and light. Here again regular feeding is absolutely necessary, and one of the advantages of the rock is that there is no danger of sodden soil. A well-planted pumice rock can give pleasure for months on end, but it is extremely slow to take hold; you will have to bear patiently with a very apathetic-looking thing for a long time after you have set the little plants in place. Unless your rock will be under lights, it is better to plant only one side; in this way there is no trouble with plants at the back having insufficient light. For a conversation piece a flowering rock set on a pebbled tray (and here use white pebbles for contrast) cannot be bettered.

African-violet specialists may well be outraged by this somewhat cavalier account of how to manage a much revered plant. But this rather casual treatment has served me very well without all that fuss, for years. For the novice nonspecialist surely that should be the main aim. If success goes to your head, then why not specialize in these plants? There are an enormous number of varieties, including the modern miniatures, and, as has been stressed in this brief account, they can all be left without water for a few days. Massed African violets, placed so that they show as a big group, are extremely effective in a small area. Don't be made nervous about trying to raise them because they are such a fetish with many growers—they are, after all, only another plant!

I also use my lights in a warm place, in the same slightly slap-happy fashion, to grow a few begonias. Good begonias for the house exist in innumerable forms, some with fibrous roots, some with rhizomes, and some with tubers. They form a rather specialized class of houseplants and, like the African violet, have hordes of devoted followers. I don't keep my window areas warm enough for begonias, most of which originated in the tropical areas of Africa or Brazil. They do best in temperatures well over 70 degrees—and I did after all originate in the British Isles! I have found begonias extremely hard to accustom to cooler conditions even when acclimatized very slowly, but they also turn into sturdier plants if they have a nightly drop of around 5 degrees.

Begonias are grown indoors for their flowers and for the many variations in their interesting and extremely diverse foliage, which comes in many colors and in many unusual textures. Beginning gardeners would do well to concentrate upon the simplest, and in my experience this is the wax begonia, the fibrous-rooted semperflorens. This does extremely well under lights and, like all begonias, does best in small pots, so quite a large display can be got onto a pebbled tray. When the plant reaches the height you want, pinch out the growing tip. This not only produces larger and longer-lasting flowers, but also forces dormant stem buds into action and keeps the plant bushy. I grow my begonias in a well-sanded compost with heavy crocking, but begonia specialists strongly recommend a mix that consists of equal parts of fine sphagnum moss, peat moss, and fine compost. This mix must also have regular feeding. Begonias dislike hard potting; they sulk and just stand still. To get the best results make sure the potting mix is very lightly packed around the roots and, if you are using a planting mix full of inert materials, do not water unless the soil feels dry. Again, like the African violet, double-flowered varieties will give you longer-lasting bloom.

Rex begonia

Another kind frequently found in the shops is the rex begonia, with its interesting green, red, and gray leaves. At one time or other most of us have tried to grow some of these, for they make wonderful additions to any plant stand. This is one of those mishandled plants about which the customer should be told a great deal more before it is brought home. Rex begonias are rhizomatous plants—that is to say, they have a strong storage root underground. They do not adjust well to the change from greenhouse to house atmosphere (though if happy they grow well under lights). If the atmosphere is not to their liking, they drop their leaves and look dreadful. For years I always threw away any that had reached the impossible stage, assuming that rex begonias were short-lived indoors. This is where I showed great stupidity, because I had not realized that the plant was falling into dormancy. Recently it was somewhat strongly pointed out to me that I was being both extravagant and showing very poor horticultural knowledge. I discovered from my critic that I ought to put any rhizomatous begonia that had gone dormant into exactly the same warm place in which I was hoarding other tropical dormant plants and treat it in the identical fashion. Chastened, I did so and the next batch of rex started back into growth in quite a short time and, by now accustomed to the house atmosphere, they gave me a long-lasting, slightly overpowering show. I hope that the retailers of these plants will make this situation clear on their labels. I should have known, and it is a black mark against me that I did not. But there is no reason why a novice gardener should realize that the collapsing plant can so easily be saved, and as rex begonias are quite expensive I consider this an unnecessary waste.

Begonias like a certain amount of sun in the winter, but they are not able to stand hot afternoon sun after the days begin to lengthen. If you are growing them in variety in a plant window, an east exposure is probably the best.

Tuberous begonia

Tuberous begonias, which delight us in the summer, are easily started under lights. Don't begin the process earlier than six to eight weeks before you can get them outside. Various curious devices are now on the market that are alleged to help the beginner start good tubers. These are mainly formed of compressed peat, a material that is extremely hard to keep evenly moist, and the pockets in which the tubers are supposed to be planted are often too small for an average-size bulb. The idea of these peat packs is that the tubers will root into the peat walls and then can be planted in a pot with the minimum of root disturbance. In theory this is a good idea; in fact it does not work out. Unless you have an extremely moist area in which the peat pots can be set, the walls will be too dry for the plant roots to penetrate, and if you have to force the tubers into the planting pocket the bulb itself will be severely injured. They grow best for me in a small "flat" (the small boxes in which annual plants are sold) filled with compost; I do not use peat moss because of the difficulty of keeping it evenly moist, yet not so wet that the tubers will rot. I bury them, round-side down, with the entire tuber just below the soil level so that the maximum amount of roots can form all over the hairy area.

Tuberous begonias are often sold with pink stem buds already showing; this gives a clue as to which side is which. If they are still unbudded, there is no cause for alarm; indeed the plant may do better for you because there will have been no chance of any injury to the small stems. Most books advise against letting water stand in the hollow area of the tuber, because it is still a very common practice to suggest that the bulb be planted with the top above soil level. Planting with soil over the whole tuber takes care of the standing water problem automatically, but you should be careful that the planting medium is kept only moderately moist until good growth is underway.

Tuberous begonias have to be pre-rooted in this manner because of the danger of rot setting in if the tubers are put into their final pots before a good root system has established itself. Once planted, set the flats under the lights or in a warm window, and wait. The root growth starts quickly, and the stems and leaves develop. You will get better, heavier rooting if you put a small heating cable in the wet aggregate in your tray and let the planted flats have what is called bottom heat. These cables come in a variety of sizes for use in these trays and in cold frames. They are designed to run off an ordinary house plug and are entirely safe even when used with wet material around them. The best kind have small thermostats that are preset for 70 degrees. You may have to search to find them, but they are inexpensive and make a great deal of difference to work done under artificial lights, particularly if the unit is set in a cold place. In the north they have the invaluable additional use of preventing an accumulation of ice in the gutters.

Many growers allow only one or, at the most, two stalks to develop in the upright varieties of tuberous begonias. I find these plants exceptionally brittle and I like a back-up system. I, therefore, usually allow mine to throw up as many stalks as they want. This reduces the size of the individual flowers, but again I prefer many medium-size blooms to a few outsized giants. What is more, a tuberous begonia with a single stalk is completely finished if, as can happen very easily, the stem gets broken.

Tuberous begonias in flats can be potted into their final pots as soon as the developing leaves have all grown to the same size. Give them plenty of crocking in a plastic bulb pan and very rich soil. Though I have not used it myself, I read that a new fish meal is wonderfully effective incorporated into the soil, and I intend to try it. To pot up the rooted tubers, knock out the side of a flat (and this is one of the reasons why I much prefer the old-fashioned wooden style of flat to the modern plastic counterpart) and slide out the block of soil in which the tubers are set. If sufficient root growth has been made the soil will remain intact. With a sharp knife, cut each plant into an even square of rooted earth. Set this block into the prepared pot and add more soil around it. Do not put any additional soil over the top of the root block. If you do, you change the level at which the plant has grown and open the door to a fearful danger with tuberous begonias—stem rot. Newly planted pots will do best if they can go back under lights with moderate watering until new growth begins once more. If you no longer have enough space under your lights, put the pots in a warm but sunless window and rotate them regularly. Tuberous begonias will not grow outdoors until the night temperature has warmed up, so nothing is gained by starting the tubers into early growth. For good development both at the early stage and later on when they can be got outdoors, the plants always need a bright location without sun, as much protection from wind as possible, and plenty of regular food. They do very well with fish emulsion, but if the leaves start to curl back strongly you are overfeeding. The other great danger is mildew on the leaves; for that reason tuberous begonias must be allowed a free circulation of air around them even at the earliest stages.

Another excellent group of summer-flowering plants that can be started and grown very successfully under lights are gloxinias. Gloxinias have begun to get a bad reputation as houseplants because of the very poor showing made by those huge, overforced plants, which appear on the market in early spring. This poor reputation is completely warranted when the plants have been forced to such an extent that they cannot possibly survive the transfer from greenhouse to house atmosphere. But gloxinias grown slowly indoors to bloom at their normal time, which is mid- to late summer, are excellent houseplants. They will reward you for weeks on end with dozens of big bell-shaped flowers in many colors and also in interesting blotched and spotted forms. The unusual types are hardly ever offered for sale commercially. But the seeds germinate extremely freely, and the plants can be successfully raised by this means under a lighting unit in the manner discussed in Chapter 11. To grow gloxinias at home from tubers, start them off exactly like the tuberous begonia, transplanting them into 5-inch pots when the leaves are really established. A soil suitable for African violets with good drainage material incorporated and proper pot crocking does best. Gloxinias will grow and bloom under lights, but once the leaves are really developing they will also be happy in an east window or in a bright, sunless place outdoors if the night tempera-

Gloxinia

Cut back

Subsequent growth

ture has warmed up. Indoors the pots must be rotated regularly for the plants bend toward the light and lose all symmetry. They are also semi-succulent, so the pots should only be watered when the top soil looks dry.

Gloxinias are plants that can only be hurried by professional growers. Those of us who raise them at home must be patient, for they need a long time to mature. Eventually buds will show, and then you can start a light feeding of fish emulsion. Always try to keep water off the leaves, for they spot very easily. If you break a leaf, and they are tiresomely fragile, razor it right back to the tuber; don't allow a juicy stalk to rot on the plant. The weight of the oncoming buds is often so heavy that the plant flops. A little discreet staking will improve its appearance. Put a small green stake against the rim of the pot at the back of the plant. (Gloxinias grown under window conditions always have a back and front no matter how regularly you turn them!) Use yarn to brace up the heavy flower stalk and tie the strands to the stake. The big leaves will hide the wool, particularly if you can gently work some of them over it. Home-grown gloxinias will reward you with an extremely long period of bloom. They are far sturdier than those flaccid, overforced spring plants, because they are blooming at the natural time of year and have not been forced into out-of-season flowers.

Gloxinias are plants whose bud formation can be controlled by the manipulation of light. In nature they will only set bud after they have had several months of very long daylight hours. Professional growers produce those enormous plants I want to discourage you from buying by bringing them on in greenhouses equipped to provide intense humidity. Here the plants are force-fed with huge doses of fertilizer and given a tremendous amount of extra daily light. As a result, in spite of the apparent wealth of oncoming buds, the plants can only fail when brought into the house. If you bought, or were given, one of these monstrosities, you can still get a little of your money back. No matter how annoyed you are, don't give in to a very natural reaction to pitch the plant out when the foliage collapses. Instead, twist off every scrap of the mushy, decaying foliage and you will often find small, healthy leaves at the very bottom of the stem that should be left. Don't worry even if there is no sign of life at all after you have taken off the top growth. Put the pot aside in a warm place and give it just enough water so that the top soil does not dry out. In an amazingly short time fresh leaves will appear, for the roots do not stop working when you scalp the plant. If you let the new leaves grow on in a warm, bright place, the plant will rejuvenate and show new buds within three months, though the flowers will not be nearly as profuse as before. I feel that the retailers should stop selling us these overforced plants. If they must persist in the practice, surely it is also up to them to tell us how such an expensive plant can be salvaged. I myself own well over a dozen excellent gloxinias rescued in recent years from angry purchasers.

All gloxinias eventually get shabby, the flowers stop coming, and the leaves yellow. When this happens the plant is falling into dormancy. Leave it alone without water for a couple of weeks and then twist off the foliage for a second time and set the tubers, still in their pots, either back under your lights, if you have sufficient space, or in a warm window. During the winter growth period a sunny window is best. Contrary to the advice given in most books, gloxinias do not need a long rest, for if they are set aside for several months without water they frequently fail to revive. But if you, again, treat the pots exactly as you treated the earlier overforced varieties, leaves will reappear quite soon. This time the plant should be repotted as it will have exhausted the soil. And you may well be horrified to discover that the overforced plants you so cleverly rescued were sold without any internal crocking. The leaf growth that follows a natural dormancy develops very slowly; this time new roots have also to form. With warmer weather the pace will quicken, and the plant will repeat its performance year after year, turning into an enormous tuber in the process. As the days lengthen, the plant must be taken out of the full sun.

Another good houseplant under lights are the achimenes. These come in a great variety of colors and are plants which like heat. Preconditioned achimenes are now available for winter bloom, and these make delightful small flowering plants on a heating cable under lights. Achimenes grow from little tubercles that look like undeveloped pine cones. They dislike transplanting, at any rate by nervous novices, so it is well to start them in the pots in which they are to bloom. To look effective, achimenes need to be crowded in their containers. For me they seem to do best in clay pots, planted on their sides, as it is impossible to tell which end is which. They are extremely susceptible to sodden or wet soil in the early stages of their development, so be sparing with water. If you ignore this advice and start the tubercles in a flat, after transplanting slip the pot into a plastic bag and seal the top. Put back under the lights; the transplanting shock, which often is otherwise fatal, will be greatly eased. After the top growth has made four leaves, a soft pinch will promote bushiness, but, if the first four leaves grow extremely slowly, you may have a variety that dislikes pinching—so watch what you are about. Once the plant is in bloom

USING A LIGHT UNIT

give more water. If the pot soil dries out, premature dormancy will set in.

With all these instructions, it must be obvious that achimenes are not plants for casual gardeners, but their ability to flower under lights in a warm place makes them excellent plants for gardenless gardeners. Once dormant, leave them bone dry in their pots for anything up to six months; don't even remove the withered foliage. When you come to repot you will usually find an enormous increase in the tubercles. The lazy man's short cut with these plants is to restart a dormant pot with water, on a heating cable, under the lights. When growth begins, remove the undisturbed root mass into the center of a newly prepared, bigger pot, and fill fresh soil around it. This produces thick, luxurious growth and saves the tubercles the trauma of division. It does, however, prevent you from increasing the number of pots of new and interesting varieties.

In this account I have concentrated entirely upon the flowering plants I use under lights, and the list is highly personal and incomplete. If you grow plants this way, you will soon work out what is best for your tastes. That is the delight of such a unit; it can be adjusted to each person's individual likes and capabilities.

11 ✿ INCREASING YOUR COLLECTION

MOST PEOPLE once they start to use an artificial lighting unit soon cannot imagine how they ever managed without it. They take up such a small space, are inexpensive to run, and can serve a multitude of horticultural purposes. They open up exciting possibilities both for the novice and the experienced grower, and are an easy way to grow and increase your plants, both through sowing seeds and taking cuttings.

Seeds

Seeds can, of course, be started indoors on a window sill, but you will need a very cool place with an unusual amount of light. Seedlings need exceptionally strong indoor light if they are not to get drawn, that is long and skinny. If a seedling is once drawn, it never turns into a good plant. A light unit is therefore particularly good for sowing seeds because of the strength of light it generates. It is best used in a cool room with a small heating cable in the tray. Though much else has changed in the modern world, the basic needs of growing plants from seed remains unaltered: for good germination and continued health, seedlings need warm feet, cool heads, and a great deal of strong light. This triple play used to be provided by making a hotbed of fresh stable manure and straw in a pit frame outdoors, with soil laid on that. As the process of fermentation set in, there followed great activity with soil thermometers until the pile settled down to even warmth. Old garden-

INCREASING YOUR COLLECTION

ing books are full of dire warnings against what they called "green heat." Nowadays, even if we could get the manure and the men to spread it, there are very few people left who would know exactly how to build such a bed or control the violence of the fermentation.

Hotbeds were in regular use at my grandfather's. In early spring the hundreds of young plants needed for the flower garden were raised in them. The fashion of bedding out—that is, setting young, annual plants into complicated patterns to make flowering designs for summer beds—was still in vogue and not relegated, as it is today, to an occasional public park or a nostalgic exhibit. Also, at that period, there were few plant nurseries selling flats of young, forced, annual plants, and the home gardener had to raise and force his own. The hotbeds steamed away purposefully all January, and by February were ready for seed sowing. The frames themselves were covered with hinged lights—the technical term for glass covers. These, of course, had to be opened and shut and generally fussed with according to the weather, so the whole process of starting and growing plants in a hotbed called for a great deal of garden help. By midsummer the piles were almost quiet; like gradually diminishing volcanoes, they were mellowing. They were then planted to melons, which at that time were something of a summer delicacy in England. In the late autumn it fell to the lot of the gardenboy, being the lowest man on the horticultural totem pole, to dig them out. This was a messy, back-breaking job in which, when possible, I joined with great enthusiasm. I still possess a rather vivid recollection of the time my nurse found me deep in the pit of a frame, struggling with a huge pitchfork, while the gardenboy offered advice from the side. To this day I really don't think that dirt upon a frilled white pinafore was worth quite the fuss that followed. In retrospect, it now seems more probable that it was the presence of a pitchfork in the hands of a four-year-old that really upset my nurse so much. In any case the scene remains firmly printed on my mind, including the duplicity of the gardenboy who vanished, leaving me to bear the brunt of the uproar!

Setting and bedding out plants into exact geometric patterns is no longer in fashion, but those of us who garden do sometimes long for a greater diversity of plant material from which to choose—both for color and type—than we are able to buy. We feel this most acutely when the seed catalogs arrive. These make the most mouth-watering reading; they come at the dreariest time of the year and are full of delightful-sounding novelties that we all long to grow, both for outdoors and for the indoor plant stand. Unfortunately, novelties take forever filtering down to local retailers, so we send for packages and optimistically decide to grow them ourselves. This is just feasible, so long as we realize, and can circumvent, the many pitfalls ahead.

For one thing it's a very long journey from a seed package to a flowering plant, and most people get overexcited about sowing their seeds and do so far too soon—in fact, around about the first warm day! Seed-sowing during this premature vernal urge may give you good germination, but that is only the start of the long haul. Each of the small seedlings has got to be moved first into a small flat, then into a little pot, and then into a yet larger pot—and all long before you can get them out of doors if sown too early. It will follow that you will be landed with trays full of badly grown seedlings on every window sill, all of which have to be misted and rotated and watered every day. The problem of light will also be serious. This can be solved by keeping your seedlings under a light unit, but the pressure on the space, as every tiny individual plant has to be potted on, eventually, makes this impossible.

If you will restrain yourself and not sow seed until six to eight weeks before outdoor growing weather, you will be able to hold most of the seedlings in their original seed flats under lights and not have to do all the additional potting up until you can get the little plants out-of-doors. A slower start will save a lot of subsequent disappointment, because no seedling, even those that later become good houseplants, is really happy indoors during the primary stages. They all do better under lights or in a greenhouse, or even in a cold frame outdoors. It is also now known that a plant that receives any kind of setback during this very early growing stage does not ever really recover. This means that inadequate light or crowded conditions must lead eventually to a poor plant—no matter how much trouble you have taken. It will also help if you restrict the amount of seed you sow; there's no need to use all the package! Apart from keeping down the number of seedlings you have to handle, germination is always a chancy business; sometimes for no particular reason nothing whatever appears. If you sow only half the package the first time, you will then have some in store for a second try. Stored seed needs oxygen to live, and this it takes out of the air around it. A seed is not an inert substance; it is a viable object with a minute amount of dried material inside the seed coat. This is stored in

INCREASING YOUR COLLECTION

a dehydrated form, but when the seed comes in contact with moisture it will swell to provide nourishment for the embryonic shoot that also exists within the seed case. Many seeds retain this dormant vitality for rather a short period. It has recently been discovered that the vital spark will remain alive much longer if the seeds are surrounded by specially oxygenated air in a moisture-proof package. Some seedmen are now marketing their seeds in foil that repels moisture, and before sealing a puff of fortified air is forced under pressure into the packet. This method of packaging the seeds keep them fresher far longer and is particularly good for those that in the past needed to be sown almost immediately after ripening if there was to be good germination. But once these foil packages are opened the air escapes. If you want to preserve some of the seed for later use, do not reseal the packet by turning the end over tightly. This deprives the remaining seeds of any air, and they will lose vitality.

This problem has not been made clear to us by those who sell seed in this new and improved packet. If, as seems likely, more and more seedmen take to using foil, the purchaser must be told that any reserved seed has to have air. It took me a couple of years to fathom why I was having such miserable germination with my saved seed. Not until I bought seed in a foil packet from an English company did the trouble become clear. On their foil envelopes were printed specific instructions about the dangers of resealing too tightly. This method of instruction should be standard practice. Since I have taken to tearing a corner off the foil envelop that is to contain saved seed, I have had no more trouble.

Sowing seed is not hard. Use any kind of shallow container so long as it is clean, has provision for drainage at the bottom, and has been properly crocked. Crocking for small seeds should consist of a layer of finely pulverized shards or an inch of perlite. If you are using a flowerpot, the crocking must reach halfway up the container. Seed can

Seed box ready for planting

Commercial soil
Compost
Sand
Crocks

be grown successfully in undrained boxes, but this is hard for the novice to manage correctly. Try to avoid using anything that has flexible sides. Seedlings and their boxes come in for a good deal of handling, and any container with flexible sides will bend and damage the roots.

Authorities differ about which medium is best for seed starting, though everyone agrees it should be sterile. This is partly to prevent rampant weed growth which might choke out tender seedlings, but mainly to eliminate the dangers of a fungus disease called "damping off," whose spores often exist in unsterilized soil. "Damping off" attacks the stalks of seedlings just above the soil level and mows them down as though they had been cut with scissors, and there is no cure.

Two or three sterilized mediums are suggested for seeds, and all are excellent. In my experience what works well for one person does badly for another, and everyone in the end must decide for himself. Milled sphagnum moss has a very large following. This is the finest grade of sphagnum moss that has been rubbed through a sieve. You can easily make your own at home, but you may well sneeze for several hours afterward, so I would advise buying a bag! Another possibility is fine-grade vermiculite, also easily obtainable. Both these materials have good water retention, which suits the emerging seed very well, and both are light and friable, which encourages a good, spreading root growth. But there is a catch: the embryonic seed case can only support the first leaves, called cotyledons. Once true leaves appear, the root system has to provide the nourishment. Plants growing in an inert, soil-less mix have to be fed regularly, and the same applies to seedlings —but in this case the solution must be extremely weak and very carefully applied. This is quite difficult for inexperienced gardeners to do correctly, nor is it willingly undertaken by the idle gardener, and the plants, in consequence, will suffer severely.

I belong to the group of people who are unwilling to be tied into an inflexible feeding schedule for their plants. Like most horticulturists I have innumerable, urgent, daily gardening chores that cannot be skipped and adding the necessity of a daily feeding for seedlings is not practical. Being a good gardener includes, among many other aspects, the ability to face up to your own weaknesses and find a way around them. I graduated to using sterile, inert mediums when I lost a lot of plants through damping off; I then lost an equal number through my own laziness about feeding. As I knew I was not going to change, and as I was equally unwilling to go through the dreadful process of sterilizing soil in the kitchen oven (which can be done but is a loathsome job), I worked out a compromise that so far has stood me in good stead. I crock a clean shallow container properly in the conventional manner and cover the crocks with a thick layer of sand. This is to hold consistent moisture under the soil surface, for I grow all my seedlings under lights where there is greater danger of drying out. Over the sand I put a layer of compost, which contains all the nourishment any young plant can possibly need, and I tamp this down. Tamping means pressing lightly with a flat piece of wood to get an even surface; seed does not germinate well on uneven ground. Over the compost I put an inch-thick layer of commercially sterilized soil, which I also tamp down. This arrangement enables me to have the seeds germinate in a sterile soil; the layer is also thick enough to discourage any weed growth from the underlying compost until the sown seeds are up and easily recognizable. It also frees me from the boring burden of that incessant feeding. There are nutrients for the initial roots in the commercial soil, and as they thrust down into the rich compost they get all the nourishment they need. Seedlings become progressively less vulnerable to damping off as they develop. This compromise method takes them through their most vulnerable stage in sterile soil but provides them with a source of nourishment from the start. There is a secondary advantage in that the richness of the compost enables me to wait longer before having to transplant. Plants grown in inert material need early transplanting no matter how well you are feeding them.

To sow big seeds, space them well apart but remember that it is the rare amateur grower who gets 100 per cent germination. So make allowance for loss but never overlap the seed. It is also much easier for later transplanting if the seed is sown, or, in this case, put in by hand, in rows. If you put them on their sides, you will have no worries as to which end is which. Spread soil over them lightly or, in a soil-less mix, cover them with whatever material you are using. But use no more than the depth of the seed. More seeds fail to germinate because they have been buried alive than for any other reason. Press the covering material lightly with the base of a pot but don't pound it down; you are not, after all, laying a concrete terrace. Think of the way nature itself sows and use a light hand so that the small shoots can break through easily. Medium-size seeds usually can't be handled individually. Shake them carefully into rows which you can make by pressing a pencil into the planting medium. You can do this either from a small tear in the side of the seed packet or—which is my method—pouring them into the palm of the left hand and distributing them along the rows between the first finger and thumb. Try to separate them in their furrows with the very sharp point of a pencil. Once again each seed should lie alone and not overlap its neighbor. Medium-size seed needs only a light dusting of soil pressed down as a covering. Superfine seeds, such as gloxinias or begonias, should be mixed with a pinch of dry sand and sown broadcast over the soil surface. The sand will spread the seed more evenly and make it go farther, and will also show you where you have missed seeding. Very fine seed should be pressed into the soil with your tamper and never covered.

After sowing seeds do not water them from overhead, for this often dislodges your careful arrangement and washes the seeds into the sides of the pan. No matter what you sow your seed in, it is always called a seed pan. Set the container into a bowl of water until moisture shows on the surface; then—which is essential—allow all the excess moisture to drain out. This will take several hours and should be done over a basin. This process of drainage drains the seed into even closer contact with the surrounding medium.

There must be steady moisture in the growing medium, and to conserve this the planted pan should be covered, for if emerging shoots find dry material around them they will die. They are, however, equally discouraged by sodden soil, and in that case they rot. For this reason, for once, I have not found man's modern boon to horticulture, the plastic bag, useful. If you put a drained seed pan right into a bag, it stays too wet. If you do use plastic, cut a length and put it only over the top of your container, making sure that there is at least an inch of air between it and the surface of the soil for proper air circulation. If a plastic strip of this sort is held taut with an elastic band, proper drainage can then take place through the vents on the bottom of the container.

Before plastic appeared gardeners covered their newly planted seed pans with a pane of glass to conserve moisture. I find I still do better with this old method. Most, though not all, plants prefer to germinate in the dark, and the novice would be well advised to take a chance on the variety that has been sown and put thick newspaper over the plastic or the glass. Most gardening books give a germination timetable, and you should check the containers regularly. They will do best in a warm place, but I would keep them off the heating cables while the pans are covered. Otherwise there may be so much condensation on the plastic or the glass that the emerging seed will be too wet. As soon as there is a sign of growth, remove the newspaper and gradually tilt the glass, or open the plastic, so that you can condition the plants to a normal atmosphere. When the curved neck of the growing seed straightens out, put the boxes into the brightest place you own, or under lights. If the lights are in a very cold place, now is the time to use a heating cable below the boxes. This is a very critical period; the new plants cannot be allowed to dry out, but they still resent sodden soil which is an invitation to "damping off." Rather than watering the growing medium all the time, I use my mister for the first few days—until I am sure the entire box has germinated.

Tiny plants should not remain crowded together. If you have had very good germination and the leaves touch, thin your plants immediately. Most books recommend pulling out the excess plants, but I find this does great damage to the remaining root systems. I cut out the surplus plants, with sharp embroidery scissors, at soil level. If you are

Thinning seedlings

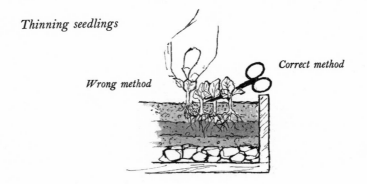

Wrong method

Correct method

not using improved F1 or F2 seeds, which are all true to size and color, and if—perish the thought—you are growing a package of seed in mixed colors, remember that the smallest seedlings are usually those which have double blossoms and the best colors. Large seedlings in mixed packages tend toward the Garden of Eden. Cut out the lusty wenches and leave the field to the dainty shepherdesses!

Even with strong-minded thinning, seedlings race ahead particularly when grown under lights, and need retransplanting when the leaves again touch. Don't delay this or the plants will never do well.

For this reason you should hold off sowing seeds until the outdoor growing season is near; otherwise the number of small pots you will have to look after takes on the aspect of a nightmare in arithmetical progression.

For transplanting, fill your flats or pots with rich, well-sanded compost but don't add any fertilizers; the young roots are still too fragile for soil additions of that sort. For a tool use something like a large plant label or an old fork. Be sure to hold the plantlet by a leaf—never the stem. At this stage the entire stem is the growing point and is therefore extremely vulnerable. Lever under and up and lift out the little plant, keeping as much of the root system uninjured as possible. Lower it immediately into a hole which you have previously made in the new flat and set the little plants about two inches apart each way.

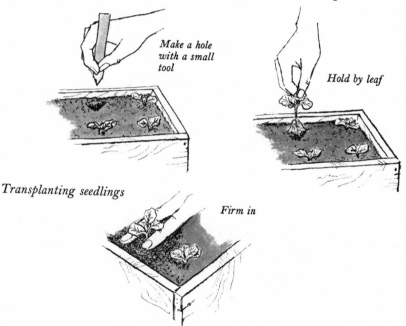

Make a hole with a small tool

Hold by leaf

Transplanting seedlings

Firm in

Now comes an essential step far too often forgotten. After the seedling is in the new location, it must be firmed in—that is, have the soil pressed closely against it. Spread your first and second fingers at each side of the stem and press the earth down firmly around it. Try not to touch the plant itself. This brings the root system into close contact with the soil. Failure to firm in newly transplanted seedlings accounts for many of the subsequent complaints of poor growth. A flat should be filled with transplants; choose a size according to the number of seedlings available. Little plants must have each other's company to thrive.

Transplanting is a great shock and, after misting the flat lightly, I usually slip a plastic tent over it for several days, keeping the whole thing out of sunlight. But a plastic-covered box can go straight back under a light unit, which is an enormous advantage. When the leaves touch again—and your patience is getting thoroughly exhausted—the plants can go into their individual pots.

I would never try to stock my garden with annuals this way; it's too long a process, and I haven't enough facilities. But I do use the light units to grow many winter houseplants from seed. Those that give no trouble except for the amount of time they need include cyclamens, gloxinias, streptocarpus (a cool-loving, close cousin of the African violet, sometimes called the Cape primrose), primulas, and schizanthus. I also raise some summer plants, which otherwise are not available, in very small quantities.

This all may seem rather more advanced horticulture than you are prepared to contemplate, but, if you will take the plunge and try a few seeds, the rewards will, I am certain, be sufficient to lead you on to try far too many the following year!

Cuttings and Layering

Sometimes after pruning a plant, you find yourself surrounded by a lot of healthy, lusty growth that calls out not to be thrown away. Most of us know that new plants are often made from just such material, but it never occurs to us to do it for ourselves. We tend to consider this a complicated horticultural process far beyond our reach. Striking a cutting, which is the technical term for rooting a severed piece of stalk, can be easily done by the novice gardener in a bright window or, particularly, under lights. This is a wonderful way to increase a plant collection.

Every piece of cut material maintains within itself a sustained urge to keep the growing point alive. To achieve this, the severed stalk must remain turgid—that is, full of water—and in a sufficiently bright but humid atmosphere so that the remaining leaves can continue the essential process of photosynthesis without losing more water than they are able to replace. A cut stalk that has wilted is one in which the proper balance between water intake and leaf transpiration has been lost. If cut stems can be given some help to prevent wilt during the first critical period, they will often regenerate and form roots.

The most obvious way to keep the stem turgid is to put the plant in water, and some plants will form roots without any further assistance. Ivy kept in fresh water, with a piece of aquarium charcoal in the jar to keep the water sweet, will root if given sufficient light, and so will the various kinds of tradescantias and the impatiens. Many amateur growers also root the leaves of African violets in water. Plants rooted in this way face a rather complicated problem when, as eventually must happen, the rooted stems are potted into soil. Water-induced roots are modified in order to extract the oxygen, which is essential to all plant growth, from the water instead of from a solid medium. Fish with their gills form an obvious analogy. When water-formed roots are transferred to soil, they suffer a serious shock. When they are taken out of water they cling together in a tight mass that is very detrimental to their growth. But, above all, they are not prepared to extract oxygen from soil until new feeding roots can be formed. A water-rooted plant inevitably stands still when potted up, while the roots struggle to readjust themselves to getting the vital oxygen in a different manner. Often this readjustment cannot take place in time to save the plant, and, at best, the growth of such a plant receives a severe check. The fact that it does not instantly collapse like a fish turns on the length of time the roots have been forced to live in water and the extent to which they have been modified. You can often tell if the process has gone past the point of no return, for roots that are entirely changed are very much thicker than their soil counterparts.

Most plants will not form roots in water; the stem end rots before new growth begins. It is better to try to create an artificially moist atmosphere in which the plant stem is surrounded by so much moisture that the leaves will not wilt. This kind of atmosphere used to be almost impossible for an amateur to produce. That is why striking cuttings was considered a job possible only for professionals. Nowadays it is much easier to provide the necessary humid atmosphere. Professional growers have an automatic misting device that surrounds cuttings with

INCREASING YOUR COLLECTION

enveloping humidity, this keeps them alive until roots form. We who handle only a few plants at a time can produce an equally humid, buoyant atmosphere through that familiar ally, the plastic bag, which holds in moisture while allowing air and light to circulate through it.

In order to form roots, the cut base of any stem must first make a callus, which can be compared to the initial scab that forms over a human wound. New roots grow around and through this healing tissue, which forms only when the cut stalk is pressed hard against a solid yet moist base. The speed at which the callus and the subsequent roots appear varies from plant to plant, but the whole process always calls for a huge expenditure of plant energy. In human beings young adults can show sustained energy in situations of stress that would defeat either an adolescent or a mature person; the same is true for plants. To be able to produce enough energy to form a callus and throw out new roots, a cutting must be neither too young nor too old. The proper stage is when the green growth of the current year has matured enough so that it snaps, not bends, when pressure is applied. Growth that is too young bends limply or tears if forced strongly downward. Wood that is too old and hard will have changed color, and the bark will be darker in color than the outer ends of the stems.

Shoots ready for cutting

Growth on which flower buds have formed is also unsuitable even if the stems are otherwise at the right stage; they will root but never turn into a first-class plant. The best plants come from cuttings made from nonblossoming side shoots. For this reason experienced growers often cut back their stock, or mother plants, in order to force just the right type of side growth for cuttings. Everything that has been said up to the present concerns plants that have thin leaves and stems and grow naturally in bushy form, but succulent material can also be induced to root, though this has to be handled a little differently, as we shall see a little later in this account.

To succeed with what we can now call by their technical name, softwood cuttings, it is best to use those little wooden flats in which annuals used to be sold. These are now, unluckily, getting as rare as diamonds, and we may have to learn to handle this work in the substitute plastic flats which, at present, I do not like as well for the process. Fill the box half full with a rooting medium; you'll need a water-absorbent material to hold the moisture, and sand or perlite for good drainage. I prefer a 50–50 combination of sand and peat moss, which works well for me, but here again other growers have different preferences. Pound this material down hard into the box to make a packed base. Experts take their cuttings with a dangerously sharp knife, and so did I for many years. The wounds, however, grew so monotonous that eventually I devised a two-part system for the mud-dle-fingered like myself. Instead of using a knife, clip off a number of suitable cuttings with your scissors or hand clippers, and let them have at least two inches of stem. Strip the lower leaves off and put the stems in a jar of water. The plant should have been well watered the evening before you go into action, so that the stems are turgid. Keep the cut material out of the sun so that there is no likelihood of wilt. To prevent mold from developing on the leaves while they are incased in plastic, avoid getting water on the foliage. As I use clippers that cut with a squeezing action, the base of the stems have been badly bruised al-though the damage can only be seen under a microscope. It is, how-ever, serious enough to prevent the formation of a callus, so I recut the material with a razor blade to make a clean cut. This second cut is made at a node, a place where a leaf once joined the stem. A callus always forms at a nodal point, and any piece of stem left below a node will only rot away. Shake a little of any of the commercial rooting powders onto a clean piece of paper and hold the prepared cutting in your left hand—these instructions, by the way, are for a right-handed person like myself. Dip the trimmed end in the powder. In your right hand have a small bamboo stake, or the unsharpened end of a pencil,

INCREASING YOUR COLLECTION

Cutting at the node

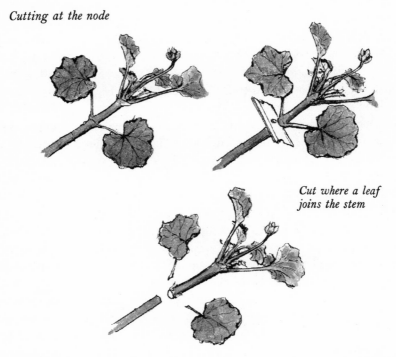

*Cut where a leaf
joins the stem*

and with that knock excess powder off the end of the cutting. With the flat end of the stick you then make a hole with a firm, solid base in the rooting material and put the cutting in it, resting the powdered end on the base. Only bury enough stem to hold the cutting upright—most people find half an inch sufficient.

There are two tricks that are essential to success in making softwood cuttings. The first is to make sure that the base you have made in the rooting medium really is solid and that the prepared stem sits firmly on it, for no cutting will form a callus if it is suspended in space. The second essential action is to firm in the cuttings. This is done in exactly the same way as with transplanted seedlings and is of equal importance, because the severed piece of plant material must be able not only to stand alone in an upright position but also be in close contact with the soil. A cutting that can rock will never root.

Once again, the small plants need company, so fill the box with cuttings but keep them all of the same material or you will run into trouble with the different speeds at which different plants will root. Don't crowd them so closely that the leaves touch, for this is an invitation to mold. With very large-leaved plants like hydrangeas, the leaves can be cut in half. Try, also, to face the cuttings the same way, for this will make it simpler for the essential light to fall upon all the leaves, particularly if the process is being carried out in a window.

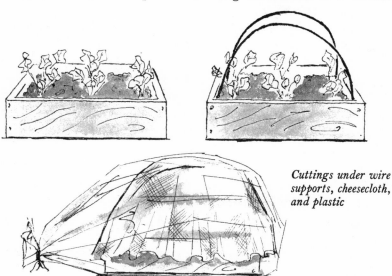

Cuttings under wire supports, cheesecloth, and plastic

After planting, water the medium lightly. The next step—and all this is nothing like as time-consuming or as complicated as it sounds—is to cut and bend wire coat hangers so that you make two little hoops which you can put in each end of the box. Drape a single layer of cheesecloth over the hoops to make a tent and let this reach down each side of the box. Finally slide the enshrouded box into a plastic bag and close the end with an elastic band. The cheesecloth provides light shade if, by chance, some sun should fall upon the plastic, and it also absorbs and recycles the moisture trapped inside the bag.

Cuttings prepared in this way can go straight under artificial lights with the tubes about two inches from the ridgepole of the box. A little bottom heat from a cable will speed the rooting process. Not only is the state of maturity of the cutting important, but the time of year when it is taken makes a difference. Under artificial lights most plants will eventually root if you have the patience, but if the mother plant has sensed oncoming cold weather, rooting will be much slower and almost impossible in a window. This does not apply to taking cuttings from evergreen plants such as yews or arborvitae, but these, after all, hardly

INCREASING YOUR COLLECTION

count as houseplants! For indoor gardeners who want to increase their plant collection, midsummer is by far the best time for softwood cuttings.

Once under the lights or in a window, the plastic will cloud over and you won't be able to see anything. After a couple of weeks, open the bag and give a cutting a tentative tug. If it comes right out without any change of appearance in the stem, put it back; you will have a considerable wait ahead. If the stem end is swollen, the callus has begun to form. Firm the cutting in again and reseal the bag; there will be roots within another two weeks with most houseplants. I usually give plants that I know have formed roots one extra week in the sealed bag; this produces much stronger growth. Then comes the period of re-introducing the cuttings, now small plants, to normal living. You do this by leaving the end of the bag open for increasingly longer periods, and normally it takes about a week more before the young plants can survive their re-entry problems without collapsing. The open-bag stage is critical, for, once the incubator is open, moisture can escape. At this time you must keep feeling the medium and adding water if it feels too dry. If the young plants wilt appallingly when the bag is first opened, which often happens with plants like chrysanthemums, close the bag until the plants revive and then start the process over.

Once the bag can remain open all day without any wilt, pull the box right out; by this time the cheesecloth will probably be rotted and can also be taken off. Keep the plants in a bright window or under lights, though not in sunlight for at least a week, but remember there is no nourishment in the rooting medium. This means you must either water with weak feeding solutions or quickly pot the new, young plants up. Depending on what you have rooted, the potting process, which is identical in method and soil content to that used for young seed plants, can be to put individual plants either into single small pots or to make a large plant by putting several rooted cuttings into a bulb pan. The latter method is a very easy way to grow your own chrysanthemums.

Occasionally a delicate plant that has rooted well looks utterly miserable after potting up. This usually is the result of a very susceptible root system having been damaged in the transfer and being unable to keep up with the moisture loss that is going on through the leaves. A plant in this kind of difficulty can usually be brought back by being put, pot and all, into a plastic bag with some small stakes to hold the plastic off the foliage and the top sealed. A week under this cover usually saves the day.

So far in dealing with cuttings we have been concerned only with the thin-leaf types which will only survive if they are given this artificially produced humid atmosphere. Succulent plants come equally easily from cuttings with far less trouble. Being full of water, succulents tend to ooze when the cuttings are taken. Slips, an old-fashioned term, of any succulent plant are less liable to rot and will root faster if given twenty-four hours unattended on a shelf in a warm, dry place to allow the air to seal the end after it has been cut with a razor. The reserve store of water is the factor that carries succulent cuttings over their first critical period. With semi-succulent plants, like gloxinias and African violets, individual leaves can be used to form new plants. Razor off a leaf and stalk and dip the end in a rooting powder. If you are taking a lot of cuttings, transfer the leaves into the usual rooting medium with a layer of sharp sand on the top. If you are rooting only one or two, crock and fill a small pot with rich compost and then put a two-inch layer of sand on top of that. Then insert a leaf stalk into the sand at an angle. The slant of the leaf prevents moisture accumulating around the fleshy stem. Semi-succulent plants are helped by a short

Succulent cuttings

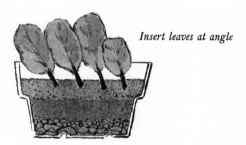

Insert leaves at angle

stay in a plastic bag, but they need this crutch only for a limited time, a week or two at the most. After that, light misting and an occasional light watering will suffice. A lighting unit is excellent for this process. With a gloxinia, a small tuber will form from the callus at the base of the leaf, and the plant must be allowed to grow on without a check for the next twelve months. That is why I prefer pot rooting from the start. African violets form new plantlets at the base of the leaf, after which the original leaf, its duty done, withers away. Cut-off crowns of African violets can also be rooted by laying, not planting, them on the

INCREASING YOUR COLLECTION

usual 50–50 mix and encasing the flat or pot in a plastic bag under lights. These crowns need to be in the plastic for a longer time. As soon as good roots form, which will be obvious from the rejuvenated appearance of the foliage, open the bag and gradually accustom the plant to the open atmosphere.

Heavily succulent leaves from plants like the crassula and sedums will root from leaf ends set at an angle, preferably in sand, but it has already been stressed that it is almost impossible to prevent these plants from rooting! They too produce little plantlets at the leaf end, but these are very slow growing and are, therefore, not so useful to a novice trying to increase his collection. It is easier to make a new plant from a rosette by merely burying the stalk in sand.

The proper stage of maturity is as important in succulent cuttings as in softwood. Geraniums are ready for cuttings to be taken when the new, green growth snaps quite audibly. Both the zonal and the other varieties should be allowed a short period in the open air to dry the razored end. Then, after they are powdered, the stems should be planted on the same firm base and in the same type of medium suited to softwood cuttings. Geraniums should not be covered with plastic. If they flag when they are first taken, mist the foliage; this will revive them. With all geraniums good roots form quickly under lights or in bright shade; sunlight should always be avoided with all cuttings.

The strongly succulent Christmas and epiphyllum cactus can also be rooted by being cut at a node and having the end dried for about a week. With these plants you may recall it is dangerous to bury any of the fleshy tissue. I make up a pot in exactly the same manner that I use for gloxinia leaf cuttings, with a pad of sand on the top. I then balance the flat, modified leaf of the succulent so that it is held upright and steady between something like two wide plant labels, with the powdered base resting on the sand. Roots form quickly and thrust down into the richer soil, but it is usually quite a long time before the new plant will remain upright without its supports. If they are taken away too soon, the leaf will fall over and tear the small new roots out of the ground. The various members of the aloe family also have to be rooted in this rather unprepossessing manner.

Plants that lose water very slowly through transpiration will also regenerate from leaf cuttings. You can, for example, cut sansevieria leaves into sections, always taking care to make sure which end is the bottom. Powder the cut ends and set them at a slant in a sandy mixture with a little damp peat moss added to it. The cut leaf ends will form small roots, and, once these are well established, underground runners form which throw up the offsets we discussed earlier. Plantlets that have been severed from the runners which attach them to the parent plant can also be easily rooted. All these methods of forming new small plants can be done in a bright window. You are, however, much more

Rooting spider plantlets

likely to have success if the work is done under a light unit. Not only will the roots form rapidly and thickly with the strong overhead light, but they can do so without the danger of scorching, which follows if sunlight strikes these little plants in their vulnerable stages. It is also far easier to grow on the newly made plants under lights than it is to try to get them to continue without a check in a window. Most windows are either too sunny or too dark. It is hard to provide exactly the correct conditions indoors.

Sometimes it is difficult to decide what to do with plants that have grown too tall and yet are not the kind that bush out easily after being cut back. Familiar houseplants which can grow us out of house and home are all the dracaenas, the dieffenbachias, the ficus, and the vining

INCREASING YOUR COLLECTION

monsteras. As was explained in Chapter 3, these plants can be be-headed, and will eventually throw new shoots, if you can bear the appearance afterward. If this is your decision, summer is again the time to swing the ax. But what about the tip you have cut off—can that be used? With dracaenas, tips can often be induced to root, if the cut end is dipped in a rooting powder and then inserted on a firm base of moist peat moss and sand and set under light.

I have not had much luck with this method of propagation, particu-larly when I have been in a hurry for new plants. The dracaenas take an enormous time to throw new roots, and a great many rot off during the wait. I have also tried to follow the instructions offered by many gardening experts to make new plants from sections of dracaena stalks buried horizontally in moist sand and kept on a heating cable or at a temperature of 75 degrees under lights. So far I have had no success at all with this method. I am still trying to discover what on earth I am doing wrong. But this is no guarantee that you won't succeed so, as an alternative to attempting tip cuttings, try chopping up the stems and burying them in sand. Don't, by the way, try to use your razor blade for this performance—a dracaena stem would make an admirable ax-handle! You'll have to use your knife or even a small saw.

I am not fond of the appearance of mutilated plants, or those in which there is nothing but a tuft of leaves at ceiling height, so when my single-stalked plants outgrow their welcome I usually take an air layer—and, for once, this cannot be done under lights.

Layering is a method by which roots are forced to form when the cambium tissue, or outer layer, of bark covering a growing stem is injured. Ground layering is used very extensively by professional and some skilled amateur growers to increase their collection of plants that do not do well from cuttings. It consists of making a cut that goes deeply into the growing tissue of a stem but does not sever the branch entirely from the parent plant. The open wound is then pegged down onto the ground, and soil, which is kept constantly moist, is heaped over the injured area. Enough nourishment continues to flow through the uninjured section of the stem to keep the half-severed branch alive. The damaged portion, which must be kept open with a small stone or wooden peg, being unable to heal itself by growing a callus to cover the entire wound, often compromises and sends out new roots from the callus it has been able to form over part of the damaged stem. In time, these roots grow sufficiently strong to turn the whole branch into a self-sustaining plant. This can then be cut away from the original parent and grown on alone.

Air layering indoors is based on the same principle and can be done by the gardenless gardener so long as he has sufficient self-assurance, the courage of his own convictions, and a good deal of patience. Choose a place on your over-tall plant where you would like the roots of your new plant to be, and pierce through the center of the stem with a penknife. I find it best to lay the plant down on its side on a layer of newspapers for this operation, for otherwise it is extremely hard to get the necessary leverage to pentrate a thin, lithe, iron-hard stem. The knife should pass through the center of the stalk and the blade show through the other side. Leave the dagger in position; then take a second knife and scrape and peel a layer of cambium half to three quarters of the way round the stem above and below the place where the knife has penetrated. This is a process called barking or ringing, and is sometimes used to force a recalcitrant tree into bloom. You must, however, take care not to girdle, that is peel off the bark the entire way round the stem. If you do, you will kill the growth above it,

Insert knife

Scrape off bark

INCREASING YOUR COLLECTION

for all the nourishment the growing tip receives is drawn up through this outer cambium layer; if the entire layer is taken off, the tip will die for lack of moisture. The effect of complete girdling can sometimes be noticed outdoors after a very hard winter. Small, starving animals, deprived of their natural food by heavy snow, sometimes survive by eating the bark off trees. In the spring, when the rest of the world revives, a totally girdled tree will die.

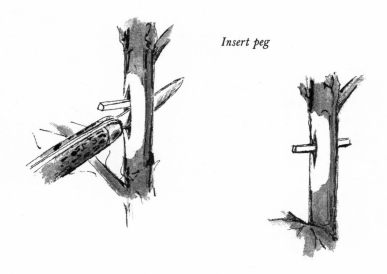

Insert peg

After you have scraped off enough bark both above and below the wound, pull out the knife but do so turning the blade sideways so that you keep the wounded area open with a peg of wood (part of a kitchen matchstick will do) that can be slipped into position while the twisted knife blade is still in place. The reason for leaving the knife in position while you ring the plant is to enable you to put this peg firmly and securely into position. If you insert it before you scrape off the cambium, it will probably fall out. Once the bark is off, the stem becomes extremely slippery, and you will find it almost impossible to get the peg into position a second time. Next, dust the pegged wound and the ringed area with a rooting powder and put a very thick spongelike pad of wet, long-grained sphagnum moss around the whole section of the stem that you have been working on. Enclose the sphagnum moss in plastic and tie it in tightly with electrician's tape above and below the wound, so that moisture cannot escape. To be successful and induce roots to form, the sphagnum moss must stay wet.

The plant should be put in a warm location and watered in the usual fashion. Eventually roots will appear in the sphagnum moss and

Cover wound with sphagnum moss and enclose in plastic bag

be visible through the plastic. It will take a long time, however, so don't get discouraged if nothing seems to happen at first. When you can see that the moss is filled with roots, cut the stem of the plant below this new root ball, and you will have a reproportioned plant. Pot it up in good soil without disturbing the sphagnum holding the new roots and use a pot that is only one inch larger than the root mass. Once the plant is growing freely again, which you can tell from the color of the leaves, you can move it up into a better-proportioned pot. A new Jack and the Beanstalk will soon start again.

Air layering is one of the oldest methods of vegetative reproduction and probably originated in the Far East. It can be seen in operation everywhere on the Indian subcontinent in a primitive form. Here, where plastic is a luxury, the older, homelier methods are used with equal success. I saw a ficus prepared in exactly the manner I have just

INCREASING YOUR COLLECTION

described, with the wounded area wrapped around with an old piece of burlap. The vital moisture was being fed into the burlap from a tin can filled with water which had a string wick coming out of the base. The can was hung from a tree a little higher than the place where the air layer was in process, and the wick was always wet. It was just as effective as our method though it needed more attention as the tin can had to be kept supplied with water. When I tried to copy the method, I had a fearful time getting the knot of the string thick enough and forced firmly down into the small hole so that the water irrigated the wick and did not just drain out of the can. But in a warm greenhouse I got an enormous dracaena back to manageable proportions this way, and I am far prouder of that achievement than of all my other air layers!

The same principle of forcing new roots to form where stem tissue is injured should be applied in early summer to long, thin philodendrons, to the syngoniums or arrow plants, and to the pothos, all of which also grow very spindly. If you are determined to save them, repot your plant into a pot large enough to have a clear inch of new soil all around the outer edges of the root ball. Wind the philodendron or other stems around the pot on top of the soil, pinning them down firmly every two inches. You will need small hairpins for the job. Straddle the stems with the hairpins and press them firmly into contact with the soil.

*Straddle stems
with hairpins*

Make sure that each place where the pins have touched the stems they have also wounded the cambium. Continue to wind all the hanging growth around and around the pot, making sure you are bruising the tissue as you pin it down. Your plant will immediately look far bushier and more interesting—nothing looks worse than one of those dreary drippers. What's more, it will very soon become a much healthier plant. New roots will form wherever you pinned the stems in, and new growing points will appear from dormant side shoots where fresh roots have formed. For a common dime-store philodendron the end result will be spectacular!

Members of the monstera family throw long, aerial roots along their stems. In nature, these grow downward toward the jungle floor like thick ropes, rooting when they hit bottom and then sending up a new young plant. You can take advantage of this capacity with your own vining monsteras. Cut off a section that already has aerial roots attached and cram the cut end and all the long lengths of aerial roots into a very small pot. You must, of course, have crocked the pot in advance, but otherwise all that is needed is to fill up the space that is not taken up by the roots with soil. Sometimes the young plant has to be steadied with a stake, as the top growth is so much larger than the pot. Put this extremely crude type of cutting into a warm, bright place and keep it well misted. In warm summer weather new, true roots will form extremely fast, and you can move the plant into a slightly larger pot in a couple of months. If you have cut off a well-proportioned top section, with big, perforated leaves, you will have a well-established gift to give away by Christmas. Your old plant, meantime, will throw out new growth where you trimmed it back, without turning a hair.

To turn a bundle of waste material or change a plant into a self-sufficient unit is an extremely heady experience. No matter how often I do it, I still have a feeling of elation when I find strong, new roots forming. Do try it for yourself. If you fail, you will only have lost material that would otherwise have gone to waste. And, as you can see, there are many ways in which this process can be managed. For limited work indoors lights are undoubtedly the way to start your further education as a horticulturist. They make it all seem so easy.

I don't think I could garden today without lights. They enable me to control the seasons and do the work when it suits me. Under them I grow plants which I would otherwise have to forego, and I experiment with seeds that would not be available for me to buy as plants. For the

INCREASING YOUR COLLECTION

gardenless gardener whose interest in growing things is strong but who has neither the place nor the time for active work outdoors, lights are the answer.

12 ❧ GETTING
OUTDOORS

MANY PEOPLE get outdoor gardening fever when the days begin to lengthen but, unfortunately, have no garden. If, however, you have a window space that you don't have to give up to that mumbling monster, the air conditioner, it is perfectly possible to make a small outdoor plot with a window box. This can be a show piece of flowers or merely a place to grow a few tomatoes. Either way, it serves an invaluable purpose by enabling the gardenless gardener to stay in contact with the soil and the natural cycle of outdoor growth. In these times of pressure and tension, this can be more important to our inner well-being than perhaps we realize.

Window Boxes

Window-box gardening is an old skill. It was used extensively in the last two centuries to decorate town houses and store fronts, and the practice still flourishes in Europe. In American cities, as town houses gradually vanished to be replaced with high-rise apartments, the use of window boxes declined. But in the country, particularly in small towns, their popularity has never waned. Now, however, they are making a general comeback even in cities. This is partly due to the fact that many new apartment buildings include balconies where window boxes, transformed into outdoor planters, are built-in features. But the

GETTING OUTDOORS

revival is not confined to new buildings. Many of the few remaining city houses have again reinstated a window box. They are also popular in less affluent districts, where a few, carefully tended, well-loved flowers, growing in a homemade box, can have a dramatic impact upon a whole neighborhood. A rather pathetic demonstration of the pleasure everyone gets from plants is the many window boxes and store-front planters in cities, such as New York, carefully and, to me, hideously filled with plastic foliage plants.

If you want to try a window box at any height from the ground, it is wise to have it constructed and attached professionally. Window boxes should be exactly level with the sill so that they neither block the light nor force you to lean over dangerously when working with them. A window box that is to be used at street level can be more easily installed by the homeowner. But these too need very strong supporting brackets for they are vulnerable not only to all the usual hazards of weight and balance, but to extra problems, such as teen-agers lounging against them, or being used as props for bicycles!

All this may make window-box gardening seem a little complicated and expensive. But a well-made box is a durable piece of equipment which should last for many years. And, though it may not produce the sense of physical coolness provided by an air conditioner, properly planted it refreshes the spirit of its owner and the passer-by. It will also pay you back for the expense and trouble you have to take to get it installed by an unexpectedly large dividend of personal satisfaction.

Don't, however, plunge into this kind of gardening without considering some of the problems ahead. First you must decide upon the kind of a box you want. The weight of a filled and planted window box is very great. Have you a place where such a heavy structure will look well and can be hung safely? In some of the new apartment houses concrete planters are now required if window boxes are to be used on a balcony. This is fine if they are provided by the management, but they are no good for homeowners except for use on a terrace—they are much too heavy to be suspended. In an attempt to solve the problem of the weight of conventional boxes, various plastic substitutes have appeared. There are, for example, fiberglass imports from England, which are imitations of the lead boxes that were in vogue in Europe in the seventeenth and eighteenth centuries. These are made from original casts and reproduce all the ornamental details of the lead, as well as the color, which blends beautifully with every kind of plant. They are feather-light and extremely attractive, but, unfortunately, they are very heavy on the purse and, unless someone is prepared to give you quite an expensive present, you are unlikely to feel you can equip all your front windows with these highly decorative boxes.

These Verein boxes, which is the trade name, are far superior to any plastic or fiberglass window box available here. The local products are usually sold in an unattractive shade of poison green, and they have the further disadvantage of being too short for most windows and too narrow to be planted attractively with a double row of plants, which is the only way to plant a good-looking window box. And, as a final blow to any possibility of their being acceptable horticulturally, many of these plastic window boxes have no drainage.

Drips from a window box onto your or your neighbor's property are a very real problem, but a solid base to the box is not the answer. I resent seeing window boxes made this way being offered for sale to unsuspecting novices. To me it amounts to a form of misrepresentation. This type of box must prove a dreadful disappointment; plants simply cannot thrive in them. New gardeners whose plants do badly are always ready to blame themselves. Naturally they do not expect to have been sold something that is useless for the purpose it is supposed to serve. When their plants die, they may feel too discouraged ever to try again, and yet the failure is not their fault. Those of us who do realize that all growing containers for plants must make provision for drainage would help our fellow beginning gardeners by commenting loudly and adversely whenever we see these horticultural booby traps on sale.

Small window boxes made of tin are also available. These are light in weight, but the plant roots will be severely damaged by the thin sides when the sun heats up the metal. The impact on the roots will, in fact, be exactly the same as if you had deliberately baked the box in an oven.

This brings us back full circle to wood as the best material to use. Window-box competitions are now sponsored by numerous civic organizations across the country, and the general consensus of all these organizations seems to be that a wooden box is the best for growing plants—partly because of the excellent insulation the wooden sides provide for roots, but also because it is the simplest for the homeowner to fit to the exact dimensions required in each individual situation.

Numerous books exist devoted entirely to window-box gardening. In

GETTING OUTDOORS

them you can find clear instructions on how to make good boxes. Redwood and cypress are the longest-lasting material, but any wood can be used. For appearance's sake, the box should be painted outside; inside it should be given a coating of a wood preservative. Don't allow anything containing creosote to be used for the interior of the box; this is highly poisonous to the roots of all plants, and the wood remains toxic for a long time afterward. If you decide to make your own box, don't take short cuts, such as nailing it together; always follow the proper directions. Among possible disasters with window boxes, there does exist the danger that, if it is shoddily made, the sides may give way under the thrust of heavy, saturated soil.

Once the hazards of construction and of getting the box securely fastened have been solved, you next must learn how best to manage the box. Obviously you will want it not only to look well when planted but also to remain in good condition during the entire outdoor growing season.

Window-box gardening is a little more troublesome than indoor horticulture, for the elements must be contended with as well as your own shortcomings. Around midsummer the men get separated from the boys where this kind of gardening is concerned, for, while some boxes look as flourishing as ever, many are tired and shabby.

Sometimes the boxes look poorly because their owners have lost interest. In that case it is much better to face up to your boredom and take out all the plants. A plain, painted box in front of a window is far preferable to a tattered box full of withered, diseased, and neglected plants. But if the box has deteriorated because you have had to go away, it should be rejuvenated with new plants; you cannot revive plants in a window box once they have started to slide downhill.

Growing plants successfully in window boxes calls for some specialized skills. You need to understand that plants in them dry out unexpectedly fast. The combination of wind and sunlight calls for daily liberal watering and frequent misting. To do well, the plants must also have regular additional nourishment both in the pot soil and applied as a foliar feed. They also need constant grooming to get rid of dead leaves and the debris that floats around in town air. If you go away a lot for weekends in the summer, window boxes are probably not for you; rain can never substitute successfully for your faithful presence with a watering can.

But, although these boxes need a lot of water, there will always be some surplus that has to drain away, and this is where the problem of those drips has to be faced. I recently read an account and saw a diagram of what seemed to be an excellent solution both of the drip problem and the daily need of the box for water. This was a box with a double bottom; the lower level, which was lined with metal, formed a reservoir for surplus water on the same principle as the saucer attached to a hanging pot. The planting, or upper, base of the box had drainage vents through which fiberglass wicks led into the lower water-storing area; and these wicks continuously fed water back into the box itself as the soil dried out. This type of box obviously is expensive to make and is even more cumbersome and heavy to hang than one of the normal kind, but it would do away with the drip and also enable its owner to go away occasionally with a calm mind.

Modified smaller types of this kind of self-watering box without wicks are already on sale, made of styrofoam and designed for raising seedlings. Obviously large, water-storing window boxes made of the same material, which will greatly help the problem of weight, could be made. And let us hope that, if they do appear, the colors will be more acceptable than those used in this material at present.

As things stand now, we have the urgent problem on our hands of how best to cope with the water overflow from the drainage vents. Window boxes are an extension of pot-growing rather than a form of outdoor horticulture; plants in them must, therefore, have some kind of internal drainage to facilitate the free runoff of surplus water. A wooden box will do best if there is a vent an inch wide running the entire length of the box. But with an aperture of this size it is also necessary to prevent a wash-out of soil, quite apart from the torrent of water that may cascade down onto the passers-by every time you give your plants their daily liberal dose of water. This can be prevented by shards used in the same way as in a flowerpot, to form a layer of structural yet open material that will hold back soil. To crock effectively such a wide vent in a window box calls for a very large number of shards, which will add tremendously not only to the bother of preparing the box but also to its total weight. It is better to borrow some tin snips from your local hardware shop and cut window-screen mesh so that it fits exactly into the bottom of the box; by this means all danger of soil wash-out will be eliminated. Over this put a two-inch layer of coarse perlite. Perlite is extremely absorbent and will release water slowly and with very little drip even if it is totally saturated.

GETTING OUTDOORS

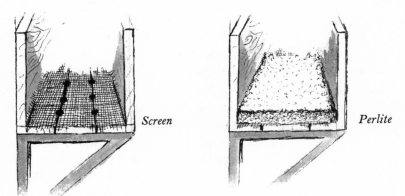

Screen   *Perlite*

With average window-box treatment there probably would be no surplus runoff at all. It also always keeps its open structure so that air can enter it; as a result the soil is in less danger from saturation. This damp layer at the base of the box is also a great help in preventing the contents from drying out. For, like the box with wicks, the material in the box itself can draw on the water that is suspended in the perlite and keep a steady amount of moisture at its heart.

And what is the material in the box to be? Many successful window-box gardeners fill their boxes to within four inches of the top with compost or with a commercial soil combined with damp peat moss and fortified with dry cow manure. Plants growing in the confined space of a window box in an outdoor exposure need all the help they can get, and a rich, water-retaining material of this kind will best help them survive over the long pull of the summer months. Unfortunately, a soil mixture weighs a great deal in itself, and enough to fill a window box is a messy, heavy nuisance to drag through the house. Also, by the end of a long, hot summer, most of the texture and goodness will have been worked out of the soil; the next year, not only will a fresh supply of earth be needed, but you will also have the extra chore of getting rid of the worked-out material.

Soil is usually suggested because growing plants prefer it. This assumes that, to do well, a window box must actually have the plants set out in the soil. But, though many excellent window boxes are grown this way, there also exists an alternative method that calls for rather less effort on the part of the grower and can produce just as good an effect. This involves using your box as a planter, rather in the manner suggested in Chapter 2, and keeping the flowers in their pots. In this way you will kill several birds with one stone. Instead of soil, the box can be filled over the perlite with coarse, lightweight vermiculite. This may not look as elegant as the peat moss that is used in the planters

Aggregate

Vermiculite

Perlite
Screen

indoors, but it is far less trouble to get wet and it holds the moisture just as well. Above all, it does not form a crust in hot weather, which is a serious danger with peat moss.

Plants, still in their pots, can be sunk right up to but not over their rims. Both the vermiculite and the pot soil can then be covered with an inch of aggregate. The aggregate serves as a mulch, conserving moisture in the box still further; it will also hide the vermiculite and prevent the disfiguring, light-colored material from splashing the flowers and foliage during heavy rain. If aggregate seems too heavy, a thick layer of firbark, which can be bought in small bags, looks well, smells delicious, and is extremely effective as a mulch.

A great deal of window-box gardening is done in towns where the air, unfortunately, is becoming increasingly polluted. As a result, many plants that used to grow well now find it hard to survive even with the most loving care. You will be able to tell if this will be a problem by the appearance of the leaves of your plants after a few weeks outdoors. If they are covered with filth and grime, the stomata will get blocked and growth inhibited. If you are unlucky enough to live where the air is poor, you will find it better to grow plants with a shiny leaf surface that can be regularly cleaned off by washing. Any plant growing under difficult circumstances in a window box will need regular and careful misting.

Air pollution, wind, rain, and radiant heat from nearby buildings make a formidable group of enemies for the window-box gardener to take on. It follows that the box can be kept looking much better if plants in trouble can be easily replaced. This is one of the advantages of keeping them still growing in their pots. A collapsed specimen can be taken out and replaced by a new plant very easily, whereas getting out a dying plant rooted into the soil can have a devastating effect upon the roots of the others growing nearby.

By keeping your plants in their pots you can also ring the changes on the seasons. Start with bulbs and pansies; move into full summer with geraniums, petunias, or whatever pleases you and suits your exposure; and end the growing season with chrysanthemums. To avoid a bare appearance in the winter use pine boughs in the box; these will look green and pleasant even when the snow flies. If you decide to sink potted plants in your box, it is important to make sure that the container is wide enough to hold a double row of pots. All window boxes look much better thickly planted: a single row of soldiers is rather a sad sight. A box is also usually more effective if the front is softened by trailing plants. The need to be able to get in enough material for a good show is one of the reasons why a custom-built box probably will give you the most satisfaction.

If you don't want to keep your plants in pots, you can still use lightweight vermiculite for the interior of the box. Knock out the plants and plant them in the usual way, keeping the pot soil level with the top of the vermiculite. Plants grow extremely well in inert material, making huge root systems. When planting this way, you will have to be even more regular and lavish with additional plant food, for the roots spread into material that has no nourishment. The filling you use inside your box and the plants put in it should all be set at least two inches below the top of the box, and the plants must also be well firmed into the surrounding medium. Wind, the enemy of all plants, is particularly damaging to any exposed this way and will rock them if they are elevated above the edges of the box. Trailing plants crouch low against this hazard, but, unless your location is particularly sheltered, you'll be well advised to stake the slightly larger plants when you set them in. This can be done perfectly unobtrusively with small green stakes and the inevitable yarn.

The number of plants that, in spite of all these gloomy warnings, will survive in window boxes is still large, and the specialized books give long lists for every kind of exposure. A box always looks better if you conform to the basic rules of display that have been discussed so many times. Concentrate on one or, at the most, two varieties of plants and, if possible, do not mix colors, other than adding the softening effect of white. White cascade petunias, for instance, combine well with anything. In the shade, the variegated vinca is equally successful in blending otherwise divergent plants. I recently noticed a most successful box planted with an extremely hard, bright red geranium that looked delightful because it had been made lacy, soft, and elegant by the single combination of a great deal of Dusty Miller.

A small box containing a combination of the various culinary herbs will grow very well in an eastern exposure, and so will a box of the scented-leaf geraniums. These would be extremely pleasant to groom, for there would be that enchanting smell as you worked with them. Window boxes need regular attention; dead leaves must be cut out, and overexuberant plants pinched back, if they are to delight us all summer long. There are plenty of foliage plants available for boxes that face north. Window boxes can also be successfully used for salad vegetables, tomatoes, or even the colored kales and cabbages for an unusual show.

The best all-purpose tool for a window box is an old kitchen fork. This will serve a multitude of purposes, including planting, weeding, and scratching in fertilizer.

No window box will look its best when first planted. It takes time before the leaves interlock and face outwards. You should also realize that much as you may enjoy working among these plants, you will not see their best face. It will be your neighbor who gets the full effect. That, in fact, is one of the charms of window-box gardening; as the neighbors realize the pleasure they derive from your plants, they too are often stirred into similar action, and the whole district may well benefit from your initial venture.

Portable Gardens

Apart from window-box gardening, you can enjoy a collection of potted plants all summer long if you have access to any open space: a patio, a balcony, or even a little area of roof. It is, however, essential to

GETTING OUTDOORS

understand that, with a very few exceptions, your indoor collection of plants will not do well or look attractive used outdoors in this manner. Most hard-working winter indoor plants need a summer of rest (described in the next chapter), and they cannot be expected to do double duty as decoration both winter and summer. The exceptions are the begonias; some of these, particularly the smooth-leaved, beefsteak begonia, like an outdoor balcony life so long as they are not put in full sun. Half a day of sun is more than enough for all the begonia tribe. Beefsteak begonias grow extremely large treated this way and look full and flourishing when brought indoors in the very early fall. These are plants that do well placed in large china containers that normally dwarf whatever is put in them. The semperflorens variety also often improves in health standing in an eastern exposure out of the wind on your balcony.

An old-fashioned screened porch does make a possible exhibition area for indoor houseplants. But, generally speaking, to enjoy potted plants during the summer it is better to use fresh material, chosen to suit the locations you have available.

Most of us at one time or another have tried to grow a few potted plants outside during the summer to liven up the place and have found the effect hardly worth the trouble, besides not being particularly attractive. Pots scattered around a terrace or whatever are undoubtedly a great nuisance to look after; they don't seem to grow particularly well and they soon become an open invitation to neglect. Outside or indoors, potted plants need the same treatment—to create a dramatic effect, they should be massed together. This, as we know, allows them to help each other, and it saves you work by concentrating them all in one place—if possible near a hose outlet. To make the best impression, you should try to use groups of the same kind of plant and have them in the same colors or at least shadings of the same color. Five pink geraniums grouped together and faced down with a few pots of ivy will look better than either five pots of varicolored geraniums or ten pots of different kinds of flowering plants dotted about the place. Do be completely realistic about using plants outdoors. If there is no faucet on your roof, don't even try to grow plants there. When the hot weather arrives, you will stop carrying watering cans!

During the summer the danger of overwatering potted plants is slight. The problem is getting sufficient water to the root ball to compensate for the accelerated loss of moisture through leaf transpiration. Plants continue to need as much atmospheric humidity as possible, just as indoors. This means that they still do best on pebbled trays —another reason for grouping the plants so that there will be a reservoir of moisture from which they can create a miniclimate among themselves. There is, however, one problem with outdoor grouping that does not occur indoors. If the plants are set where they get very wet when it rains, they should not be put so close together that there is no free circulation of air around them. Mildew and mold are summer diseases that attack the leaves of outdoor plants when they are crowded too closely. These problems are most likely to occur during hot, humid weather. For this reason it is extremely important to water outdoor plants in the morning so that the leaves can dry off before night. Also be careful when you water with a hose not to drench all the foliage. Not only does this set in mold, but water on flower heads inevitably ruins them. Many books recommend spraying plants during hot weather. I am of the opinion that hose spraying of flowering plants does much more harm than good; if you are going to use a spray at all, let it be your mister.

Potted plants growing and flowering out of doors are working extremely hard and need regular feeding. They also need constant cleaning up. A nearby broom is an essential piece of equipment, for all kinds of odds and ends drift in among the plants, bringing a slightly littered look unless daily sanitary measures are taken.

I find that summer potted plants all do better in plastic pots. These, of course, hold moisture longer and retain the additional fertilizer. But, as any excess cannot leach out through the sides of a plastic pot, it is better to feed regularly but very lightly rather than give an occasional massive dose. Yellowed leaves must also be cleared off regularly. This I do every evening after the lights are turned on, for plants out-of-doors look just as attractive lit up as they do inside. It is a quiet, restful time, when the other pressing duties of the day are over, to hover around the plant stand, sharing the light with innumerable moths, culling the dead and admiring the living. Plants look better by night and, absurd as it may seem, appear to respond extremely well to extra attention given to them at that time. Let me again repeat that under no circumstances should they be watered during this evening session of mutual admiration—that is the road to mold and mildew. Dead-heading, the cutting off of all seed pods, is another of my evening chores and is absolutely essential if you want the plants to remain in flower.

GETTING OUTDOORS

The exposures you have available are not too important. Plants that will make an attractive show exist for almost every outdoor position. A windy roof with full sun is the most difficult location, but if you are a really determined gardener you will find some heat-lovers that can survive even there. In general, plants classed as sun-lovers prefer morning sunlight rather than hot afternoon sun. If your location is a shady or northern one, there are many foliage plants and ferns that can be arranged for a very cool-looking effect. I also use the covered portion of a shaded porch, in a place which gets very little very early morning sun, for my gloxinias. Here they bloom extremely well and last a very long time. The same location suits the achimenes after they have come into bloom. I do, however, grow these into bud in a rather lighter place.

You must never overlook the danger of wind. Apart from the obvious damage it does to potted plants by knocking them down, it also does more subtle harm. It pulls the moisture out of the leaves faster than the roots can replace it; it rocks the plant stems, thereby injuring the feeding roots; and it burns the tender tip growth. You will grow much better outdoor plants if you can combine two essentials: sufficient circulation of air and a location near water with protection from the prevailing wind. You can do this by putting your plants against a wall or backing them up against a hedge. If you have no hedge or possible wall space, try to provide an artificial windbreak with a piece of lattice, a piece of plastic sheeting tacked over a frame, or even an old storm window braced to form an angle with the house. The change in the appearance of the plants when shelter of this sort is provided will be spectacular.

I stage plants on pots or on planks set on cinder blocks, and I use a great deal of ivy to soften the general effect. Up to now I have been

*Staging and windbreak
for summer porch*

rather lukewarm about the use of ivy in pots, but for an outdoor display this is an invaluable plant. Ivy and white petunias can be attractively combined in a single pot for a pleasant effect. The petunias give the ivy the slight shade they prefer against full sun, and the plants, being in a larger pot, are less likely to get forgotten when watering. I have found that small pots tucked into a plant group have a hard time attracting attention and getting enough water. If you want to continue to use one of these combined pots indoors later, cut out the petunia plants when the pots come inside. The ivy will soon overwhelm the space.

GETTING OUTDOORS

If you buy annual plants to pot up yourself, try to get young plants that have been grown separately, in what, technically, are called plant bands but which are often individual peat pots. Grown singly this way, the plants are more expensive but suffer far less of a setback when they are potted on. Make sure that the annuals you buy have been properly grown. Don't, for instance, buy petunias that look pale of leaf and starved in appearance, particularly if they have only one single, unpinched stem. To make these miseries useful for a pot, you would have to cut them back heavily, which will delay flowering for at least a month. It is worth reiterating that any seedling that gets off to a bad start is never going really to recover.

To make a good show of potted annuals buy them as early in the season as possible, plant two or three in a bulb pan with a very rich soil —there will be a lot of competition for nourishment among the roots— and bring them on slowly in good light. Nice as it is to make up your own pots, it will take much longer to make a fine show. For the novice gardener I think it is better to buy plants that have already been well started professionally and are in their final pots. In this way you will get the maximum period of bloom, and, if you search around enough, you will find a great many retail outlets that sell excellent potted annuals.

If you are using special containers for your outdoor potted plants, and there are now a great many of these on the market ranging from cement planters to wooden or asbestos bowls, always be very sure that there are drainage holes bored at the base. If not, put in a deep pad of stones to make the usual dry well. Undrained containers have to be carefully watched; they fill up not only with overwatering but also after heavy storms. The excess must, therefore, be continuously emptied. Big containers with drainage holes are excellent, but they do demand large and bushy plants; a small geranium in a large cement vase is a silly sight.

One of the advantages of massing your outdoor plants against some kind of background is that the plants will all turn toward the open area and, for once, face you. They interlock pleasantly with each other and should not be rotated. In the shade this interlocking effect can be extremely interesting if some of the plants have variegated leaves. Coleus is an admirable plant for such a location; this plant is a close relative of the European stinging nettle, a horticultural menace that every child learns, painfully, to avoid. The stinging nettle is to me what poison ivy is to you, and only recently have I been able to talk myself out of an aversion to its cousin, the coleus. The loss was entirely mine, for this is a good-natured plant that comes in a tremendous diversity of leaf color. It does need severe pinching-out to keep it bushy; outside it normally remains free of that pest, the mealy bug, which pursues it relentlessly indoors.

The sphagnum-covered plank garden, which was described in the chapter on succulents, can also be used as an excellent outdoor growing panel. Succulents themselves delight in a summer out-of-doors in containers, or on the plank, but they must be accustomed slowly to the brighter intensity of the light or their leaves will scald. Planks can also be planted to petunias. For this you should buy small F1 cascade plants, wash all the soil off each individual root ball, poke a hole through the wire into the sphagnum, and insert the plant deeply so that part of the stem is also buried. Then replug the hole with more wet sphagnum. As the plants start to expand, give them several hard pinches. Hung on a wall, and carefully watered, these turn into generous panels of bloom. For lasting flowers the panels need regular food and as always must be laid on their backs when this is given. I have also grown flowering planks of marigolds that were not really an esthetic success for, though they grew very well, they looked a little like angry matchsticks. For early summer bloom I have planted planks with pansies. Planks obviously can be used for many annual plants, and it would be rather a challenge to try many varieties—though not, of course, all on the same plank. The essential requirement is to get the annuals set into the sphagnum while the root system is still small enough to be got through the wire without injury, and to water the sphagnum daily.

Plants that can be grown in pots for outdoor use are very numerous, but those we can actually buy are unfortunately much more limited. After a good many years I have narrowed my choices down to marguerites, felicias, crotons, petunias, and the annual chrysanthemums for full sun, with Dusty Miller and some varieties of ivy as excellent softeners. For a half-day of sun all the geraniums will thrive, and the ivies and petunias will, in fact, do better. For bright shade I use upright fuchsias and tuberous begonias: the impatiens or busy Lizzy and the wax or semperflorens begonia. In quite deep shade I make tropical groupings of ferns and philodendrons and some of the winter, self-heading monsteras. Fatshederas also look well grouped in the shade.

Most books list a far larger variety, but looking realistically at what

GETTING OUTDOORS

the novice can find at the local retailer and what seems most likely to survive, these possibilities are probably the best—or so they have proved to be for me.

One of the most useful pieces of gardening advice, which I have followed faithfully since I first heard it, was given by the late Lord Abercrombie, himself a famous horticulturist. Asked for a useful slogan for new gardeners, he came up with one which I think we should all use. He suggested, "Find out what you can grow well and grow lots of it." I have yet to come upon any horticultural advice more succinct, more sensible, or more applicable to growing potted plants outdoors in the summer.

13 ❧ PESTS AND PROBLEMS

WITH THE ARRIVAL of warm weather most of us get bored with houseplants. We have had to look at them and fuss over them all winter long, and the sight of flowers in bloom outdoors adds to our disinclination to have anything more to do with indoor plants.

The ritual of an annual spring house cleaning is now largely a thing of the past. With modern equipment we keep our houses sufficiently in order, so that it is no longer necessary to carry all the soft furnishings outside and beat and shake off the dust. But old habits die hard. As the sun shines more brightly indoors on our possessions, most of us still feel compelled to try to revive our houses and keep them in trim with the fresh feeling of spring. To anyone perking up her house, probably the most depressing and uninspiring sight is the appearance of the plant collection! No matter how much care we may have given plants during the winter, spring sunshine will show up every defect. The over-all appearance is often made worse by pests and half-dead plants that can take our style of living no longer. It is impossible to improve the situation by buying a few new plants: this is too much like new wine in old bottles—more fundamental treatment is necessary.

The first reaction to inner convictions that houseplants are a nuisance is often a vague feeling of embarrassment. You feel a little guilty for not cherishing them through thick and thin, awful as they may look. But this is an absurd reaction, for you did not buy your plants for better or for worse. Plants owe you nothing, and sentimentality over them will only lead to your disliking them even more intensely. So take advantage of your hard-boiled feelings and throw a great many of the less expensive ones away. Psychologically this will lift a considerable burden from your shoulders and make you more willing to try to do

PESTS AND PROBLEMS

something about the more important specimen plants. Furthermore, it is not sound horticultural practice to try to keep small potted plants alive when they are already brown, tattered, and shabby after a winter indoors. If they look poorly now, just imagine how they will look at the end of the summer. The plants that should be junked are withered ferns, long, thin, and almost leafless philodendrons, mini-skirted fat-shederas, and all those yellowed ivies. Your room will immediately look better in their absence, and with the collection reduced your problems of summer care will be simplified.

Spring is the moment when pests proliferate. These probably have existed in small quantities on the plants throughout the winter, but the stronger sunlight of spring, added to dry house air, and, almost certainly, much less attention from you than earlier in the year, brings into view the attacks of a great many insects. This is an additional reason for throwing out small inexpensive plants. Cleaning the pests off them is never worth the effort. And don't, by the way, feel that you have failed as a gardener because your plants are under attack. It is a rare and extremely fortunate indoor gardener who has never been confronted with some kind of insect invasion.

In spite of our temporary disillusionment with indoor plants, we all have some that are too good and cost too much to be thrown away. Now is the time to make a very cold-eyed appraisal of their condition preliminary to carrying them over the summer. For me, plants worth saving would include all large and costly foliage specimens, citrus plants, bays and rosemaries, and all the succulents. Also I expect to save specimen flowering plants such as azaleas, clivias, spathiphyllums, and anthuriums. Among the hanging plants the epiphyte cactus, the hoyas, and the tradescantias are all worth preserving. Plants like the winter-flowering geraniums by now will have played out their roles and should be thrown away.

If you have a corner of the garden where all these deplorable plants can be knocked out and piled up, you will also have the start of a compost pile. I am not one who believes that everything that goes into such a pile needs to be free from all disease. The heating process, which breaks down this vegetable matter into usable soil, takes care of most of the problems that may have inflicted themselves upon your plants. Compost is so valuable, and its equivalent so hard to buy, that those of us who have room to make a pile should do so. No matter how primitive our methods may be, the natural elements eventually will turn this rubbish into rich, dark soil. So just go on piling it up. I realize that compost-making is a great art and that soils of varying nutritional value can be made by more elaborate methods. If you are unable to do heavy outdoor work, the family compost pile can take on a very simplified form—nothing special needs to be done other than throwing vegetable matter in a heap and leaving it alone. Organic gardeners will not like this short cut to compost production, and I agree that results do not come as quickly with this do-nothing treatment as they do with careful stacking and turning. But the end product is still enormously better than any commercial soil you can buy, and, if you burrow into the center of one of the devil-may-care heaps, you will always find good, rich soil year after year.

Gardenless gardeners cannot turn to compost-making, though I have heard of dedicated organic gardeners who pile armfuls of wet leaves into garment bags and allow them to rot down in these on their balconies over the winter. But those of us who have garden space are compounding one of the very many sins of our generation against the environment in which we live if we do not return to the soil the organic matter we take out of it. Conserving waste vegetable matter, whether it is weeds, old plants, or even the scrapings from the preparation of our vegetables should be a primary duty for all interested in protecting our land.

At the end of the indoor growing season all clay pots should be washed. Many of them will be covered with green scum. You'll need steel wool, a vegetable brush, and hot water, which will not hurt the plants and will halve your labor. Next, go thoroughly over each plant looking for dead wood and withered leaves. If some of the leaves have died off at the tips, cut off the dead section; eventually the whole leaf will die, but the immediate effect will be better! You must also clean the leaves. The plants of the most dedicated housekeepers get covered with dust both on top and on the lower surface of the leaves, and the effect on the unhappy plant is the same as outdoor air pollution. It feels as though it had perpetually blocked sinuses! You can wash the leaves of big plants individually, but you must take care to clean both sides. Some indoor gardeners, faced with the need to clean a plant with small leaves (an azalea, for instance), put a pad of newspapers in the bathtub, stand the plant on them, and turn on the shower. The downpour refreshes the plant and cleans the tops of the leaves—it also makes the most frightful mess. But it won't clean the underside of the leaves

PESTS AND PROBLEMS

or dislodge the debris that always lodges in twiggy plants. If you can get outside, it is better to clean each plant individually with a very strong jet from a hose. If this is impossible, crumple foil over the top of each pot (here, by the way, actually is a use for that horticultural horror) to prevent the saturation of the soil inside the pot or having all the soil wash out. You can then take the covered pot to the sink, turn it upside down, and run a forceful spray of water underneath and into the heart of the foliage. This cleans and invigorates the entire plant, and it will also dislodge some of the bugs that have accumulated—but nothing like all of them. The power of a fragile object, such as an aphid, to withstand the pressure of a heavy spray, angrily directed upon it by an indignant horticulturist, is quite amazing. The next step, therefore, has to be a close inspection.

To do this effectively, get your plant up at eye level on a table and look it over very thoroughly. Ideally we should keep a sharp look-out for pests all winter long and catch trouble before it starts. But even with this suspicious watchfulness on our part, pests suddenly increase late in the indoor growing season and can build up into a mammoth infestation in a very short time. If this happens, the control methods have to be rather drastic.

Violently infected plants are not worth saving no matter how large or expensive they may have been. You can never destroy all the invaders, and the plant will spread its troubles to those in the neighborhood with great speed. Also a violent infestation of any sort usually does irreversible damage to the plant itself. But valuable plants won't get into a serious state of this sort without giving you warning, so long as you really do look them over quite regularly. It's the smaller plants that suddenly spring upon us massive invasions, hidden under leaves and along the stems.

The most frequent nuisance for indoor gardeners to combat is the aphid, a tiny, ephemeral-looking insect that sucks the life out of the plant. Aphids come in a great many varieties and colors, like the plants they live on, and are sometimes called plant lice. They colonize at a frightening speed once well established, and not only are they plainly visible to the naked eye but they also exude a sticky secretion that gives the whole plant a shiny appearance. Ants use some types of aphids as milch herds, leading them onto the plants and milking them of these secretions. The aphids that appear on indoor plants are not usually brought in that way; they have always existed in small numbers. For that reason, and because of the danger of other pests, many books suggest isolating plants when first bought from a commercial green-house to be sure that they are, in a horticultural sense, clean. This is excellent for those willing to take the trouble. In my case, I invariably forget to water a plant isolated in another room, and, though I do examine my new plants carefully when I buy them, I am not prepared to go further than that.

If you have a valuable plant that (obviously in your absence) has become covered with aphids, try this simple treatment. Mix up a lather of soap (not detergent) suds in a large bowl of lukewarm water and add, if you wish, a little concentrated nicotine. This, like many plant remedies, is a deadly poison and must be used with great care in exactly the proportions suggested by the manufacturer. It should be kept, like all your plant poisons, safely under lock and key. I myself first try plain soap and water, and only if that fails do I give a second treatment with nicotine. Operation Plant-Wash consists again of cover-ing the top of the pot with foil, upending it, and swishing the infested foliage through the warm soap suds. Be sure to rinse the plant off very thoroughly afterward in a bowl of clear, cold water. Most of the aphids will then be found to be gone. You should, however, keep a sharp eye out for those veterans of the treatment who, like Captain Bligh, can survive impossible hazards. Destroy them instantly with your fingers wherever they may show.

Nowadays all kinds of sprays are available that claim to get rid of every kind of pest. I am extremely wary of these, particularly for use indoors, for many of them contain ingredients about which too little is known. We don't, for example, know enough about the long-term effect of some of these materials upon ourselves when, as inevi-tably happens, we inhale the fumes as we spray the plants. But we do have appalling evidence of the damage that one of them, DDT, has done, and is continuing to do, to birds, fish, and mammals all over the globe. We also know that some of the sprays used to control pests in our fruit orchards leave a deadly residual poison unless used in exactly the correct proportions. And I do not wish to experiment upon myself. Properly handled, these sprays may be essential for the production of the world's supply of food, but regular and casual use indoors cannot be desirable for anyone. Some of them are also lethal to many plants they are supposed to be saving.

Sprays which are harmless to humans are those based on pyrethrum and rotenone, both derived from natural vegetable materials and used by the South American Indians to poison the fish that they then eat with no ill effects. More sprays based on these two products are now being marketed. These you can use quite freely, as long as you remember to put the goldfish in another room. But please make it an unbreakable rule always to read the label on any pest spray before you buy it. If it contains materials of which you have never heard, regard it with suspicion. There is also an organic spray made with a hemlock base that is a delight to use. This is called Cedoflora and is not nearly well enough known. It is water-soluble and can be used in a mister. It takes some rather violent shaking before the material combines with the water, but it produces the delightful smell of pine woods, is harmless to humans and animals, and has a highly lethal effect on almost all plant pests. Who could ask for more? Cedoflora is very effective used undiluted against the mealy bug, another common houseplant pest.

The mealy bug looks like a dot of cotton wool and is usually found either in a leaf axil or along the stems of plants. On camellias and gardenias it also lurks around the necks of the buds. Generally it prefers areas that are not exposed to bright light. This makes the mealy bug less immediately obvious than aphids. It does not spread quite so quickly, but, being a large, sucking insect, it does a great deal of damage to the host plant. Mealy bug can also be stopped cold with cotton dipped in alcohol. With expensive plants, a careful, daily inspection looking for those white, woolly dots is really very much in order. If mealy bug is allowed to spread into all the crevices of a plant, it is much harder to eradicate. Caught early, it is easily treated. Any badly infected small plant with soft leaves that is harboring mealy bug—the African violet, for example—should be thrown away, for the insects are almost unreachable. Clivias, which are prone to this trouble, will be killed if the pests get into the growing heart of the plant. If you have had to treat a clivia very extensively, wash the leaves off afterward so as not to leave too much residue of the cure.

The third common sucking pest is scale. This is frequently found on citrus plants, ferns, jasmines, and the bay. It starts life as a small, neutral-colored crawling insect, and at this stage is very hard to spot. Later scale grows a hard, brown shell, something like the covering of a minute tortoise. During this stage of its life cycle scale attaches itself permanently, either to the stems of the plants, or to the veins of the leaves, where it draws voraciously on the life sap of the plant—safe under its hard covering which no wash or spray can penetrate. Most of us scratch off scale when we find it with our fingernails, but the more fastidious can scrape it off with the back of a knife. This is another pest that must be treated by hand once the outer shell has hardened.

If your plants have taken on a gray, webby look with pale foliage, they are probably being attacked by mites—in particular, the red spider mite. This is a microscopic insect that feeds on the undersides of leaves and revels in the dry atmosphere of our houses. It has increased seriously as a pest in the postwar years, and it is suspected that some of its natural enemies may have been eliminated through uninformed use of DDT. Badly infected plants must be thrown out. Those you want to save should be taken outdoors and given a very forceful hosing on the undersides of the leaves with cold water; if you have really strong pressure on the spray of your kitchen sink you can use that. A badly attacked plant takes a very long time to recover. This, by the way, is one of the ailments that hits the ivy plant indoors. Proper atmospheric moisture, together with regular misting of your plants, is the best way to prevent this serious trouble striking your collection.

Many of the summer flowering plants, particularly Martha Washington geraniums, ivy geraniums, fuschias, and achimenes are highly susceptible to a minute sucking insect called white fly, which rises up in clouds when the plant is touched. I use a strong spray of cold water for mild cases of white fly, and for greenhouse use there is available, I believe, a vapor-emitting cartridge that can be suspended and will eliminate this trouble. But any such preventives can only be used in a greenhouse; do not allow yourself to be persuaded to use them indoors.

As I can still get my plants outdoors, if the white fly attack is really serious, I use the modern poison malathion. This is the safest of the new pesticides because it leaves very little lasting residue in the ground. It is the long-lasting residue of the modern spray materials in the ground, rivers, lakes, and even oceans that has caused such widespread damage to all wild life. But I use it with considerable precaution and only out-of-doors. I choose a calm day so that no residue will be blown back into my face, and I always wear gloves and a mask. Perhaps I err on the side of super-caution, but I would far rather be safe than sorry. I was very much startled to read in a bulletin that goes to many gardeners the advice to dip plants into a vat of malathion to cure them of any summer-accumulated pests before returning them indoors. Maybe it would cure them of the pests, but I am not at all sure

PESTS and PROBLEMS

that breathing over the vat would be at all good for the gardener.

There has now appeared on the market another method of dealing with the problems caused by sucking insects. This method involves treating the soil in which the plant grows so that toxic material can be absorbed by the root system. The poison is a granular powder of high potency, and it has to be spread in a carefully measured amount over the moistened topsoil of the pot. It can then be scratched in lightly with a small stick or a plant label and the pot well watered. I find this material extremely effective if it is used as a preventive and watered into the topsoil of valuable plants before trouble strikes, or if a bit is put into the bottom layer of soil at repotting. I give most of my summering houseplants a dose when I put them out and another before I bring them back in. When wet, the poison gives off a rather sinister, onionlike smell. The plant slowly draws it up, in a dissolved form, into its tissues and throughout the entire stem and leaf system. Here it lodges and is toxic to all sucking insects, though harmless if given in the proper proportions to the plant itself. If a plant is already badly infected, I have not found this systemic control, which is the technical term, entirely effective, but it does work very well as a preventive. The directions for using it are extremely specific and must be followed exactly. Again, I wear gloves, which I normally loathe when gardening, and, when I handle any of these poisons, I measure out the amounts into a cheap, plastic spoon which I then break. There is hope that the fungus ailment that is destroying our elms can be controlled by this systemic method by eliminating the elm bark beetle. Without wanting to overemphasize caution, I would point out that the men who use systemic material on trees wear the equivalent of wartime gas masks. This is why I use all these potent insect killers so infrequently and so carefully. Good growing habits and a little ruthless determination about sick plants ought to prevent the need for any such violent poisons.

After taking all this trouble to clean up your plants, you must next turn your attention to the plant stand. The pebbles should be scraped up and sterilized in a bowl of boiling water, and the trays and saucers washed with a disinfectant. Bugs in pre-emergent stages live in the debris of leaves and soil which washes down during the course of the winter. Gardening books always emphasize how important it is to make sure that your stands are completely clean before you take your plants indoors. But when the moment comes to bring in the plants, or even refurbish an existing collection, somehow you will always be in a rush and unable to do the clean-up properly. It is far better for the health of the plants if the pebbles and trays can be cleaned off in this way twice a year. The other important time is during the short days of midwinter when many plants are slightly dormant and highly susceptible to pests. Let me, at the cost of being a repetitive bore, suggest that you also have two periods in which you throw out poor plants—in the late spring and after the Christmas slump.

The summer repair season is also the time for any light pruning or reshaping that may be needed. It is also the proper moment to take stock of the growing requirements of the plants you intend to keep. You must decide whether repotting is necessary. If the roots are bursting out of the pots in all directions, some action obviously will have to be taken. You will have to choose between the various possible actions discussed in Chapters 1 and 3. If there seems no particular reason for repotting the plant, and yet the pot soil looks exhausted, lean, and hungry, and overfine, top dress it with the richest material you have available. All plants recover better from any kind of root shake-up if it is done during the early months of the summer, for they have a long period of strong daylight hours in which to reclothe themselves and heal their wounds.

After all this washing, pruning, and pinning you have, in early summer, to face the decision of what to do with your plant collection during the hot weather. If you have access to a garden, the problem is relatively simple. Except for African violets, which always do better left indoors, most plants thrive best if they can be got outside as soon as there is absolutely no danger of frost. But I do want to stress again the point made in the last chapter that houseplants that have worked hard for you all winter should not be expected to be able to be used for decoration in the summer. The aim of getting them outdoors, where this is possible, is to give them a greatly needed period of rest and recreation where they can revive from the indignities they have suffered growing indoors and gain strength to go through all the same problems the following winter

Putting out the houseplants that you wish to save is an action that has to take place in two stages. When any of them first go out, they must be put into deep shade. It is extremely important that their initial contact with the much greater intensity of outdoor light is not sunlight. It doesn't matter whether they were in a sunny window before;

PESTS AND PROBLEMS

sunlight out of doors will scald the leaves and spoil the appearance of the plant forever. After a couple of weeks you can move them, still in their pots, into their permanent summer location which, ideally, should be in dappled shade. Not all of us have a place of this sort, but full summer sunlight does not suit many potted houseplants. If you have no broken or dappled shade, set the plants on the north side of the house. Big plants are extremely likely to get knocked over by the wind. Don't try to avoid this difficulty by taking them out of their pots and planting them in the ground. They may thrive and be much less trouble to look after during the summer, but, released from the strait jacket of the pot, the roots will spread out in all directions. When fall comes and the plants have to be got back into pots, the shock of digging up rampaging roots and cramming them back into a pot that is a reasonable size to use indoors often kills them. Repotting of this sort should never take place just before the unhappy plant has to undergo the worst period of its life—living through the winter indoors with you.

Some books advocate digging holes in the ground and burying the plants, pots and all, up to the rims. If you have the energy this is a fine idea, but it is also an extremely exhausting job. I use a less tiring method. I take old wooden boxes, orange crates, or whatever I can get from the market, and knock out the bottoms. I stand the bottomless box on the ground and put a heavy layer of shards at the base. This provides internal drainage and discourages wandering roots. It also

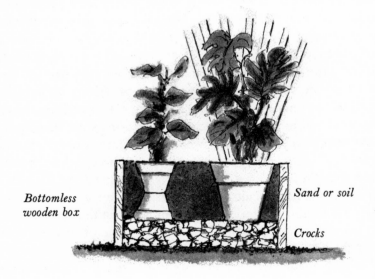

Bottomless
wooden box

Sand or soil

Crocks

serves as a slight protection against foraging worms. After the period of acclimatization in deep shade is over, stand the large plants on the shards in the boxes and put in small plants on upturned pots, very much in the style of the planter boxes mentioned in Chapter 2. I try to site my boxes near trees. This both gives them the right dappled exposure and gives me something to which I can tie the larger specimens. The boxes are filled in around the pots, though not over their rims, with sand, soil, compost, or whatever organic material is handy. This fill anchors the pots against the wind and acts as an insulating agent to prevent the pots from drying out too fast if you should want to take a short holiday. For continued good health you must water and feed these summering plants very regularly. If you have plenty of space and know that you will be around all summer, it is also possible to set your indoor plants on planks and bricks that give them much better protection against worms. Hanging plants can be hooked onto the branches of trees or put on a shelf that is high enough off the ground to allow the foliage to fall without getting damaged. If you go away a lot, hanging plants should be left on tall, upended pots and soil banked around them to serve as an insulation against drying out. They will survive better left alone this way for short periods than if they are left suspended.

All plants that have been summered outdoors will need cleaning up before you bring them back indoors before frost. And do be really dispassionate as you look them over and be sure they are really worth saving! Submerge overnight in a bucket of water the entire pot of those that you do decide to keep; this will destroy the worms.

If you cannot take your plants outside, you should use them differently indoors during the summer. Pull them back from bright, summer sun and group them elsewhere in the room. Take down your hanging plants and let them have a rest from their peculiar growing problems by being stood on upturned pots on a pebbled tray. Only take houseplants out onto a porch or balcony if it has shade, or only very early morning sun. If the place where you put the plants indoors during the summer has very poor light, give them extra artificial light. This need not be given when you are around and when it may heat up the room. Use your timer and have the lights come on in the night when it won't bother you but will give the plants the extra boost they may need.

Most plants do well with air conditioning so long as they are not in a direct blast from it and the room is not kept too cold. What does kill

PESTS and PROBLEMS

them is the economical kind of air conditioning that allows the room to heat up intolerably during the day, and then drops it twenty degrees in a great rush a couple of hours before you get home.

But even the most dedicated horticulturists have to go away sometime, and what about the plants? This, once more, is the moment for the plastic bag. Water your collection and put three stakes slanted at an outward angle into the side rims of each pot. The stakes are intended to hold the plastic off the foliage. Choose plastic bags that are not perforated; for large plants, use garment bags. Put the staked plant inside and seal the top tight with an elastic band. So long as these shrouded plants are kept in a light place, where no sunlight falls on the bags, they last happily encased in this manner for weeks on end with no attention. Plants that are too big for this treatment can have the pots

themselves wrapped in plastic with only the stem protruding, and the plastic taped tightly around the stem with electrician's tape. This is a more makeshift arrangement and will not keep the plant healthy for so long, but it will serve your purpose for a short holiday. To me, one of the advantages of the plastic bag method is that I am in control of the situation and can uncover my plants at leisure. Somehow it is curiously irritating to have to rush to water your plants when you return from a trip before you even have time to unpack your suitcase!

A couple of warnings may be in order about using this particular method of taking care of plants. Don't decide that the poor thing needs a lot of extra water before you leave it, and saturate the soil and spray the foliage in a mistaken idea of kindness before putting it in the bag. Moisture cannot pass through plastic—that is why the plastic-bag method works in the first place—and if the plant is over-wet when it goes in, the saturated soil will rot the roots, and the wet foliage may well rot off also. Also, don't put any plant still standing on a saucer into a plastic bag. The water that will collect in the saucer may also produce over-wet pot soil. Set the plant, simply in its pot, and with normally moist soil, into the bag and there should be no rot problems. Your plant may enjoy the close moist atmosphere so much, particularly if it is a humidity lover in the first place, that it resents the return to the normal indoor atmosphere of a house or apartment. Ease it back into the harsh realities of indoor life by opening the top of the bag for a couple of days, but leaving the plant still in it. This half-and-half treatment serves as a sort of horticultural decompression chamber and can ease the shock. But a plant in an open bag needs water, so don't forget it during this stage. It can usually be put back on its normal pebbled saucer without any violent reaction if you will take the re-entry problem a little slowly.

Earlier I mentioned the importance of bringing plants indoors again while the days are still warm and the house windows are wide open. This is a sensible practice no matter how lovely the fall weather. The slower the plants can readjust to indoor life, the better they will do.

And the next year they will flourish still more. You will be far less tense and apprehensive about them; you will have discovered which plants you like, which you handle the best, and which plants do, in fact, bore you. You will be realistic as well as optimistic, and that is the hallmark of a good gardener. Enthusiasm wedded to common sense gives everyone a head start in making things grow.

RECOMMENDED PLANTS AND GROWING CONDITIONS

ANY PLANT list always brings trouble on the compiler. Plants are much more flexible than we realize and very often overlap in the categories, being equally at home in several locations. This, therefore, is not suggested as a final definitive list of where and how to grow certain plants. It is merely the record of the houseplants I grow and the locations in which I have found they do best in my house. Your own list will soon show variations from this one, just as mine is not the same as that of many other horticulturists. The comforting thought is the fact that we are all correct. What does well for us is the way we should grow it.

The key is very simple:

* means that this is not really a houseplant (I use it on a summer porch or heated winter porch)

Warm is a night temperature in the 70-degree zone

Cool is a night temperature in the 60-degree zone

Cold is a night temperature in the 45-degree-upward zone

Sun is full winter sun

Winter sun is for plants that cannot take sunlight indoors in the summer

Bright sunless is a window area that faces east or north

Medium light is an area that gets light from a window but is not a window sill

Poor light is an area that is set back in the room

RECOMMENDED PLANTS AND GROWING CONDITIONS

African violet (*Saintpaulia ionantha*)	warm; winter sun
Aluminum plant (*Pilea cadierei*)	warm; bright sunless
Amaryllis (*Hippeastrum* species)	bulb; cool; sun
Aphelandra (——— *squarrosa*)	warm; bright sunless
Apostle plant or toad lily or walking iris (*Neomarica northiana*)	warm–cool; medium light
Arrow plants (*Nephthytis*) (*Syngonium*)	warm; medium–poor light; high humidity
Azalea (——— *indica*) (——— *kurume*)	cold; sun
Bay (*Laurus nobilis*)	cold; sun
Begonia (rex) (——— *rex*) (hairy-leaved) (——— *scharffiana*) (tuberous) (——— *tuberhybrida*) (wax) (——— *semperflorens*)	warm; bright sunless
Boston daisy (*Chrysanthemum frutescens chryaster*)	cold; sun
Box (*Buxus sempervirens*)	cold; sun
Browallia (——— *americana*)	cool; winter sun summer; light shade
Busy Lizzie (*Impatiens sultani*)	cool; winter sun
Cactus (*Christmas*) (*Schlumbergera bridgesii*)	cool; bright sunless
(*desert varieties*) (*Cactus*)	cool–cold; sun
(*Easter*) (*Schlumbergera gaertneri*)	cool; bright sunless
(*Thanksgiving*) (*Zygocactus truncactus*)	cool; bright sunless
Caladium, fancy-leaved (——— *candidum*)	warm; medium light

Calamondin orange (*Citrus mitis*) — warm–cool; sun–bright sunless

Calathea (———) — warm; medium light; high humidity

Camellia (——— *japonica*) * — cold; bright sunless
(——— *reticulata*) *

Cape primrose (*Streptocarpus*) — warm–cool; bright sunless

Carrion flower (*Stapelia gigantea*) — cool–cold; sun

Cast-iron plant (*Aspidistra lurida*) — warm; medium–poor light
(——— ——— *varie-gata*)

Chinese evergreens (*Aglaonema pseudo-bracteatum*) — warm; medium–poor light
(——— *pictum*)

Chrysanthemum (——— *morifolium*) — cool; sun

Clockvine or black-eyed Susan (*Thun-bergia alata*) — cool; sun

Crocus (———) — cold; sun

Croton (*Codiaeum variegatum*) — warm; sun

Crown of thorns (*Euphorbia splendens*) — warm–cool; sun

Cyclamen (——— *persicum giganteum*) — cold; bright sunless

Daffodil (*Narcissus*) — cold; sun
(paper-whites) (——— *tazetta*)

Donkey-tail sedum or burro's tail (*Sedum morganianum*) — cool; sun

Dracaena — warm; medium light–bright sunless; will survive poor light if artificial light is added
(Florida Beauty) (——— *godseffi-ana*)
(——— *margi-nata*) (*gra-cilis*)
(——— *warnec-kii*)

RECOMMENDED PLANTS AND GROWING CONDITIONS

Dumb cane or mother-in-law's tongue (*Dieffenbachia* "Rudolph Rhoers") (——— *picta superba*) — warm; medium light–bright sunless

Echeveria (———) — cool; sun

Ferns (Bird's-nest fern) (*Asplenium nidus*) — warm; high humidity; medium light–bright sunless
(Deer-foot fern) (*Davallia*)
(Maidenhair fern) (*Adiantum*)
(Mother fern) (*Asplenium bulbiferum*)
(Golden polypody fern) (*Polypodium aureum*)
(Sword or Boston fern) (*Nephrolepis exaltata bostoniensis*)
(Staghorn fern) (*Platycerium bifurcatum*)
(Table or brake fern) (*Pteris cretica*)

Fiddleleaf fig (*Ficus lyrata* or *pandurata*) — warm; light-tolerant

Flaming sword (*Vriesia splendens*) — warm; bright sunless

Flamingo flower (*Anthurium andraeanum*) — warm; medium light

Friendship plant (*Pilea involucrata*) — warm; bright sunless

Fuchsia* (——— *speciosa* [*hybrida*]) — summer plant; bright sunless

Gardenia (——— *jasminoides veitchi*) — warm; bright sunless

Geranium — cool; sun
(zonal) (*Pelargonium hortorum*)
(ivy-leaved) (——— *peltatum*)
(Martha Washington or regal) (——— *domesticum*)
(Scented)
peppermint (——— *tormentosam*)
lemon (——— *crispum*)
rose (——— *graveolens*)
nutmeg (———*odoratissimum*)

Recommended Plants and Growing Conditions

Gloxinia (*Sinningia speciosa* hybrids)		warm; bright sunless or artificial light unit
Golden sedum (*Sedum aureum*)		cool–cold; sun
Gorgon's or Medusa's head (*Euphorbia caput-medusea*)		warm; sun
Grape hyacinth (*Muscari*)		cold; sun
Grape ivy (*Cissus rhombifolia*)		warm; bright sunless
Herbs		cool; sun or artificial light unit
basil	(*Ocimum*)	
chive	(*Allium schoenoprasum*)	
chive, garlic	(*Allium neopolitanum*)	
cress	(*Lepidium sativum*)	
dill	(*Anethum graveolens*)	
fennel	(*Foeniculum vulgare*)	
marjoram, sweet	(*Origanum majorana*)	
mustard	(*Brassica*)	
mint	(*Mentha*)	
nasturtium	(*Tropaeolum majus*)	
parsley	(*Petroselinum hortense*)	
sage	(*Salvia officinalis*)	
thyme	(*Thymus serpyllum*)	
watercress	(*Radicula nasturtium-aquaticum*)	
Houseleek (*Sempervivum*)		cold; sun
Hyacinth (*Hyacinthus*)		cool; sun
Hydrangea (mophead) (———— *macrophylla hortensis*) (lace-cap) (———— ———— *tricolor*)		cool; bright sunless; winter dormancy

RECOMMENDED PLANTS AND GROWING CONDITIONS

Ivy (English) (*Hedera helix*)
(Baltic) (*Helix baltica*)

cool–cold; sun

Jade tree (*Crassula argentea*)

cool; bright sunless

Jasmine (*Jasminum officinale*)

cool; sun

Jerusalem cherry (*Solanum pseudo-capsicum*)

cold; sun

Kaffir lily (*Clivia miniata*)

warm–cool; bright sunless

Kalanchoe (———— *blossfeldi-ana*)
(panda plant) (———— *tomentosa*)

warm–cool; sun

Lantana (upright)* (———— *camara*)
(weeping)* (———— *montevi-densis*)

summer plant; sun

Lemon tree (Meyer lemon) (*Citrus limo-nia meyer*)
(American wonder lemon)
(———— ———— *ponder-osa*)

warm–cool; sun–bright sunless

Lemon verbena* (*Lippia citriodora*)

cold; bright sunless;
winter dormancy

Lily of the Nile* (*Agapanthus*)

outdoors; sun; grows large,
most suitable for tub culture

Lobelia, hanging* (———— *gracilis*)

summer plant; bright sunless

Maple, flowering (*Abutilon hybridum*)

cool–cold; sun

Marguerite, white (*Chrysanthemum fru-tescens*)

cool; sun

Monstera, self-heading (*Philodendron sel-loum*)

warm; medium–poor light

Moses-in-a-boat (*Rhoeo discolor*)

warm; light-tolerant

Night-blossoming cereus (———— *epi-phyllum oxypetalum*)

warm–cool; bright sunless

Nut orchid (*Achimenes*)   warm; bright sunless or artificial light unit

Orchid cactus (*Epiphyllum* hybrids)   warm–cool; bright sunless

Otaheite or Tahiti orange (*Citrus taitensis*)   warm–cool; sun–bright sunless

Painted arrow (*Vriesia mariae*)   warm; bright sunless

Painted fingernail (*Neoregelia spectabilis*)   warm; bright sunless

Painted nettle (*Coleus blumei*)   winter: sun
summer: bright sunless

Palm (*Chamaedorea elegans neantha bella*)   warm; medium–poor light

Panda plant: *see* Kalanchoe (——— *tomentosa*)

Pansy* (*Viola cornuta*)   cold; sun; not really a houseplant

Partridge-breasted aloe (——— *variegata*)   cool; sun

Peperomia (——— *obtusifolia variegata*)   warm; medium light
(emerald ripple) (——— *caperata*)
(watermelon) (——— *sandersii*)

Pepper plant (*Capsicum annum*)   cold; sun

Petunia* (*Petunia* F1 hybrids)   summer plant; sun

Philodendron, trailing (*Philodendron cordatum*)   warm; medium–poor light; does well with artificial light

Pilea: *see* Aluminum plant (——— *cadierei*) *and* Friendship plant (——— *involucrata*)

Pineapple plant, dwarf (*Ananas anan assoides nanus*)   warm; bright sunless

RECOMMENDED PLANTS AND GROWING CONDITIONS

Pittosporum* (——— *tobira*)   cold; sun; can grow quite large

Podocarpus (——— *macrophylla*)   cold; light-tolerant

Poinsettia (*Euphorbia pulcherrima*)   warm–cool; sun

Pothos, variegated (*Scindapsus aureus*)   warm; bright sunless or artificial light

Prayer plant (*Maranta*)   warm; medium light; needs high humidity

Primrose (*Primula*)   cold; sun
    bunch (——— *polyanthus*)
    fairy   (——— *malacoides*)
          (——— *kewensis*)
    poison (*obconica*)

Purple heart (*Setcreasea purpurea*)   warm–cool; bright sunless

Queen's tears or lady's eardrops (*Billbergia nutans*)   warm; bright sunless

Rosary vine (*Ceropegia woodii*)   warm; bright sunless; always stays very small

Rosemary (*Rosmarinus officinalis*)   cold; sun

Rubber tree (*Ficus elastica*)   warm; light-tolerant; can grow very large

Sedum (———)   cool–cold; sun
    (——— *seiboldi*)
    see also Donkey-tail sedum
        (——— *morganium*) *and*
        Golden sedum (——— *aureum*)

Snake or mother-in-law or bowstring plant (*Sansevieria*)   warm–cool; light-tolerant

Spathe flower (*Spathiphyllum floribundum*) with large leaves (——— *clevelandii*)   warm; moderate light; bright sunless for bloom

Spider plant (*Chlorophytum elatum vittatum*)   warm; medium light

Star-of-Bethlehem (*Campanula isophylla*)   cold; sun

Swedish ivy (*Plectranthus australis*)   warm–cool; bright sunless

Swiss-cheese plant (*Monstera delicious*)   warm; medium light

Ti plants (*Cordyline terminalis*)   warm; medium light; bright sunless

Toad lily: *see* Apostle plant (*Neomarica northiana*)

Tree ivy (*Fatshedera lizei*)   cool–cold; winter: sun

Umbrella tree (*Schefflera actinophylla*)   warm; medium to bright sunless

Vase plants (Bromeliads in variety)   warm; medium to bright sunless

Vinca (———— *major variegata*)   summer plant; bright sunless

Wandering Jew (*Tradescantia fluminensis*) (*Zebrina pendula*)   cool; bright sunless

Watermelon peperomia: *see* Peperomia, watermelon (———— *sandersii*)

Wax plant (*Hoya carnosa*)   cool–cold; sun

✿ INDEX

A Note About the Author

THALASSA CRUSO was born in 1909 and spent most of her childhood in Guildford, Surrey. She was trained in archaeology and anthropology at the London School of Economics, where she took an honors diploma in 1931. After apprenticing under Sir Mortimer Wheeler at Verulamium (St. Albans) and Professor Christopher Hawkes at Colchester, she excavated and published a report on the Iron Age Fort at Bredon Hill in Worcestershire. From 1931 to 1935 she was an Assistant Keeper at the London Museum in charge of the Costume and Nineteenth-Century Collections and the author of a book on costume. During World War II she served at the British Consulate in Boston, where she has lived since her marriage in 1935. Throughout her varied career she has maintained an active interest in horticulture. In the fall of 1967 she launched a very successful television career with the 54-show series "Making Things Grow" on WGBH-TV (Boston), which is still running on public television across the United States. Since then her public television work has included the 36-show series "Making Things Work," a 6-part show on the "Small City Garden," WGBH Specials on the Boston Flower Show in 1969, the Arnold Arboretum in 1972, and the Cape Cod Dunes in 1974, and, in 1974-75, commentary for "Family at War," a 53-part series sponsored by the Eastern Educational Network. In addition to her books she has written as a regular columnist for the *Boston Sunday Globe*, the *Boston Globe Calendar* and *McCall's* magazine and as a contributor to *Country Journal*. She is a Fellow of the Society of Antiquaries of London, a member of the Royal Archaeological Institute, the Royal Horticultural Society, the Garden Club of America, the Garden Federation of Massachusetts, and a trustee of the Massachusetts Horticultural Society. An accredited horticultural judge, she is herself the winner of many gardening and greenhouse awards, including, in 1969, the Garden Club of America's Medal of Merit, and, in 1970, the Horticultural Society of New York's citation for distinguished horticultural service and the Garden Club of America's Distinguished Service Medal.

A Note on the Type

The text of this book is set in Monticello, a Linotype revival of the original Binny & Ronaldson Roman No. 1, cut by Archibald Binny and cast in 1796 by that Philadelphia type foundry. The face was named Monticello in honor of its use in the monumental fifty-volume *Papers of Thomas Jefferson*, published by Princeton University Press. Monticello is a transitional type design, embodying certain features of Bulmer and Baskerville, but it is a distinguished face in its own right.

Typography and design by Ken Miyamoto